LA POTINIERE
AND FRIENDS

For all our friends

... particularly the special
ones!

To Margaret and Jim
with love from
David and Hilary.

August 1990.

LA POTINIERE
AND FRIENDS

David and Hilary Brown

CENTURY
London Sydney Auckland Johannesburg

ACKNOWLEDGEMENTS

We should like to thank the following friends, new and old, who have made this book possible.

The young ladies at Century, especially Sarah Wallace, for being so patient and helpful with such demanding authors.

Susan Fleming, for making editing so painless.

Nick Price for his dedication, co-operation and contribution, and for being a constant pleasure to work with.

Jill Henderson for transforming some illegible handwriting into neatly typed pages.

And we are particularly grateful for the generosity of Jack Knox and Johnny Apple; the former for allowing us to reduce and reproduce his delightful drawing of a vine, which hangs in the restaurant and gives so much pleasure, and the latter for his kind and understanding foreword, and his support and encouragement over the years.

That such special people should all so willingly assist us makes us feel special too.

Text copyright © David and Hilary Brown 1990
Photographs copyright © Nick Price 1990
Illustrations copyright © Jack Knox

First published in 1990 by Century Editions,
an imprint of the Random Century Group Ltd,
20 Vauxhall Bridge Road, London SW1V 2SA

Random Century (Australia) Pty Ltd,
20 Alfred Street, Milsons Point, Sydney,
New South Wales 2061, Australia

Random Century New Zealand Ltd, PO Box 40-086,
Glenfield, Auckland 10, New Zealand

Random Century South Africa (Pty) Ltd,
PO Box 337, Bergvlei, 2012 South Africa

British Library Cataloguing in Publication Data
Brown, David
La Potinière and friends.
1. Food: French dishes – Recipes
I. Title II. Brown, Hilary
641.5944

ISBN 0-7126-2043-5

Photography Nick Price

Editor Susan Fleming

Art Direction David Brown

Typeset by SX Composing Ltd, Rayleigh, Essex
Colour separation by Colorlito, Milan
Printed and bound in Spain by Graficas Estella

CONTENTS

FOREWORD

David and Hilary Brown's extraordinary restaurant in East Lothian, La Potinière, is no bigger, no more expensive and no fancier than necessary. Those who judge eating places by the thickness of the carpet, the complexity of the food, the steepness of the prices or the pretentiousness of the waiters would be well advised to go someplace else. Here, you eat what Hilary has cooked, without choice, served by David with intelligence and charm, and you pay 1970 prices. I haven't ever noticed the carpet, if they have one.

The simplicity of their approach arises not out of provincial ignorance but out of their own modesty. David and Hilary travel on the Continent every year, usually concentrating on France and Italy, delighting their friends with postcards commenting on meals eaten, wines drunk, churches visited and landscapes seen. But they have no desire to recreate Jamin (or, for that matter, the Waterside Inn) in the shadow of the Lammermuir Hills.

Instead, the Browns have carefully judged how much they themselves can do, with the occasional help of a washer-up, while maintaining consistency in food and service and preserving their own sanity. Within those self-imposed limits, it seems to me, La Potinière approaches perfection. Certainly it is one of the half-dozen restaurants in the world I think of when someone asks, 'If you could have dinner anywhere in the world tonight with a few good friends, where would you go?'

With soups, with mousses, with textures and seasonings in general, Hilary has an astonishingly sure hand. One seldom says, while eating at Gullane, 'the balance is a little off here' or 'I would have added a pinch of x.' She makes the most remarkable, succulent, diet-busting scalloped potatoes. But what has always astonished me, particularly in the early days, was how many changes she could ring on the humble chicken. Only my Ohio grandmother, a great small-town cook, ever made me look forward to chicken as Hilary does.

It shows what you can do when you don't need to show off.

R. W. Apple Jr.
Washington, D.C., 16 February 1990

INTRODUCTION

When we started this book, 'La Potinière and Friends' was just a working title, no more than a throwaway line in preference to the 'La Potinière Cookbook' or whatever. As the project progressed, however, we realised more and more how appropriate a name it would be, for by far the greatest reward of our years as restaurateurs has been the number and variety of friends we have met in or through the restaurant. We were led into this profession by our pleasure in entertaining friends at home and we have been so fortunate in the vast majority of our clientele that what we do still feels a little like that.

We retain and cherish friends from the days before we had a restaurant, although our commitment to the restaurant and its anti-social hours restricts our opportunities to see them. Their appreciation of our amateur entertaining encouraged us to go further.

We also have many restaurateur friends. Naturally they are the most sympathetic people with whom to share the problems and pleasures of our daily life and work. Only they can understand properly, and it has been a constant reassurance to us to be so close to such special people. There are some restaurateurs whom we regard as friends although we may not know them. They are those who have, or still do, run their own restaurants, be they humble or grand, with honesty and generosity, who are openly encouraging to newcomers to the profession, and who believe that the future of good cooking can best be assured by sharing, not by secrecy. I have often felt that a chef with 'secrets' is a chef with something to hide.

The 'secret' of the cooking at La Potinière is that there is no secret, no short cut. Cooking is a labour-intensive occupation and requires time and care. It used to annoy me that there are some who wait until the moment we serve lunch or dinner to telephone 'because they know we will be there', apparently without any comprehension that we have been there all day preparing. It still annoys me because it is an inconvenient time to telephone, but if there are those who think that there is some magical way of having a meal ready for a restaurant full of people, that's all right by me.

There should be some element of magic anyway about eating in a restaurant. How many of us think of ourselves as merely filling a seat which was occupied earlier that day, and will be occupied again the next by another eating similar food, off the same plates, with the same cutlery, and that this goes on all week, all year. Surely, while you are eating in a restaurant that moment is, or should seem, unique. The whole dining room and kitchen exist only for you and the others who are there at the same time as you. This, at least, is how it is for us when we eat out. We may know the reality better than most, but the restaurant we are in only exists for the time we are there. The more special the place, the more this should be the case. If you are made aware of the routine aspect or feel part of a production line, something is wrong.

Because we are sensitive to this romantic aspect of eating out, we are very conscious of it in La Potinière. However we may feel physically or psychologically at any time, for some or all in the restaurant it is a unique moment. Even on a miserable January day, when the single table booked for lunch stands between us and some more comfortable alternative, we will do all we can for them. We philosophise that it is not their fault that they are on their own, but the fault of all the others who didn't book for that lunch, and we genuinely sympathise with them because we have been that single table elsewhere and have been treated abysmally at times.

Doubtless it is easier for us to take this approach because of the clients themselves. It is necessary to book, and it can be difficult at times to get a table. We are some distance from Edinburgh, the nearest source of significant numbers of our clientele. Our meals are at set times and, although the menu changes daily, there is no choice. All this conspires, although it was never calculated to do so, to ensure that almost everybody who sits down in La Potinière has gone out of his or her way to do so, and really wants to be there. It is a very positive start to any relationship.

From such promising beginnings have emerged not only many happy clients, but many good friendships. These we develop outside the restaurant, because we should always like friends to be able to come to La Potinière on their own or with others without feeling obliged to involve us. They encompass a wonderful divergence of ages and walks of life. The only common factor need be some interest in eating well, which brought them through the door originally, and this does not exclude many. It is a very great compliment and encouragement to us that people sufficiently enjoy and appreciate what we do professionally to want to know us socially.

This book, a compilation of many of Hilary's recipes which have formed the basis of the success of La Potinière, plus a few thoughts of my own, is offered both as a useful cookery book and as a souvenir of the fifteen years we have been at La Potinière. It is also an expression of our gratitude to all those who have inspired, helped and supported us along the way.

'Little by Little'

We met when we were still at school and our desire to spend as much free time together as possible quickly put paid to our previous individual athletic success. Yet we were never very attracted by dancing or partying, preferring to go to the theatre, the cinema or for long walks, or, and it is very difficult to remember when this first emerged, out for meals. It is curious that, although we were both fortunate to have mothers who cooked well and believed in real rather than convenience foods, neither of us had any experience or tradition in our upbringing of dining out, and the only sight of a bottle of wine might have been a Spanish Sauternes (yes, they could actually label wines like that in those days) with Christmas lunch. In fact, I remember the first bottle of wine I ever bought was just that, and for that purpose. It cost six shillings.

Any further interest in wine was to wait a while, but our introverted obsession with eating out progressed from the local steakhouse, to a good Italian restaurant some twenty miles away, and then to Houstoun House, the domain of Keith and Penny Knight. We still remember clearly our first visit to Houstoun. It was a winter's evening and snowing heavily. Hilary had passed her driving test and had borrowed her mother's car, but was frightened by the conditions, so I drove although still a learner. It is a very beautiful sixteenth-century Scottish tower house and it never looked better than that night, floodlit in all its restored glory in the dramatic white landscape. I suppose that occasion was a turning point for us. This was more interesting and exciting food than we had hitherto encountered, and in such an environment took the pleasure of eating out on to a new plane. Although we had no conception of where it was to lead us, a seed was sown that night which was to influence the rest of our lives. The menu, as Hilary recalls it, was mushroom and cheese *piroski,* mussel soup accompanied by lovely little warm rolls, chicken in a mustard sauce, an interesting cheese trolley, and a dessert called Tortoni.

It was at this time that we first became aware of the *Good Food Guide,* whose founder, Raymond Postgate, had just entrusted it to a new editor, Christopher Driver. We eagerly digested the entries and started to plan trips to interesting sounding restaurants. In fact, from then until the present day, all our holidays and journeys have been planned to include eating places of special note.

By this time I was studying at Glasgow School of Art and Hilary, who had gone to Glasgow College of Domestic Science to study dress and design, had changed course to food and nutrition. As she became more involved in cooking, we started inviting friends round for meals inspired by our eating-out experiences and the cookery books we were avidly collecting. These suppers were always accompanied by wine, but very simple stuff.

We married when Hilary began teaching, and I was a postgraduate student, and we honeymooned, of course, in Paris. By now our interest in food was becoming passionate.

We cannot remember any particular moment of decision that we should like to run a restaurant, but we know that by 1974 we were looking at properties with that thought in mind. The only possibilities we considered were in or around Glasgow. That was our home town and where we knew best, and we naturally thought that we should start our restaurant there. It was not to be. We found ourselves in the impossible position of competing with Chinese buyers who seemed to have limitless funds, in cash.

Meantime we continued our weekend jaunts to places in the *Good Food Guide*. It had become our bible and we had become regular contributors to it. On one such excursion to the other side of Edinburgh, we had lunch in the tiny La Potinière in Gullane. We knew that it was on the market and by way of conversation asked the lady who owned it if she had sold it yet. 'No, but I would sell it to you,' was the reply. Of course, I assume she would have sold it to anybody (we were later to find how unattractive the trading figures were), but her words started us thinking.

By the middle of that evening we were telephoning from home to state our interest, and three months later we moved to Gullane. It was a Wednesday, the last day of September. With the help of some friends we packed a van with all our belongings from our Glasgow flat, and drove east. The proceeds from the sale of our home had helped pay for the restaurant, but we had been fortunate to obtain the lease of the cottage next to La Potinière. So, with most of our possessions still in tea chests, we opened for lunch the next day, on October 1st, 1975.

We have often speculated since, that, if we had been more sensible and allowed a week or two of planning, preparing and reorganising we might well have taken cold feet. It was a combination of enthusiasm and naïvety which made us jump right in at the deep end, and fortunately we kept swimming. We learned as we went along, our only guide being our own standards and attempting to offer in terms of food, wine and environment, what we ourselves should like to be offered. One friend and former colleague had made the point, and I thought it very sensible at the time, that being self-employed required self-discipline and that if we didn't put in a full eight-hour day we weren't working hard enough. The irony is that we never needed to remind ourselves as we quickly found that we had adopted a profession where double that was to be the norm!

Within a few months of opening we were approached by the now defunct Edinburgh *Tatler* for a recipe or two to accompany a small article on La Potinière. In our innocence we were very flattered and excited. Eventually, of course, we were asked if we should like to accompany the article with an advertisement and we realised that we had been gently 'conned'. We agreed to buy the smallest space available and advertised for the first and last time. Any subsequent press coverage has only been strictly without strings attached. Looking back, however, we find it reassuring that the simple wording of our intent so many years ago should be just as valid today.

> Imaginative table d'hôte meals at a leisurely pace
> and distinguished wines at a reasonable price.

Very quickly our Saturday dinners began to fill up three or four weeks in advance. The lead time continued to extend until by the early 1980s there was not an available table on a Saturday evening for a full two years! In fact it has fallen back to about eighteen months now, but this remarkable, if somewhat bizarre situation has certainly caught the public imagination, often to our detriment. For example, although this very distant booking applies only to Saturday evenings and, to a lesser extent, Sunday lunchtime, there are many who think every day is full months ahead. As a result there are those who might come, but feel that unless they have booked a long way ahead it is not possible. This misconception and its effects were typified one midweek lunch when, although in the middle of summer, we had only three tables. A lady at one of them, oblivious to the irony in her words, said that she was surprised to see us so quiet when she tells all her friends not to bother trying to come because we are always full!

Some question whether dinner at La Potinière is worth such a long wait. Of course it is not. I feel that the reason so many people are prepared to book so far ahead is simply that they know that they can rely on the standard to be the same. It will still be the same cook taking the same care. If the restaurant is open, she will be cooking everything that is being served. If she is not there the restaurant will be closed. How many places are there of which this can truthfully be said?

Doing this on our own is physically very demanding, apart from anything else, and there is little good argument for Hilary peeling every potato, and the time I spend polishing glasses or ironing napkins. There are countless chores which others could do just as well as ourselves, yet we selfishly cling to the original ideal of a scale and a style which we can handle between us. Then, if any appreciation of our efforts is expressed, we really can feel that it is all our own work. We are very lucky to have an occupation where we enjoy, at first hand, every process from concept to consumer reaction. And this whole creative and fulfilling cycle takes place every day we are open.

'Take It or Leave It'

The little building which houses the restaurant was constructed in the twenties at the entrance to a coalyard. The coal merchant built it for his sister, who lived in the part which is now the kitchen and utility area, and ran the front part as a confectionery shop and café. It was christened the 'Central Tea Room'. In the thirties the shop aspect disappeared and it became 'The Wishing Well', serving lunches, teas and morning coffee. As such it remains a fond memory of many who lived in Gullane or holidayed in the area during its thirty-year life span. In the early seventies it metamorphosed into La Potinière in the hands of a

French North African lady. If we were starting again today we would not give our restaurant a French name, simply because we are not French. I do not know whether we would have chosen a French name in 1975, but the fact that it had one did not offend us, and there was too much of greater importance demanding our attention to bother changing. By the time we were more able to attend to such matters it was too late. La Potinière was us.

We owed so much to France for inspiration that being thought of as a 'French' restaurant was not inappropriate. We further extended the myth by writing our little menu in French. This again is something we should not do if we were starting now, but fifteen years ago we saw nothing wrong with it and it does contribute to the theatre, the fantasy aspect of eating out. Furthermore, it helps make our written menu, always so simplified as to give a minimum of enlightenment, even more obscure. We deplore menus which lovingly describe every last detail of a dish, leaving nothing to surprise or to the imagination, much preferring to explore and discover for ourselves. I of course happily disclose anything asked of me about a dish either before or after serving, yet I prefer our guests to taste and think first.

In a similar way the modesty of the exterior of the restaurant is something we have not tried to disguise. Apart from creating more of a surprise on opening into a pretty little rustic dining room, the simple facade gives us an anonymity which we are glad of. We are on the village main road, yet it is of no advantage to us, since we are rarely, if ever, in a position to accept passing trade. In fact, we have been nurturing a willow tree in front for all the years we have been here and are slowly disappearing from view under its spreading arches. We really only want to be found by those who want to find us.

I'm sure there are many local people who think we are still a tea room which never seems to be open. We remember with great pleasure one day when a local repair man was working on our cooker. Apparently there had been an item on television the previous night about that year's newly published *Good Food Guide*. 'Did you see the telly last night?' he asked. 'There was a bit about the "best" restaurants in the country and they showed a photograph of this place by mistake!' Suitably put in our place, we smiled and said nothing.

Yet such an unremarkable building has inspired a great deal of remark over the years; and at times it seems that food or travel writers go out of their way to find a new disparaging description. A *Sunday Times* writer with a vocabulary and imagination to match his experience and knowledge of food could only muster 'small'; but it has been variously likened to a scout hut, a bus shelter, a garage, a rust brown settler's hut and, would you believe, an artistic bungalow of the 1890s. This verbose and pompous description, typical of its author, is undermined by its architectural inaccuracy. Not too surprising, perhaps, when the same observer described a collection of original paintings and drawings as prints!

'Yesterday's Papers'

Writing about food or wine has been one of the real growth industries of recent years, and now it seems that any newspaper or magazine, no matter the size or scope of its circulation, has to have a resident gourmet. There are some very perceptive food columnists, thank goodness, but there is also an awful lot of rubbish written. The obvious flaw is that the majority of food and travel writers have no qualifications or credentials to justify their opinions. This might be fair from a consumer's viewpoint since the articles are primarily for an audience similarly unqualified, but the deception is that the writer is looked on as an expert because his words are printed in a newspaper. Journalists must realise this awesome responsibility, yet rarely stress their amateur status. Anybody well versed in any subject handled by the media must be aware how shallow and inaccurate the general standard of reporting is, and will yet believe what is printed about subjects of which they know less. I often wonder if this absolute faith in the press is universal or if it is peculiarly British. It used to be said that those who can, do, and those who cannot, teach, which I always thought unfair. Today, however, I think it could be said with some justification that those who can, do, and those who cannot, write about it. I hasten to add that I am not writing out of pique, as most of the words printed about La Potinière have been kind or kindly meant – until now!

The independent guide books, on the other hand, deserve to be taken far more seriously. We rely on independent guide books when travelling abroad or in unfamiliar parts of Britain, and are grateful for their help. On the whole they recognise their responsibilities and are fastidious in their judgement. They are not infallible, but who could expect otherwise. There is no doubt whatever that they are largely responsible for the general improvement in standards in hotels and restaurants over the last 20 or 30 years, and that they set the ball rolling by making both cooks and customers more demanding, ambitious and enthusiastic about restaurant food.

They're not, of course, perfect. *Michelin* is too tight lipped, the *Good Food Guide* is too garrulous. Those in between in style, combining symbolic ratings with brief prose, are the most comfortable for traveller and restaurateur alike. *Michelin*, nevertheless, commands an unwarranted respect in this country because of its legendary dominance in France and because of its classic red hardback cover, which has been mercifully untampered with in decades. The other guides, all at an aesthetic disadvantage thanks to regular ill-advised 'facelifts', better reflect the British scene. It is to be a paradox that many of the most proudly British chefs still seem to want a French *étoile* more than anything else.

From whatever source, as long as the guide is genuinely independent of influence from the restaurateur and requires no payment from him, awards, be they stars or other symbols, are of great importance. Most good cooks are sensitive people and appreciation of their efforts is vital for morale. Some sort of 'official' appreciation, particularly early in one's career, can be so encouraging. We shall always have a soft spot for the AA who in 1977 were the first to give us a rosette for cooking. A member of their inspectorate telephoned to say that he wanted to come to see us about an award. Not realising in those days that none of the guides tell you about awards before publication, we became very excited at the thought of being told we had won a rosette. Our faces fell when the AA representative arrived and told us that the special colour feature of that year's guide was to be called 'Dining in Style', and along with six others, 'The Most Elegant', 'The Most Modern', etc, we were to be 'The Prettiest' restaurant in Britain. No doubt many would have been delighted with the appellation, and the poor man must have been confused by our disappointment, but the food was what really mattered to us. When the guide was published, to our delight we found we had also been awarded a rosette!

That same year saw our first entry in the *Good Food Guide* which had been our guiding light in Britain since we began eating 'seriously'. It also gave us an award, in this case a wine glass symbol, for a limited but well-chosen wine list. This meant that, thanks to us, Gullane was in bolder print than Edinburgh on the map of Scotland, which we thought great fun. The point is, however, that for a young couple in the early days of running their first restaurant, such things were a tremendous boost to morale, and an inspiration to try even harder.

The *Good Food Guide* continued to be good to us and the next year the wine glass had grown into a bottle which was joined by a mortar and pestle the following year. So it remained until the mortar and pestle symbol was abandoned in favour of silly numerical ratings. I have always wondered why the G.F.G. turns out so well on the whole when there are such obvious potential pitfalls in relying on consumers' reports. When anyone who cares to write can be a self-appointed restaurant critic, it must take a discerning editor to sort out the fools from the sensible. It is always with trepidation that we open at our entry, a feeling reminiscent of receiving one's school report card. However, despite the hurt feelings and controversy which always accompany a new edition, it remains the most useful and interesting guide for keen native eaters.

For foreign travellers whose English may well not comprehend some of the *Good Food Guide*'s flowery prose, the Egon Ronay and AA guides will be of most help, although, as with all guides in all countries, the more cross-referring one does the more likely one is to succeed. The comparatively new *Ackerman Guide* is regularly criticised for being 'restaurateur friendly' by food writers. It is a curious complaint which reflects more on the writers than on the guide.

'2000 Man'

I have a nightmare vision of the year 2000 in which nobody is capable of tasting and thinking for themselves any more. Everybody eats, drinks and pays according to some numerical rating bestowed by a self-appointed expert. It happens already, as demonstrated by the Robert Parker phenomenon in the USA. He publishes a journal in which his opinions of wines are expressed by a mark out of one hundred. It is such an absurd concept, that surely nobody would take it seriously. Yet not only is it taken seriously, but many wine drinkers accept Parker's personal ratings as gospel. Even in this country I know wine merchants who are asked to supply some customers according to the Parker scores. It doesn't matter what the wines are as long as they are 'not less than eighty out of a hundred' or whatever.

Personally I think numerical ratings are as inappropriate for wine and restaurants as they would be for paintings or theatrical performances. It is impossible to be wholly objective in one's judgement of such things and I should not wish it to be otherwise. Obviously a large proportion of the public, unsure of their own opinions on such subjects and dreading social blunder, disagree, and embrace definitive guides. Armed with those, and the confidence of other people's opinions, their cultural status is assured. They know that they are drinking a great wine and eating in a great restaurant because it is written that this is so. If they don't actually like the wine or the food, they know that they must be wrong and, again dreading *faux pas*, agree how marvellous it all is. So, if thinking and tasting and thinking about taste can be socially dangerous and uncomfortable, why bother?

Perhaps the time has come to compile a guide to the paintings and sculptures of the world with percentage ratings!

'Star Star'

One of the marvellous things about the restaurant business is the wealth of example, past and present, to learn from.

Our annual visits to La Pyramide in our early French travels showed us the importance of generosity of spirit in a restaurant. Everything there contrived to shower us with hospitality. The welcome, the flowers, the food and the attention of the staff were all abundant and genuine. Of course it was expensive, that standard of cuisine and environment has to be; but having accepted that, one got so much more than one paid for. He must have been a great man who created such a place and generated such a willing commitment in his staff, and she was a great lady who maintained it after his death. It was easy to believe that Fernand Point's old quip about the diners at La Pyramide being his guests and as such he could not charge them: 'I only ask that you give me a little money so that I may take care of my guests tomorrow' came very close to his real feelings.

A similar wholehearted generosity and a dedication far beyond the bounds of duty is to be found in Francis Coulson and Brian Sack at Sharrow Bay on Ullswater. If there was any justice then Francis should have had a knighthood by now, and I'm sure that someone in another industry who achieved and maintained such international respect would have long ago. In a business where one has to prove oneself daily in public, he has done so for forty years and with typical self-effacement will claim that 'anyone could do it'. Such humility becomes a restaurateur.

Dedication to the highest standards and the very best of taste are the hallmarks of Jean-Claude Vrinat, who for me is the greatest restaurateur in the world. Taillevent is the epitome of discreet elegance, the epitome of Vrinat. It might be possible to eat better than at Taillevent, but very rarely. There might be better wine cellars, but precious few. There may even be more refined interiors, but I doubt it. What there is not, to my knowledge, is anywhere else which achieves such excellence in all of these aspects, and the synthesis approaches perfection.

It has become usual for outstanding chefs to have their own restaurants. As recently as 20 or 30 years ago comparatively few chefs were known by name in the public domain; but men like Bocuse and Guérard changed all that and now most of the great restaurants in France and many in other parts of the world are better known by the name of their chef proprietors than any other. Yet a great chef is not necessarily a great restaurateur. Claude Deligne of Taillevent is an unfamiliar name to many, although he is one of the elite seventeen three-star chefs of France. Maybe he would make a good restaurateur, but he prefers to concentrate on his kitchen and be a great chef. So Taillevent remains the prime example of a restaurant where owner, chef and staff dedicate themselves to the glory of the establishment rather than a pursuit of personal fame. While others are off publicising themselves Mr Deligne is in the kitchen and Mr Vrinat is in the dining room. We dine at Taillevent once a year, on Hilary's birthday, and always leave inspired. We are proud to know it so well and to be known by it.

Dedication, generosity and humility glow from within each of these establishments and are patently bound together by love. Love of what you are doing and respect for those for whom you are doing it is the single most important criterium for running a restaurant, and probably anything else. One attention-seeking young London restaurateur claims that those who say they do it for love are liars and that the only motivation is money. I pity not only him but his customers and, despite his talents as a chef, I am not surprised that I have never enjoyed eating in his restaurant. As so succinctly put in Nicolas Roeg's *Eureka*, 'there is only one golden rule, do unto others as you would have them do unto you. The rest is conversation.'

A refreshing trend of the British hotel and restaurant scene is the continual inflow of enthusiasm and talent as people give up often very successful careers in other fields, because of their interest in food, and open their own establishments. In our experience these places tend to be natural and hospitable environments where the cooking has life and taste. The proprietors are people who have learned from travel and experience and have tried to create the sort of restaurant or hotel they would like to eat or stay in, rather than attempting to provide what they think the public want or expect. Some are simple, some are grand, but all are special.

Since this was how we started at La Potinière, we have a natural rapport with those others and many have become dear friends. They include Arthur and Jean Butterworth, who created White Moss House, Eric and Betty Allen of Airds Hotel, Fred and Gunn Brown at Altnaharrie Inn, and Paul and Kay Henderson of the wonderful Gidleigh Park, a place with such high standards that we leave not only inspired by the cooking, but wanting to redecorate our own house!

When we began, though, there was no more influential force on us and on the British restaurant world during the seventies than John Tovey at Miller Howe. Fortunately, the English Lakes are within our reach for a day trip and we regularly made forays to the various culinary highlights which that area seems to breed so successfully. We had been to Miller Howe two or three times for dinner but had always driven home after ('ooh, you mean Scots', I can hear John saying).

On the Queen's Silver Jubilee we had lunch at Sharrow Bay followed by dinner at Miller Howe. Such celebration was not because we are avid royalists but because it happened to be the day after Hilary's silver jubilee and we had been to the Box Tree at Ilkley the night before. When I was paying the bill in the office at Miller Howe, John was there and it emerged that we had a restaurant. With genuine interest he asked where, and when we told him he instantly recognised that we were in the *Good Food Guide*.

We did not drive home to Scotland that night. Instead we were scooped up by this remarkable man and taken back, with a bottle of Louis Roederer Cristal, to stay at his house. Such an immediate and enthusiastic reception for a virtually unknown couple of restaurateurs by such a celebrity made a great impression on us, and we hoped that we might be capable of emulating such kindness to beginners in later years. John has been a dear friend ever since.

About this same time, a new star was emerging in Fife. We had heard plenty about the Peat Inn, but had never met David and Patricia Wilson. When at last we did, we discovered that we had so much in common – our Glasgow origins and another graduate of the Art School in Patricia, our mutual passion for the restaurants and wines of France and our determination to improve Scotland's culinary status. At every opportunity we met to eat and visit vineyards in France, or taste old wines together at home, and just to talk. There is nobody with whom, over the years, we have shared more hopes, frustrations and gastronomic experiences, and the talk never runs out, as many a 4 am bedtime will testify. It has been with great affection, pride and admiration that we have watched them fulfil all their ambitions.

'In Another Land'

It was not food that first drew us across the channel. Thanks to the films of Jean Renoir, Claude Chabrol, Eric Rohmer and Claude Lelouche which we saw at Glasgow's 'Cosmo', and the wealth of nineteenth- and twentieth-century paintings in Glasgow's Art Gallery, we were in love with France even before our first visits together in the late sixties. Our earliest experiences of Paris, made possible by the very cheap short holidays available through Paris Travel Service at that time, convinced us that, for us, it was the essential city, and to this day we have to return at least once a year or we should feel very deprived.

So many aspects of French life appealed to us. The light. The unique blend, everywhere, of practicality and style. The respect for the old, be they people or buildings, coupled with the relentless pursuit of the future in fashion, architectural and automotive design. The well-behaved children, the love of cats, the cinema, flowers and, of course, food and wine. The French are arch chauvinists, certainly, particularly, and not surprisingly, when it comes to that last duo; but they will readily adopt and cherish what appeals to them from other cultures. Nowhere else are Mickey Mouse and Woody Allen so appreciated.

With so much natural empathy for the French (our first car had to be an old Renault 4, which we loved, despite the puddle splashes coming through the floor), it is not surprising that we so readily absorbed their obsession with gastronomy. The street markets and cheese shops were a revelation to us at a time when courgettes, aubergines and peppers were looked on as 'unusual' vegetables at home, and anything other than very ordinary Cheddar was rarely seen. We are still very excited by these places and envy those who have the opportunity to draw their daily inspiration from such abundance and quality.

We began in the bistros and inexpensive restaurants of Paris, but it was not long before we'd ventured further, armed with *Michelin* and *Gault-Millau*. Fortunately, our palates and pockets sufficiently developed in time to appreciate some of the great days of La Pyramide at Vienne and Pic at Valence, to rush to Eugénie-les-Bains when Michel Guérard started the revolution of new-wave cooking and to eat regularly at L'Archestrate in Paris where Alain Senderens brought it to the peak of refinement.

Having been so spoiled, we are not likely to be easily impressed, but we have lost none of the old excitement and anticipation as we head for restaurants new or familiar. They are, of course, carefully chosen. It is now many years since we spent much time or money looking for hidden gems here or abroad. If they are real gems their lustre is unlikely to have been ignored, and we are unlikely to be the first to spot it. Our free time is too limited and too precious to waste on unremarkable food, and our money too hard earned. If we do not have somewhere special to go, we prefer to eat at home or at a friend's table; and if there is no restaurant of particular interest when we are travelling, we simply do not have a meal. We have often settled for a carton of *fromage frais* and an apple in a French hotel room.

Although we have eaten in all the three-star restaurants of France and most of the two-stars, such necessary extravagance is to some extent balanced by sleeping in modest hotels and avoiding meals altogether, unless we feel there is something to be learned from them. If this sounds rather joyless, I can assure you otherwise. Misery for us is the regret of having consumed a meal of little nutritional value and no educational value, far less having had to pay for it!

The sad fact is that eating out today, even in a 'cheap and cheerful' establishment, is an expensive pastime, and, although it may sound self-defeating, I wonder at the number of people who do it regularly. For the price of a mediocre meal out, one could feast at home. For the price of two mediocre meals one should be able to eat out very well. I see no comparison in terms of value, and yet there are thousands of mediocre restaurants.

Our continual visits to the best restaurants of France, Italy and Great Britain are, we believe, of fundamental importance to our profession. We have learned most of what we know about running a restaurant from them, and continue to add to this knowledge with every trip. Rather like paying one's own way through university, it has been expensive and, at times, very wearing; and although the course has lasted twenty years already, there is still so much to discover. We do not expect much sympathy for having to eat in yet another special restaurant, or taste wine in yet another cellar, and we would not wish to suggest that we do not enjoy it; but it would be easy to slip into the complacency of having 'seen it all before' and settle for a restful, economical holiday. If the day comes when we could do this without feeling guilty, it might be time to give up the restaurant, and I think we shall realise it.

Meantime, it is our duty and our desire to see and taste and keep in touch, taking from each experience what we like and rejecting what we do not. Even to apparently stand still in this business one must continually evolve, if only subtly, and to seek inspiration and example is vital. Self-evident this may be, yet despite our protestations, not one of those gastronomic fact-finding missions is subsidised by a single penny of tax relief. I can only describe this as short-sighted and narrow-minded, and just a little pathetic.

We have never come home empty-handed from our trips to France, and apart from interesting bottles and foodstuffs we invariably have some porcelain, glassware, cooking utensils, antiques, *objets d'art*, cutlery or various useful or ornamental items for the house or restaurant crammed in the back of the car. Some day, perhaps, we shall take them all back again.

'Satisfaction'

I have often argued that cooking is a craft rather than an art. This is not an attempt to denigrate cooking but to define it. It does not mean that a cook cannot be an artist but it does mean that he or she does not have to be. The promotion of the ideal of the chef as an artist has done great harm to the craft of cooking in recent years, and has produced countless banalities. If cooking is art then it must look like art seems to be the justification for the childish pastiches which often result. Let the beauty be in the freshness of the natural colours and textures of good ingredients.

It is not possible at this stage in time to discuss or write about restaurant food without some reference to the much misunderstood 'nouvelle cuisine'. Let me therefore say what this means to us, rather than avoid the term because it has become such an international embarrassment. Although they originated before we were born, we look on the principles which Fernand Point established at his restaurant La Pyramide as being what the new cooking was and is all about. Firstly it is careful selection of good ingredients, then it is combining and cooking those ingredients sensitively so as to retain or enhance their attributes rather than lose or disguise them. Paul Bocuse, who was an apprentice of Point at the time of this revolution, refers to the previous concern in French cuisine with 'ostentatious effect which had little to do with cooking' and dishes which had to be prepared by someone who had 'the talent of a painter and an architect'. Does this not strike a disturbingly familiar chord as one reviews much of the cuisine promoted by restaurants, books and magazines over the last decade?

It is not surprising that there is a new wave of simplified, almost peasant cooking sweeping through the fashionable and the influential restaurants of the western world as we enter the nineties. From the point of view of food and flavour this is a relief, because it is not too late to revive or rediscover some glorious dishes which should never have been forgotten. However, the hallmark of much of this cooking is simplicity of ingredients and preparation, and it is questionable how appropriate this is in a smart and expensive restaurant. It is food that we love, and it is the style of food which we more often than not eat at home. It is the backbone of Italian cooking, and to some extent Californian cooking. It triumphantly reasserts the importance of taste over presentation; but it does seem very pretentious to offer it at three-star French restaurant or London prices.

It seems that some top chefs and restaurateurs are already recognising this dilemma and opening secondary bistro-type restaurants to indulge their inclinations in a more appropriate environment. Already Guy Savoy, Michel Rostang and Alain Doutournier in Paris have done so, and Georges Blanc in Vonnas is about to. I suspect that we shall see a whole flood of such alternatives open in the next few years.

One of the problems for today's young chefs is the pressure exerted by books and magazines to make food look good in photographs. Food photography as more than mere illustration is a comparatively new phenomenon, although it has already produced some masters of the art. It does not, however, care what the dishes taste like. Beautiful food photography can be very inspiring for a cook, and brings the various cuisines of the world to one's own doorstep, but it cannot teach one about taste or smell or the beauty of the ingredients. To understand such things one has to travel. Real Italian food, for example, has an inner beauty which, though apparent in reality, generally disappears in photographs leaving a somewhat unsightly plateful.

Unless a cook has travelled and tasted extensively, he is at a severe disadvantage, and it will come as no surprise that his food may be as superficial as a photograph. Again the media do not help by constantly having to discover new talents and inflating them to stardom before they have time to gain experience. Film stars and pop stars also seem to get younger every year, but I have yet to see the acting improve or hear the music improve.

Although I have questioned cooking's pretension to being fine art, there is no doubt that there are many parallels between running a restaurant and being involved in the performing arts. More and more, dining in a restaurant is an evening's entertainment and the metaphors of dining room as theatre, menu as programme, courses as acts and cook as star are all too apparent. The tingling anticipation of the empty restaurant just before the arrival of the 'audience' and the curious silent loneliness of the restaurant the morning after are also, I believe, familiar emotions to theatre people. On the same theme, I feel that the audience is entitled to expect that the publicised star should be performing for them, and if only a 'stand-in' is available, they might reasonably expect at least to be warned in advance.

The most meaningful comparison, however, is the vital feedback from audience to performer. Without the encouragement of appreciation we could not possibly continue. We want to give pleasure and are only really happy when we feel that we have done so. I have to keep Hilary informed of reactions in the restaurant, as I continually adjust from relatively calm dining room to frantic kitchen. By serving the coffee she has a chance to meet everyone, which she values because she can then visualise them the next time we are planning a menu for them, or when she is preparing their meal. Without trying to sound too sentimental or idealistic, this is, for us, what it's all about. We hope that this book, also, will give pleasure.

EQUIPMENT

Anyone who has been in our kitchen (and most who come to La Potin-ière have) knows that it is really rather small and homely, as opposed to large and stainless steel. As far as equipment is concerned, the only difference between my kitchen and most domestic ones is that I have a large six-burner, two-oven cooker. I am sure that I have more pots and pans and bowls, etc, than a domestic kitchen, but there is no need for you to feel that you cannot tackle my recipes through lack of equipment.

There are certain things which I consider vital, however.

1. *Sharp knives* are a must. Sabatier style knives in various sizes for various jobs. I find my small one the handiest. Many a time I have frantically looked for it if it has been misplaced, as no other knife will do the job so well.

2. *Food processor*. Invaluable as a time saver, for slicing vegetables, making hollandaise, and essential for some desserts. I like to have a separate bowl for oniony uses, as I daren't risk an onion smell tainting desserts.

3. *Balloon whisks* are super for smoothing out any type of sauce. I also like to use them for whisking egg whites, because it is easier to tell what stage they have reached than it is if using an electric hand-held or free-standing one.

4. *Mouli-legume*. This is like a sieve on a stand with a handle and a flat scraper which is used to sieve vegetables to make a purée. After liquidising my soups, I rub them through the finest mesh, which traps any skins, pips, etc, which would detract from the smoothness of it. A sieve could be used instead, but it would take longer to press the soup through it.

5. *Liquidiser*. I much prefer the results when soup is liquidised as opposed to being puréed in a food processor. The texture is much smoother.

6. *Rubber gloves* are so useful when handling hot dishes, pans, etc, apart from the obvious use of protecting your hands from soap, water, chemicals and foods which may cause an allergic reaction.

7. *Hand-held electric beater*. I particularly like to use it when making shortcrust pastry, when adding cream to mousselines and when whipping cream.

8. *White porcelain*. We have a wide selection of ramekins, *pot-au-crème* dishes, shallow round and oval gratin dishes, etc. Most of these are available with a pattern, but we prefer the understated style of plain white and, in general, prefer unpatterned china to show food off to its best advantage.

9. *Copper bowl*. The way to achieve the best results from whipped egg whites is to whisk them in a copper bowl, using a balloon whisk. This is especially important when you want them to expand and rise as for a hot soufflé, as it is easier to stop whisking them at just the right moment.

10. *Le Creuset terrines*. I use these for certain desserts, breads and, of course, terrines, as the shape of the slice is a pleasant, squarish one which I like.

11. *Scissors* which can be taken apart for cleaning are a good idea.

12. *Chopping boards*. Thick polythene boards are preferred to wooden ones from a hygiene point of view. Keep one for onions, leeks and garlic, and one for raw meat, as well as one for bread, etc.

13. *Crinkle-sided flan tins* with removable bases in various sizes make serving a tart, quiche, etc, so much easier and more attractive.

Naturally I have a wide selection of wooden spoons, spatulas, large metal spoons, bowls, pyrex dishes, baking and roasting tins, sieves, etc, but as you can see, there are not any pieces of equipment which are not available to the home cook, apart from my cooker.

PASSING THOUGHTS

While writing this book, I have noted down some points which I think are worth mentioning. There is no definite order to this list.

1. Before using utensils such as wooden spoons or chopping boards, check that there are no lingering onion or garlic smells.

2. If using cream in mousselines, or if whipping it, make sure that it is cold. Use straight from the refrigerator.

3. Once you start whisking egg whites, you must continue and then use them straightaway. If you leave them, they will start to separate and re-whisking will not do any good.

4. Use a balloon whisk to make sauces smooth and shiny.

5. Check your oven temperatures with an oven thermometer, as they all vary a little. Fan-assisted ovens are much hotter, therefore the setting will need to be adjusted according to the recipe and the manufacturer's instructions. The recipes in this book are assuming that they will be made in a conventional oven.

6. Take care over presentation. Do not waste time, money and ingredients by spoiling it at the last minute with heavy-handed presentation. A little effort shows your guests that they are important to you and that you care about them. At the same time, don't spend so long on it that the food becomes cold or your guests wonder if you have given up and gone to bed!

7. Do not guess at quantities. I weigh out and measure everything, as this is the only way to ensure consistency and accurate results.

8. As good stock is so useful, make up a large quantity and freeze it in small amounts, so that you always have some around when you want to make a reduction sauce.

9. Write lists and plans. Make a note of the proposed menu and plan what can be made ahead. Make a rough plan of action, working out the

best order of work. Write down the required ingredients and score them off as you get them.

10.   Use a timer with a loud ring, so that you can hear it easily. When you have many things to do, it is possible to get so involved that you lose track of time.

11.   Use bowls which are suited to their use. Do not use a bowl which is too small when whipping cream, for example. If it hasn't enough room to expand as air is beaten into it, cream will become very solid and will turn from lightly whipped to being over-whipped in seconds.

12.   Wear comfortable shoes. You will feel tired much quicker if your shoes are too high. I wear Scholl sandals when working and they really do make a difference to how I feel.

We do not intend to preach about raw ingredients or be dogmatic about what one must use. These are important issues on which one has to decide for oneself, and the arguments, ethical, gastronomic, conservationist or whatever, are too big to approach here and are more eloquently discussed elsewhere.

For example, not everyone has the opportunity, as we do, to buy eggs and poultry straight from local farms, but there is little reason these days for not buying free-range eggs from your local shop since they are now so readily available. Free-range poultry might be more difficult to come by and, unless you have a reliable supplier, you may find that what you gain in flavour is more than lost in tenderness. We always use wild salmon during the season, but we do not scorn the farmed variety. We would much prefer to use good-quality farmed salmon in the winter months than no salmon at all. Again, while our preference is for wild deer, farmed venison is no doubt an excellent product.

That meat and fish should be fresh goes without saying, but beyond that the most important criterion is quality. This is our prime concern when shopping for ingredients. The price is incidental. We have never costed a single meal for the restaurant. We feel this would take much of the joy out of planning and preparing menus; and as long as at the end of each year the balance is in our favour we are happy to remain in ignorance. If you base your choice of ingredients on cost you are defeated before you begin.

THE FIRST COURSE

SOUPS

Soups can be wonderful, and there are few foods which provide such warmth, comfort and satisfaction. Made with care, they can be served at any occasion, from simple supper to grand dinner party, and they do not have to be expensive to be really good.

The basic ingredients for my soups are vegetables, butter, dry sherry or fruit juice, and herbs. I avoid using stock for a number of reasons: firstly, I feel that enough flavour is derived from the vegetables; secondly, when I make stock I would rather reduce it, and use it as an invaluable addition to sauces; and thirdly, the flavour is cleaner (for, unless the stock is made the day before, allowed to become cold and then the fat removed, the soup can often end up tasting greasy). Most of the soups at La Potinière are smooth vegetable ones, and because they are stock-free they are suitable for vegetarians.

Herbs, fresh or dried, can enhance soups dramatically. Dried ones are perfectly good for cooking with, but fresh herbs as a garnish look very pretty. They are much easier to obtain now from food specialist shops and supermarkets, and are also fun to grow yourself.

Presentation, as with every dish, is important, and a little effort can make a simple soup look appealing and attractive. At La Potinière we serve the soup in individual bowls at lunchtime, but at dinner a tureen and ladle are left on each table for guests to help themselves. Top each bowl or the tureen with a little lightly whipped cream and perch a sprig of fresh herbs on top. This, by the way, is the only cream in my soups as I feel that adding it to soup softens the flavour too much and makes it too rich. (The *crème* of the French titles of the recipes is intended to describe the *texture* of the soups.)

29

When it comes to the seasoning and consistency, both are very personal. I prefer them to have plenty of flavour and body. Always taste before serving to check that the seasoning, temperature and consistency are perfect, and add salt and water if necessary. (If you are anti-salt, use a low-sodium salt substitute.)

Soup does not require an accompanying wine. It is much more important to concentrate on a good choice of aperitif, which could, if necessary, carry on with the soup course. My first choice is always champagne. It is vital, however, that it should have at least a year or two's bottle age to begin to develop its unique potential. Many of the inexpensive champagnes available through supermarkets are excellent products which have economised on the extra cellarage required (the great champagne houses do not release their wines until they are beginning to drink well). If one has appropriate storage conditions and patience, these will prove great value, but without that additional age they tend to be foamy and characterless and best suited to Buck's Fizz or Kir Royale. You would be better with a well-made *méthode champenoise* Saumur.

Spirits as a rule are inappropriate aperitifs, but it is the traditional place of some fortified drinks such as the intriguing blend of cognac and grape juice called *Pineau des Charentes* or, of course, sherry. A light dry *fino* or *manzanilla* is a drink which can happily cross over from aperitifs to partner a soup, and some such as San Patricio have recently been improved by dropping a couple of degrees of alcohol, bringing them much closer to the type of *fino* drunk in Jerez. Dry sherry must always be fresh and chilled.

Chambery vermouth, again chilled, is an excellent start, as is the pretty and popular Kir (dry white wine with a little *Crème de Cassis*); but I still prefer to begin with a wine. If not champagne, how about a good German Riesling, the ideal opportunity to enjoy the delicate refinement of these wines; or a mouthwatering Sauvignon from the Loire; or a fresh young Sauternes, where the undeveloped sweetness is merely softening the wine rather than dominating it, or, and I keep coming back to it, whatever you fancy. It is, after all, an opportunity to look at a wine without the complication of food, and it all comes down to personal taste.

Crème de Tomate et Menthe

Tomato and Mint Soup

This intriguing soup can be made all year round using the ripest (but still perfect) tomatoes you can find. It is an ideal way of using up a glut if you grow your own.

6 servings

2 oz (50g) unsalted butter
8 oz (225g) onions, peeled and finely sliced
2 lb (900g) tomatoes, the redder the better
3 fl.oz (85ml) dry sherry
1 tablespoon caster sugar
1½ rounded tablespoons dried mint or 3 rounded tablespoons chopped fresh mint
seasoning

Garnish
sprigs of fresh mint, plus a little lightly whipped cream

1. Melt the butter in a medium-sized saucepan. Add the onion and cook gently until softened but not coloured. Stir from time to time with a wooden spoon.
2. Add the tomatoes whole, with skins and stalks, the sherry, sugar and mint. No water is required at this stage. Stir together, cover with a lid, then simmer for 45 minutes to an hour. Stir occasionally.
3. Ladle the mixture into a liquidiser and blend until smooth.
4. Pour the soup through a mouli into the rinsed-out pan.
5. Stir together, then add enough water to correct the consistency. Season to taste, about 1-2 teaspoons salt. It should have plenty of body so do not add too much water. The tomatoes should have created enough liquid.
6. Reheat the soup when wishing to serve, and ladle into warmed soup bowls or one large tureen. Garnish with a little lightly whipped cream, topped with a sprig of fresh mint.

Potage St Germain
Pea and Mint Soup

This is one of my favourites. Its striking colour and delicious flavour are dependent on careful cooking and on using the correct peas (I use Bird's Eye Country Club).

6 servings

2 oz (50g) unsalted butter
8 oz (225g) onions, peeled and sliced
4 oz (100g) lettuce, trimmed and chopped
1 lb (450g) frozen peas
1 heaped teaspoon dried mint
or 2 heaped teaspoons chopped fresh mint
2 oz (50g) *petits pois*
seasoning

Garnish
sprigs of fresh mint, plus a little lightly whipped cream

1.   Melt the butter in a medium-sized saucepan, and add the sliced onion. Cook gently until the onion is softened but not brown.
2.   Add the lettuce leaves, and stir together with a wooden spoon. Add 10 fl.oz (300ml) water, and simmer for about 40 minutes.
3.   Liquidise until smooth. Pour through a mouli into a bowl.
4.   Place the peas in the same pan, cover with 10 fl.oz (300ml) water and bring to the boil as quickly as possible. As soon as the water comes to the boil, remove from the heat, pour into the liquidiser, add the mint, and blend until smooth. Pour through the mouli into the bowl containing the onion and lettuce mixture.
5.   Stir together, season to taste, add water if necessary, and return to the rinsed-out pan. It should not be too thin or it will lose its character.
6.   When ready to serve the soup, reheat it over a medium heat. Add the *petits pois*. Do not allow the soup to boil for more than a minute or two as the colour is easily impaired. Serve in warmed bowls or in a tureen, garnished with a little whipped cream and fresh mint.

(clockwise from left) *CREME DE POIVRONS DOUX, CREME DE CAROTTES ET ORANGE, POTAGE ST GERMAIN*

BOUILLON D'ECOSSE EN GELEE

Crème de Carottes et Orange

Carrot and Orange Soup

Choose bright, juicy carrots for this to ensure as dramatic a colour as possible. For a change, use a teaspooon of the ground spices on p.106 instead of the coriander.

6 servings

2 oz (50g) unsalted butter
8 oz (225g) onions, peeled and sliced
1 lb (450g) carrots, peeled weight, finely sliced
finely grated rind of 1 orange
3 tablespoons frozen concentrated orange juice or
10 fl.oz (300ml) orange juice
½ teaspoon ground coriander
1 garlic clove, peeled and crushed
seasoning

Garnish
lightly whipped cream, plus fresh dill or chervil

1. Melt the butter in a medium-sized saucepan, add the onions and cook gently until softened but not browned. Stir now and again with a wooden spoon.
2. Add the sliced carrots to the onions along with the orange rind, orange juice, coriander and crushed garlic. Stir together, cover with a lid, and sweat gently for about 5 minutes.
3. Add enough water to cover the vegetables, cover and simmer gently for an hour. Stir occasionally, adding more water if it dries out too much.
4. Ladle the mixture into your liquidiser and blend until very smooth. Pour back into the rinsed-out pan, through a mouli or sieve.
5. Reheat, adding more water or orange juice to bring it to the correct consistency. Add 1-2 teaspoons salt to taste.
6. Serve in warmed soup bowls or one large tureen, with a little lightly whipped cream topped with a sprig of fresh dill or chervil.

Crème de Poivrons Doux
Red Pepper and Orange Soup

This is a lovely bright orange-red soup. Add extra orange juice if you want to heighten the orange flavour. Be very careful when liquidising or pouring it, as splashes will stain cloth permanently.

6 servings

2 oz (50g) unsalted butter
1 lb (450g) onions, peeled and finely sliced
1¼ lb (550g) red peppers, cored and seeded weight
3 fl.oz (85ml) dry sherry
finely grated rind of 1 orange
1 tablespoon caster sugar
1 level teaspoon ground coriander
4 fl.oz (120ml) frozen concentrated orange juice
seasoning

Garnish
lightly whipped cream plus fresh coriander or chervil

1. Melt the butter in a medium-sized pan, add the onions and cook until softened, stirring now and again with a wooden spoon.
2. Having removed the stalks and the seeds from the peppers, slice them finely. I use a food processor for this, which produces a more moist result than chopping by hand. This also means that I do not have to add much extra liquid during the cooking process.
3. Add the peppers and all the remaining ingredients to the onions, stir, cover and simmer gently for 45-60 minutes.
4. Liquidise until smooth, then pour through a mouli or sieve into the rinsed-out pan.
5. Reheat, correct consistency by adding more water or orange juice, and season to taste.
6. Serve in warmed bowls, garnished with a teaspoon of whipped cream, and a leaf of fresh coriander or chervil.

Crème de Marrons

Chestnut Soup

Ideal to serve at Christmas time, although it can be made all year round. It is filling, so do not make it too thick if it is part of a large meal.

6 servings

2 oz (50g) unsalted butter
4 oz (100g) back bacon, cut into fairly small pieces (optional)
4 oz (100g) onion, peeled and sliced
6 oz (175g) carrots (peeled weight), sliced
4 oz (100g) potatoes (peeled weight), sliced
1 medium leek, cleaned and sliced
2 celery sticks, washed and sliced
1 teaspoon dried rosemary
3 fl.oz (85ml) dry sherry
1 lb (450g) tin unsweetened chestnut purée
3 fl.oz (85ml) medium Madeira
seasoning

Garnish
2 oz (50g) streaky bacon, finely chopped
lightly whipped cream and parsley

1. Melt the butter in a medium-sized pan, add the bacon and cook until browned. Add the onions, stir in well and cook until softened.
2. Add the other sliced vegetables along with the dried rosemary and the dry sherry. Stir together, cover and sweat for 5 minutes over a medium heat. Add 1½ pints (900ml) water, stir, then simmer for half an hour. Potatoes tend to stick, so stir now and again, going right down to the base of the pan.
3. Add the chestnut purée, breaking it up a bit and continue to cook, covered, for another 30 minutes. Add more water if it becomes too dry.
4. Liquidise the soup, then pour through a mouli or sieve into the rinsed-out pan. Reheat, add the Madeira, and season to taste.
5. Fry the finely chopped bacon in a little extra butter and drain on kitchen paper. Serve the soup in warmed bowls, decorated with a teaspoon of whipped cream, the bacon and freshly chopped parsley.

Bouillon d'Ecosse en Gelée
Jellied Scotch Broth

Having said that I use my stocks for sauces rather than for soups, there is one exception to this. If I have made more lamb stock than I need, I use it to make a quick version of Scotch Broth for ourselves. It is so warming and delicious, and if I omit the barley and pulses it is very low in calories!

Root vegetables such as carrots, leeks, onions and celery are cut into ¼ in (6mm) dice and are cooked in lamb stock until nearly tender, then skinned broad beans are added. Served with lots of fresh mint, it is wonderful, particularly if the lamb stock was strong and clear.

For a true Scotch Broth, barley and split peas would be added along with a piece of mutton and cooked for hours. When we visit my parents, they always make a huge pot of lamb broth for us, which contains root vegetables, barley, split peas, lentils, lamb shank and their own broad beans. It is simmered for hours and becomes a wonderful, hearty, comforting soup which is almost a meal in itself. Such humble ingredients, but such a great soup!

This jellied version is made in the same manner as the quick and hot version, and is allowed to become cold and set in soup bowls. It is imperative that your stock is strong, jelly-like and clear. If not clear, you will need to simmer the stock with a couple of lightly whisked egg whites and their crushed shells for 15 minutes, before pouring through a muslin-lined sieve into another pan. The egg whites trap all the impurities in the stock which would have spoiled its clarity.

I think that this is rather a nice notion, an elegant Scotch Broth, which shows that with any dish, however 'ordinary', care and imagination can turn it into something special.

4 servings

1 pint (600ml) fat-free jellied lamb stock (see page 139)
3 oz (75g) carrots peeled weight, cut into ¼ in (6mm) cubes
3 oz (75g) white part of leek, rinsed and cut into ¼ in (6mm) cubes
1 oz (25g) celery, wiped and cut into ¼ in (6mm) cubes
3 oz (75g) courgettes, trimmed and cut into ¼ in (6mm) cubes

3 oz (75g) shelled broad beans, blanched and skins removed
2 lamb cutlets, 'eye' of the meat removed and cut into
¼ in (6mm) cubes
1½ oz (40g) pearl barley, simmered in water for 20 minutes and
drained
seasoning

Mint cream
½ oz (15g) mint leaves
2½ fl.oz (65ml) double cream, chilled

1. Decide whether the stock is the correct consistency. For this, it is
best if it is lightly set, forming a soft jelly. If it is too stiff, add a little
water, and if it has not set enough, it will need to be reduced a bit
longer. In this case, use 1¼ pints (750ml) and reduce. Unfortunately
you cannot tell its consistency without letting it chill again, so I hope
you will not need to do this.
2. Place the stock in a pan with the carrots, leek and celery. Bring to
the boil, turn down and simmer for 10 minutes. Add the courgettes
and, after another 3 minutes, the broad beans and diced lamb. Cook for
another 1½ minutes, then remove from the heat.
3. Add the cooked barley, stir together, then taste to check seasoning. Add salt if necessary, remembering that the colder a food is, the
more subdued the flavour; add enough to give the soup plenty of flavour without tasting salty.
4. Pour into a large bowl and stir occasionally while it cools.
5. Ladle into four pretty soup bowls, place on a tray and transfer to
the refrigerator. Chill until set.
6. For the mint cream, bring the mint leaves to the boil in a small pan
of water. Boil for a minute, then pour through a sieve. Rinse in cold
water to set the colour. Pound the blanched leaves in a mortar and
pestle until smooth.
7. Combine the mint purée, the cream and a pinch of salt in a bowl.
Add 2 tablespoons of very cold water and whisk until it becomes thick
and fluffy. Cover and refrigerate until required.
8. To serve, dip two dessertspoons in boiling water, shake dry, take a
spoonful of the mint cream and shape it into a neat oval, using the two
spoons. Place it carefully on top of the jellied broth. Repeat with the
others and serve immediately.

Potage de Lentilles à l'Oseille

Lentil and Sorrel Soup

Every spring I look at our wonderful, healthy crop of sorrel and wonder what on earth to do with it. It has such a strong flavour that a little goes a long way, so even if I use it shredded in a sauce, only a small amount is needed. Then I develop this soup which uses what seems like a lot – especially if making it for a full restaurant. Like spinach, a whole panful will reduce to next to nothing when cooked.

6 servings

2 oz (50g) unsalted butter
8 oz (225g) onions, peeled and finely sliced
4 oz (100g) brown lentils, washed
3 fl.oz (85ml) dry sherry
5 oz (150g) sorrel
seasoning

Garnish
lightly whipped cream and a little raw sorrel

1. Melt 1½ oz (40g) of the butter in a medium-sized pan, add the onion, and cook until softened, stirring with a wooden spoon.
2. Add the lentils, dry sherry and 1 pint (600ml) water. Simmer gently for 40-45 minutes.
3. Meanwhile, shred the sorrel. Place the leaves on top of each other, roll up like a Swiss roll, then, using a sharp knife, cut across to form thin strips. Cook these strips in the remaining butter until wilted, which will only take a few minutes.
4. Add most of this cooked sorrel to the soup mixture, then liquidise until smooth. Pass through a mouli or sieve into the rinsed-out pan.
5. Reheat, add the remaining sorrel, correct the consistency and add salt to taste.
6. Serve in warmed bowls, garnished with a teaspoon of whipped cream topped with a little finely shredded raw sorrel.

Crème Dubarry
Cauliflower Soup

This combination of ingredients produces a lovely flavour, but because the soup is so pale, serve it as part of a meal which has plenty of colour about it!

6 servings

2 oz (50g) unsalted butter
8 oz (225g) onions, peeled and finely sliced
1 medium garlic clove, peeled and crushed
1 heaped teaspoon mustard powder
5 fl.oz (150ml) dry sherry
1 medium cauliflower, trimmed and broken into florets,
or 1 lb (450g) florets
seasoning

Garnish
fresh herbs and lightly whipped cream

1. Melt the butter in a medium-sized pan, add the onions and cook until golden brown.
2. Add the crushed garlic, mustard, 3 fl.oz (85ml) of the sherry, and the cauliflower florets. Cover and cook for 5 minutes.
3. Add 1 pint (600ml) water, re-cover and simmer for an hour. Add more water if necessary. The cauliflower should be soft but not discoloured by this time.
4. Liquidise until smooth then pour through a mouli or sieve into the rinsed-out pan.
5. Reheat, correct consistency and season to taste. Just before serving, add the remaining dry sherry.
6. Serve in warmed bowls, topped with a teaspoon of whipped cream, decorated with chopped parsley or dill. Alternatively, mix a little Meaux or grainy mustard with the whipped cream.

Crème Flamande
Potato and Onion Soup

This is a very simple, but delicious, soup, which can be made when your store cupboard is looking very bare. All you need are potatoes, onions, butter and a little cream. Fresh herbs as a garnish do, of course, make all the difference to the appearance and if you have a supply to hand, so much the better. Cook the onions slowly and carefully so that they begin to turn golden and translucent without burning, as this is what gives the soup its character.

6 servings

2 oz (50g) unsalted butter
1 lb (450g) onions, peeled and finely sliced
1 lb (450g) potatoes, peeled weight
seasoning

Garnish
a little double or whipping cream, lightly whipped
any fresh herb in season, such as flat parsley, thyme or sweet cicely

1. Melt the butter in a medium-sized pan, add the onions, then cook gently for 20-25 minutes, stirring frequently. They should become translucent and golden brown, but not in the least burned, as this will give the soup a bitter flavour.
2. Remove a tablespoon of the buttery onions which will be added later once the soup has been liquidised.
3. Add the potatoes and 1¾ pints (1 litre) water. Bring to the boil, stirring occasionally to check that the potatoes are not sticking. Lower the heat, cover and simmer until the potatoes are soft, about 40 minutes.
4. Pour into a liquidiser and blend until smooth. Pour through a mouli into the rinsed-out pan.
5. Reheat, adding the reserved onion slices, 1-2 teaspoons of salt, and some water if it seems too thick. If you like pepper, add a little freshly ground black pepper. Taste to check if flavour, temperature and consistency are correct.
6. Serve in heated soup bowls, decorated with a teaspoon of lightly whipped cream and decorate with fresh herbs.

STARTERS
AND
FISH

This section contains many different styles of starter: mousselines, soufflés, vegetable and pasta dishes, as well as various fish dishes. Most of them can be made larger and served as a 'main' course or as the main part of a simpler meal, preceded by soup and/or a sweet to follow. Quite a few are suitable for vegetarians, particularly demi-vegetarians who eat fish. All of the ingredients, apart from the *foie gras,* are easy to get and are available all year round.

When planning a starter, as with any other course, choose one which provides contrast in colour, texture, shape and taste to the rest of the meal.

For the starter or fish course, the Alsatians are supreme. They encompass all styles from the comparatively light and dry to the very rich, and despite their alluring floral bouquets they are masterpieces of balance, dry yet with muted acidity, and while sufficiently robust to cope with food, remaining elegant and subtle. I often hear people proposing 'crisp' wines with high acidity to 'cut through' the richness of a dish, but in my opinion such confrontations are likely to upset the balance of the cooking and the wine-making. An attempt to complement rather than contrast is a better ploy.

Try a Riesling with fish and shellfish, moving to *Reserve Personnelle* or even *Vendange Tardive* qualities as the dish gets richer. This is the Alsatians' noblest grape, but the Gewürztraminer is a godsend for spicy, fruity or highly flavoured dishes. And the Pinot Gris or Tokay d'Alsace, an unfairly neglected grape, has a staggering ability to age and develop, which in the great wines from the great years resembles the secret of eternal life.

Soufflés aux Courgettes
Courgette Soufflés

Soufflés which have been cooked very quickly in a very hot oven rise dramatically, but they also sink just as dramatically. Because these ones are cooked fairly slowly in a bain-marie, they rise slowly and evenly and then behave reasonably well as long as you serve them immediately. I have been making them for years, and they are thanks to a recipe in Elizabeth David's *French Provincial Cooking*.

When whipping egg whites, you must use a spotless, grease-free bowl. I use a copper one which I clean by rubbing with salt and a cut lemon, then rinsing and drying thoroughly.

7 servings

1 lb, 6 oz (625g) courgettes (choose small dark green ones)
seasoning
2 oz (50g) unsalted butter
1½ oz (40g) plain flour
5 fl.oz (150ml) milk infused over gentle heat with a slice of onion
1 oz (25g) Parmesan cheese, freshly grated
1 oz (25g) Cheddar cheese, grated
2 egg yolks, size 2
4 egg whites, size 2

1.　Remove and discard both ends from the courgettes. Weigh out 1 lb (450g) and slice these very thinly. (A food processor is good for this.) Place in a colander or sieve and sprinkle with 1½ teaspoons salt. Mix in well then allow to drain for at least an hour.

2.　Cut the remaining courgettes into dice ¼ in (6mm) square. Salt and drain these also.

3.　Melt 1½ oz (40g) of the butter in a medium-sized pan, add the flour and cook over a gentle heat for about 5 minutes, stirring occasionally. This will cook the starch in the flour. Set aside.

4.　Meanwhile place the drained sliced courgettes in a pan with 5 fl.oz (150ml) water. Bring to the boil, and cook for about 5 minutes.

5.　Liquidise until smooth, then add, along with the flavoured milk, to the roux (the cooked flour and butter mixture). Use a whisk or electric hand-held beater to ensure a smooth mixture.

6.　Place on a low to medium heat and cook for about 20 minutes, whisking frequently. At this stage the mixture is fairly thick and as it tends to form large bubbles which burst, sending splashes of courgette mixture flying, half cover with a lid. By the end of the cooking time, it should look and feel slightly thinner which means that the starch has cooked and the floury taste should have gone.

7.　Place the grated cheeses in a bowl, add the hot mixture and whisk together. Allow to cool for 2-3 minutes, then add the egg yolks, whisking them in thoroughly. Allow to cool down slightly before using.

8.　Melt a little of the remaining butter in a small pan and cook the drained diced courgette until browned slightly but still fairly firm.

9.　Preheat oven to 350°F (180°C) Gas 4. Brush six to seven ramekins (5 fl.oz/150ml capacity) with butter. Sit in an ovenproof dish which will hold enough water to come half-way up the sides of the ramekins.

10.　Correct the consistency and seasoning of the courgette mixture. Very little, if any, salt will be needed due to the salt added earlier on. The consistency is very important. If it is too thick the soufflé will be too heavy and will not rise well; if too thin, the mixture will spill over the edge when cooking. The consistency should be fairly soft, like lightly whipped cream. Add more liquid, milk or water, a little at a time, until the correct consistency is reached.

11.　Place the egg whites in a spotless, grease-free bowl, and whisk until stiff. I prefer to use a balloon whisk as it gives one more of a feel of the stage that they have reached. Over-whipped whites become dry and lose their ability to rise. Whisk them until a pixie's hat shape is formed when the whisk is lifted out with the whites still clinging to it, then turned upside down.

12. Add a quarter of the whites to the mixture, whisk in thoroughly, then carefully fold in the remaining whites, using a large metal spoon.

13. Half-fill each ramekin, using a ladle. Divide the diced courgettes between them, then cover with the remaining soufflé mixture.

14. Place the container on the front of the middle shelf, fill with enough boiling water to come half-way up the sides of the ramekins, then slide it into the oven.

15. Bake for 25-30 minutes, undisturbed, until risen and golden brown on top. It is all right to have a quick peek, but close the door very gently afterwards.

16. Place on serving saucers or plates and serve immediately.

Tarte au Soufflé
Soufflé Tart

This makes an interesting change from quiche. A soufflé, flavoured with cheese and fresh chives, is baked inside a pastry case, cut into wedges and served with a creamy tomato and mustard sauce. Use a 9×1 in (23×2.5cm) flan tin with a fluted edge and removable base, and line it with pastry the day before you wish to use it. I prefer to make my pastry, line the flan tin straightaway, then relax it overnight in the refrigerator. It is important to relax pastry before baking it, as this should prevent it from shrinking during the baking process.

6-8 servings

9×1 in (23×2.5cm) pastry case, baked blind (see page 198)
1 rounded tablespoon Moutarde de Meaux or other grainy mustard

Soufflé
1½ oz (40g) butter
1½ oz (40g) plain flour
12 fl.oz (350ml) milk, infused over gentle heat with a slice of onion

3 oz (75g) strong Cheddar cheese, finely grated
3 oz (75g) fresh Parmesan cheese, finely grated
4 egg yolks, size 2
seasoning
2 tablespoons finely chopped chives
5 egg whites, size 2

Tomato and mustard cream sauce
7½ fl.oz (225ml) double cream
1½ teaspoons Dijon mustard
1½ teaspoons tomato purée

1.   For the soufflé, melt the butter in a small pan. Add the flour, stir together and cook gently for about 5 minutes.
2.   Remove from the heat and gradually add the strained warm milk, whisking as you do so. Use a spatula to make sure that all of the butter-flour mixture is incorporated as it may stick to the corners of the pan. Beat or whisk the mixture well to remove any lumps.
3.   Replace on the heat and, whisking occasionally, cook for about 20 minutes by which time the mixture should have lost its floury taste.
4.   Remove from the heat, and whisk in the grated cheeses a little at a time, heating if necessary until the cheese is melted.
5.   Pour into a bowl, allow to cool for a few minutes, then beat in the egg yolks. Season to taste with freshly ground black pepper and a little salt (you will not need much due to the saltiness of the cheese), then add the chopped chives. Whisk now and again while it cools, as this will prevent a skin from forming. At this stage the cheese mixture can be left, covered, for a few hours until required. It is best though if it is still warm when the whites are added.
6.   When ready to complete, preheat the oven to 350°F (180°C) Gas 4, and place the oven shelf below the centre.
7.   Spread the cooked pastry case, still in its tin, with Moutarde de Meaux or other grainy mustard.
8.   Check the consistency of the cheese mixture. It will have stiffened as it cooled down and may have to be thinned down with a little milk. If it is too thick, the soufflé will be heavy and it will not rise well, but if it is too thin, it will rise to the height of the pastry case, then spill over. The consistency should be like lightly whipped cream.
9.   Place the egg whites in a fairly large spotless bowl (see page 42).

Beat the egg whites until stiff, using a balloon whisk or an electric hand-held mixer. Using a balloon whisk will give a greater volume of whisked whites, and you can gauge the stage that they have reached more easily. Over-beaten whites become dry and do not rise well as the air that you have been beating into them is knocked out. It is the expansion of the trapped air during cooking that makes a soufflé rise. Beat until they are stiff and if some is lifted out of the bowl on the beater or whisk and turned upside down, a floppy pixie's hat shape will be formed.

10.   Spoon a quarter of these on to the cheese mixture and whisk in. This will loosen it, making it easier to fold in the remaining whites, without knocking out the air. Fold these in gently, using a large metal spoon. Make sure that they are thoroughly blended, but stop mixing the moment that they are.

11.   Ladle or pour the soufflé into the pastry case. It should nearly fill the case. Do not spread the soufflé out, but using the handle of a small knife, form a channel between the edge of the pastry case and the soufflé mixture. This helps the soufflé rise straight upwards.

12.   Place on the oven shelf, remembering to allow space for it to rise, and bake for 25-30 minutes until risen and golden brown on top. The ideal cooking time will produce a soufflé which is cooked just enough to cut into wedges, but which is still moist and delicate inside. As ovens vary in temperature, you will have to use your own judgement. Testing with a skewer would at least show you if it was too soft inside.

13.   While the soufflé is cooking, prepare the sauce. Place the cream and ¼ teaspoon salt in a smallish pan. Bring to the boil, then simmer for 2-3 minutes until it starts to thicken, watching it carefully as it likes to boil over when you are not looking! Add the mustard and the tomato purée, whisk together and set aside until needed.

14.   Remove the soufflé from the oven, carefully balance the tin on a drum of salt or other suitable object and let the outside rim of the tin slide off. Place the soufflé pie (including the metal base) on a serving plate and serve at the table, or cut into wedges using a serrated knife, place on warmed plates, top with a tablespoon of the reheated sauce and serve straightaway.

Soufflés à l'Italienne
Parmesan Soufflés

These soufflés do not require last-minute whisking of whites which can be awkward when entertaining. This stage can be done well in advance, then all that is needed to be done at the last moment is to slip them in a hot oven for 10 minutes. Always, always use fresh Parmesan in preference to the pre-packed powdered type. I buy a large chunk, and grate small quantities, as needed, in my food processor. Try eating thin slices of it – it is wonderful.

6 servings

2½ oz (65g) unsalted butter
1 oz (25g) plain flour
12 fl.oz (350ml) milk
1 teaspoon salt
2 egg yolks, size 2
3 egg whites, size 2

To serve
9 fl.oz (275ml) double cream
3 oz (75g) fresh Parmesan, finely grated

1. Melt the butter in a small to medium pan. Add the flour, stir together and allow to cook over a medium heat for 4 minutes. This process bursts the starch cells, getting rid of the floury taste.
2. Add the milk gradually, whisking it in with a balloon whisk to ensure a smooth mixture. Bring to the boil, turn the heat down to low, and let the sauce bubble gently for 4 or 5 minutes, whisking now and again.
3. Remove from the heat, and whisk in the salt and egg yolks. Pour into a bowl and allow to cool slightly, whisking occasionally.
4. Meanwhile, brush six non-stick tins (each with a capacity of 5 fl.oz/150ml) with a little extra butter. Line the bases with rounds of Bakewell paper cut to fit exactly, then butter these also. Place on a baking tray. Pre-heat the oven to 400°F (200°C) Gas 6.

5. Whisk the egg whites in a spotless bowl (see page 42) with an electric or balloon whisk.

6. Whisk a quarter of the beaten whites into the cool mixture, then gently fold in the remainder, using a large metal spoon.

7. Divide between the six tins (they should be nearly full and rounded – do not level them with a knife), then bake for 10 minutes on the middle shelf. They will have risen well.

8. Remove from the oven. Now, they will transform in front of your eyes from well-risen soufflés into sunken wrinkled disasters, but do not worry! These are magical soufflés.

9. When you wish to serve them, which could be hours later, preheat the oven to 450°F (230°C) Gas 8. Pour the cream into six shallow round white porcelain dishes (I use Apilco 5½ in/14cm ones).

10. Gently run a round-ended knife around the inside of the tin, turn the soufflé out on to your hand, remove the paper, then place it carefully, the same way up, on to the cream. Repeat with the others. If they refuse to come out, place in the oven for a few seconds only, to melt the butter.

11. Sprinkle the Parmesan over the soufflés and the cream. Arrange on two baking trays. This can be done a little ahead of time.

12. Bake for 10 minutes, on two shelves, by which time they should have puffed up again and the cheese and cream will be golden and bubbly.

13. Remove from the oven, and serve immediately. They will be easier to handle if you sit each one on a larger, cooler plate. Sprinkle with freshly chopped herbs if you wish.

TERRINE D'AUBERGINES

SOUFFLES AUX COURGETTES

Pâtes Fraîches

Fresh Pasta

Providing that you have a food processor and a pasta roller, you should find pasta both easy and rewarding to make. There really is no comparison between home-made pasta and the bought type, even 'fresh'. I find it very satisfying to make and serve, rather like pastry. Pasta rollers come with spaghetti, tagliatelle and tagliarini cutters. Sheets of pasta can be used for ravioli, lasagne, cannelloni, tortellini, etc. Although it does not take long to make, you need to allow time to rest the dough and to allow the pasta to dry to a certain extent.

It seems a pity to mask the flavour of home-made pasta with over-elaborate sauces, so keep them simple. A lovely, but very rich, example is spaghetti dressed with grated lemon rind, fresh Parmesan and cream. You could use Greek yogurt for a lighter version, but it will not be quite so delicious!

4 servings

6 oz (175g) strong plain flour
1 teaspoon salt
1 teaspoon olive oil
1 egg, size 2
2 egg yolks, size 2

1. Place flour (don't sieve it), salt and oil in your food processor fitted with the cutting blade. Blend for a few seconds, stop, and add the egg plus the yolks. Blend again until the ingredients mix and just come together to form a ball. Turn out on to your work surface and knead gently into a smooth ball. Wrap in cling film and rest in the refrigerator for at least an hour.

2. Attach your pasta roller to a suitable work surface. Set the rollers to the widest setting.

3. Flatten the dough slightly and feed this between the rollers while you turn the handle. Fold into three, flatten again and feed back through the rollers. Repeat about six times until the dough is smooth. Flour the work surface and leave it to rest for 15-30 minutes.

4. Set the rollers one step closer. Roll out the pasta once. It will have stretched after this, so cut it in half across the way. Move the rollers another step closer and roll out again. Again it will have stretched, so cut in half to make handling easier. Lay these strips out side by side on your floured work surface. This thickness will probably be the right one for spaghetti, but if you are making ravioli or lasagne one more rolling will be needed. Of course, pasta rollers may vary, so use your discretion, but remember that during cooking, the pasta will swell. Many recipes say to roll out the pasta at the thinnest setting possible for ravioli, but this setting on my roller is so close that the pasta is 'chewed up' and tears.

If making ravioli, fill while the dough is still damp, but if cutting into spaghetti, tagliatelle, etc, allow it to dry out for half an hour, which will prevent it from sticking together. Do not leave it too long before cutting, or it will become too brittle.

Pâtes Fraîches au Caviar
Fresh Pasta with Caviar

Our introduction to caviar was such an indulgent one! Jean and Arthur Butterworth (formerly of White Moss House at Grasmere), David and I were treated to an enormous amount of caviar by our friend John Tovey at his Lakeland home. He served it with chopped hard-boiled eggs, raw onion and parsley (and iced vodka!). I think that we all surprised John by consuming it so eagerly, and he had to open another large tin of it. This was followed by *foie gras*, another of life's luxuries. I remember loving every mouthful, but by later that afternoon I also remember the room spinning around me at an alarming rate, due to the small (but obviously too much for me) amount of vodka. On another occasion in Paris, and again with John, we had a sampling of Beluga, Sevruga, Oscietra and pressed caviars at Caviar Kaspia in the Place Madeleine. Each was very different and the comparison was very interesting. This time I avoided the vodka!

We prefer Oscietra, but it can be difficult to obtain, so I sometimes use Mandarin Beluga which is less expensive than its Russian equivalent. I like to serve this in a large bowl at the table, tossing it in front of our guests, so that they can see the striking contrast of white pasta, blackish caviar and green parsley. It does not take long to make, so have your plates and serving bowl heating.

4 servings

1 quantity fresh pasta (see page 49)
seasoning
5 fl.oz (150ml) double cream
finely grated rind of 1 lemon
1 oz (25g) unsalted butter

Garnish
2 oz (50g) caviar
flat parsley

1.   Bring a large pan of water to the boil. Add ½ tablespoon salt.
2.   Pass the pasta strips through the spaghetti cutters, and drop the spaghetti into the boiling water. Bring back to the boil, being careful that it does not boil over. Boil for 3 minutes, or until *al dente*.
3.   Pour through a sieve or colander into the sink, and return to the pan. Add the cream, lemon rind and butter. Bring to the boil, gently mixing together with a wooden spoon. At this stage, keep the seasoning delicate as the caviar is very salty. One can add more at the table if necessary.
4.   Transfer to the warmed bowl (I use a large white porcelain salad bowl), spoon the caviar carefully over the top and quickly decorate the pasta with leaves of flat parsley. Serve immediately and mix together gently at the table.

Pâtes Fraîches au Citron avec Légumes Croquants

Fresh Pasta with Lemon and Crisp Vegetables

Grated lemon rind combined with pasta, cream and Parmesan gives a lovely, fresh flavour. For contrast of colour and texture I team the lemon pasta up with crisp strips of vegetables which are seasoned with fresh tarragon and crushed coriander. The pasta on its own is delicious, but visually is more striking if served on top of the vegetables. As with quite a few of my starters, this is suitable for vegetarians.

4 servings

1 quantity fresh pasta (see page 49)
2 large carrots
2 large leeks
2 medium courgettes, rinsed and dried
16 mangetout peas, rinsed and dried
2 oz (50g) unsalted butter
2 teaspoons whole coriander seeds, lightly crushed
seasoning
1 tablespoon fresh tarragon leaves
finely grated rind of 1 large lemon
5 fl.oz (150ml) double cream
2 oz (50g) fresh Parmesan cheese, grated
ground nutmeg

Garnish
flat parsley or fresh coriander leaves

1.   Prepare and roll out the pasta as described. Allow it to dry out on a floured surface until required. I like to cut it just before cooking, as that eliminates any possibility of it sticking together. However, if you want to prepare it well in advance, let it dry out for half an hour to an hour, depending on the temperature of your kitchen, then cut it using the

spaghetti cutter and place on a baking sheet sprinkled with flour. Alternatively you can hang the cut spaghetti over a wire coat hanger.

2. Put a large pan of cold water on to boil.

3. Prepare the vegetables. Wash, dry and cut the carrots into straight-sided blocks, 4 in (10cm) long. Cut these into thin slices, 1/16 in (1-2mm) thick.

4. Trim the root end off the leeks, and cut the tougher green leaves off so that the remaining leek is 4 in (10cm) long. Cut into quarters lengthwise then rinse under cold water to remove any earth. Shake dry.

5. Top and tail the mangetouts. Cut the ends from the courgettes, then cut lengthwise into thin slices, 1/16 in (1-2mm) thick.

6. Melt ½ oz (15g) of the butter in a large frying pan over a medium heat. When sizzling add the carrots and leeks, and cook for 5 minutes, stirring all the time. When cooked, but still firm, add the courgettes, the mangetouts and the crushed coriander seeds. Season with a little salt. Cook until warmed through but still crisp and firm. Remove from the heat, and add another ½ oz (15g) butter and the tarragon leaves (chop or leave whole).

7. While the vegetables are cooking, add ½ tablespoon of salt to the boiling water. If still uncut, pass the pasta through the spaghetti rollers, and throw the cut pasta into the boiling water. Bring back to the boil (be careful that it does not boil over), and cook for 3 minutes. Test by carefully removing a piece and biting it. It should be *al dente* – still with a bite left in it without it being either too soft or too hard.

8. Pour through a large sieve or colander into your sink, shake dry and return to the pan. Add the remaining butter, the grated lemon rind, cream, Parmesan and a little salt, a few turns of the pepper mill and some grated nutmeg (about an eighth of a whole one).

9. Return the pan to a medium heat and stir the ingredients with a wooden spoon. When the cream bubbles and a sauce is formed, remove from the heat. Taste to check the seasoning.

10. Divide the vegetables between four warm plates, making sure that everyone has their share of each vegetable. Flatten them out so that they are spread out over most of the plate.

11. Using a tablespoon and fork, shape a quarter of the pasta into a barrel shape by spinning it around the fork which is held perpendicular to the bowl of the spoon. Place this upright on top of the vegetables, pressing down gently to steady it. Repeat with the others. Scatter fresh flat parsley or fresh coriander over the pasta and serve immediately.

Terrine d'Aubergines
Aubergine Terrine

I have been making some dishes for years, but this recipe is a new one. I have always avoided meaty terrines as I do not find them very interesting, and they are usually rather heavy at the beginning of a meal. At the same time, terrines are very useful when entertaining as they are best made in advance, they are easy to serve, and one large terrine will provide enough for up to ten servings.

This terrine, which is made up of slices of fried aubergine, cumin and a red pepper custard, is colourful and delicious. Decorated with a little ratatouille, it makes a very elegant party dish. If you or any of your guests are vegetarian, it is ideal.

This quantity is enough for a 2 lb (900g) loaf tin. (I use a Le Creuset cast-iron loaf tin as I like its shape, but any other would do.) If you would rather make a smaller one, halve the quantities and cook for 10 minutes less.

8 servings

2¼ lb (1kg) aubergines
olive oil for frying (I use half virgin olive oil and half refined olive oil such as Pacchini. You will probably need about 5 fl.oz/150ml)
seasoning
8 oz (225g) red peppers
2-3 teaspoons ground cumin
2 eggs, size 2
3½ fl.oz (100ml) double cream

To serve and garnish
1 quantity Ratatouille (see page 145)
virgin olive oil infused with a small whole unpeeled garlic clove

1. Peel the aubergines and slice lengthwise into strips ½ in (1cm) thick. Cover a tray with a double layer of kitchen roll.
2. Heat 2 tablespoons of the oil in a large non-stick frying pan, and place in as many pieces of aubergine as you can side by side. Use tongs

or wear rubber gloves as this can be very hot work. Season with a little salt. When brown on one side, turn over. Pour a little more oil into the pan and shake hard so that the undersides all get their share. Once again, fry until golden. If the slices do not feel cooked, turn over and cook until they feel soft when pierced with a skewer. Transfer on to the kitchen roll, then repeat with the remaining slices.

3. Preheat the oven to 350°F (180°C) Gas 4.

4. To prepare the peppers (if you have a gas hob), pierce the stalk end on to a long fork and rest this over a high flame. Keep turning the pepper until it becomes completely blackened, then place in a plastic bag. Repeat with the others. Allow them to sit in the enclosed bag for about 10 minutes, then rub under cold water to remove the skin. Pull out the stalk and wash out any seeds. Cut into medium-sized pieces. (Always use a fork which is not valuable for this technique, as after a few uses it will become very marked.)

If you cook by electricity, bake the peppers in as hot an oven as possible until black, or place under a hot grill and turn until black all over. Then repeat the plastic bag and rubbing procedures.

5. Heat a tablespoon of olive oil in the frying pan, add the chopped peppers and cook gently for about 5 minutes, stirring occasionally.

6. Lightly brush your chosen loaf tin or terrine with oil, then line it completely with cling film.

7. Place a few slices of aubergine in the base of the terrine, and sprinkle with ½ teaspoon ground cumin. Repeat with the remaining slices – you should have five layers altogether.

8. Place the peppers in the liquidiser and blend until smooth. Add the eggs, a teaspoon of salt and cream and blend for a few seconds only – any longer will make the custard too frothy.

9. Pour the custard over the aubergine slices, lifting them slightly so that the custard pours down evenly through the terrine.

10. Place in a container such as a roasting tin, pour in enough boiling water to come half-way up the sides of the terrine, and carefully place on the middle shelf of your preheated oven.

11. Bake for 40-45 minutes or until a skewer, when inserted, comes out dry. Allow to cool, cover with cling film and chill.

12. To serve, turn out on to a board, trim off the outside ends and slice into ¾ in (2cm) slices using a serrated knife. Arrange on serving plates with a little mound of ratatouille to one side and then dribble a teaspoon of flavoured virgin oil around the terrine.

Foie Gras

We first experienced real *foie gras*, as opposed to *pâté de foie gras*, at La Pyramide restaurant in Vienne. Although now closed, we have a great deal of affection for this restaurant, originally run by Fernand Point and latterly by his wife Mado. It taught us so much and we feel privileged to have known it when we did.

Foie gras is one of life's luxuries, along with caviar. It is expensive, rich but absolutely delicious. Normally, fresh *foie gras* is cooked with seasonings and alcohol such as Madeira and/or Armagnac, in a terrine, and served in slices when cold. It can also be sliced when raw and pan-fried. As it is very, very high in fat, cooking it can be tricky. The first time that I tried to cook it was following a Troisgros recipe, in which it was blanched in boiling water, cooked for a minute and allowed to cool in the liquid. When I looked into the pan, in amongst a sea of grease floated my *foie gras,* now the size of a golf ball!

The method I now use is much more reliable, but it does still need care and attention. We prefer duck to goose *foie gras* as it has more flavour.

8 servings

1 fresh duck *foie gras*, 1½ lb (675g) in weight
2 teaspoons salt
½ teaspoon freshly ground white pepper
1 teaspoon caster sugar
2 tablespoons Bual Madeira
toasted sultana brioche (see page 206)

1. Place the liver in a bowl of ever so slightly warm water. This makes it more pliable and therefore easier to handle.
2. After an hour, remove it and gently break the two lobes apart. The next stage is very time-consuming, as the tubes and veins have to be removed without damaging it too much. To do this, make cuts down the side of the lobe which had been joined, and using a very sharp knife, work out the tubes and veins. It is very tedious, and just when you think that you have removed them all, you will probably find another network of them.
3. Scrape off the outer membrane which covers the liver.

4. Mix together the salt, pepper and sugar and sprinkle over the surfaces of the liver, turning it to make sure they are evenly spread. Sprinkle the Madeira over, also as evenly as possible. Fit the two lobes back together again and press into a 1-1¼ pint (600-750ml) terrine, with the smaller lobe underneath. Press down gently, cover with cling film and refrigerate overnight.

5. Next day, remove and allow it to stand at room temperature for an hour. Preheat the oven to 225°F (110°C) Gas ¼.

6. Sit the terrine in a roasting tin which you have lined with a few layers of newspaper. Fill the tin with 2 in (5cm) cold water.

7. Place on the middle shelf and cook, still covered with the cling film, for 40 minutes. By this time there should be about ¼ in (6mm) of fat floating on the surface.

8. Remove from the oven, and lift out the terrine. Cut a piece of card which will cover the *foie gras* exactly. Cover the *foie gras* loosely with a fresh piece of cling film, sit the card on top, and weigh it down with a light weight, say 7 oz (200g), which should be heavy enough to submerge the liver under the fat. When it begins to set, remove the weight and cling film, re-cover and refrigerate when cool.

9. The *foie gras* should be left like this for at least 24 hours to allow the flavours to develop.

10. To serve, remove from the refrigerator half an hour to an hour before it is needed, depending on the weather. If it is too cold, the flavour will be too subdued, but if too warm it starts to soften and becomes rather unpleasant.

11. Cut into slices ⅜ in (9mm) thick, and serve a slice on a large plate, accompanied by a couple of slices of toasted sultana brioche.

Instead of serving the *foie gras* with brioche, a thick slice of hot, salted potato is rather good. Peel large potatoes and cut into ½ in (1cm) slices, one per person. Score the flesh to form a diamond pattern ¼ in (6mm) into the surface, sprinkle liberally with salt and leave for an hour. Wipe off any excess salt and cook in a little oil or butter in a non-stick frying pan, turning over frequently until golden brown outside and tender inside. Cook fairly gently to avoid burning the outside before the inside is cooked.

We first enjoyed this contrast of cold smooth *foie gras* and hot crispy potato at Arpège in Paris, the home of one of France's most inspired young chefs, Alain Passard.

Gâteau de Foies de Dindes, Sauce aux Poivrons Doux

Turkey Liver Gâteau with Red Pepper Sauce

This is a typically Burgundian dish, although there they usually serve it with a crayfish sauce. I serve it with a red pepper sauce which contrasts well with the colour and taste of the gâteau. I use turkey livers which are firmer and larger than chicken livers, but either could be used.

6 servings

6 oz (175g) fresh turkey livers, trimmed weight
2 eggs, size 2
1 oz (25g) onions, peeled and roughly chopped
½ oz (15g) parsley
12 fl.oz (350ml) double cream
½ – 1 teaspoon salt

Sauce
½ oz (15g) unsalted butter
3 oz (75g) onion (peeled weight), finely sliced
1 large red pepper or 4 oz (100g) prepared weight
4 fl.oz (120ml) double cream
½ teaspoon salt

Garnish
4 oz (100g) turkey livers, trimmed and cut into thin slices
fresh parsley or chervil

1. Trim livers and carefully cut away any greenish parts (bile). You will need 6 oz (175g).
2. Place the eggs, onion and parsley in your liquidiser and blend until smooth. Add the livers and once again blend until smooth, then add the

cream. Blend until mixed, then add the salt. Stop after 5 seconds as the salt has a thickening action. If you leave the liquidiser on longer, the mixture becomes thick and gooey. Use straightaway, or pour into a bowl, cover and set aside until needed.

3. To make the Red Pepper Sauce, melt the butter in a small pan, add the onion and cook until softened. Stir occasionally and do not allow to brown.

4. Wash and dry the pepper. Cut the stalk out, cut in half, remove the seeds then slice finely. Add to the onions and cook gently for 10 minutes. Stir now and again.

5. Add the cream and the salt, stir together, then allow to simmer gently for 30 minutes, by which time the vegetables will be soft.

6. Pour into the liquidiser and blend until smooth. Rub through a sieve into the rinsed-out pan.

7. Set aside until needed. Preheat the oven to 350°F (180°C) Gas 4.

8. Brush six individual 5 fl.oz (150ml) non-stick tins with a little butter. Cut rounds of Bakewell paper to fit the base exactly. Fit in, then butter these also. Sit the tins in an ovenproof container which will hold enough water to come half-way up the sides of the tins.

9. Give the liver mixture a stir, then pour it into the tins. Place on the front of the middle shelf, fill the container with enough boiling water to come half-way up the sides of the tins, then slide it in carefully.

10. Bake for 25-30 minutes until firm and, if a skewer is inserted, it will come out cleanly.

11. Melt a little extra butter in a small frying pan and when hot add the liver slices. Turn over quickly to seal both sides. Depending on their thickness, this may be all that is required as they should only be lightly cooked. Keep warm until needed.

12. Reheat the sauce and check the seasoning and texture, adding a little water if it is too thick. It should lightly coat the back of a spoon.

13. Remove the tins from the oven, run a round-ended knife round the edge, then invert them on to warm serving plates.

14. Spoon some sauce either over or around them and top with a slice or two of fried liver. Decorate with fresh herbs such as chervil or parsley. Serve immediately.

Crèpes Florentines
Chicken and Spinach Pancakes

The filling for these pancakes has had many a customer guessing – most have been convinced that they are filled with broccoli as the combination of the chicken and spinach looks rather like it.

Serve one pancake as a starter, or two as a main course.

Makes 10-12

Pancakes
3 oz (75g) plain flour
salt
1 egg, size 2
1 egg yolk, size 2
4 fl.oz (120ml) each of milk and water, mixed
½ oz (15g) unsalted butter

Filling
1 oz (25g) unsalted butter
6 oz (175g) onions, peeled and finely chopped
1 garlic clove, peeled and crushed
9 oz (250g) chicken breast, skinned and boned weight and cut into strips
1½ lb (675g) frozen leaf spinach, defrosted, or 3 lb (1.4kg) fresh spinach, washed and thick stalks removed
4 fl.oz (120ml) double cream

Sauce and topping
8 fl.oz (250ml) dry white wine
10 fl.oz (300ml) double cream
2 oz (50g) Parmesan cheese, freshly grated

1. *The pancakes.* Place the flour, a pinch of salt, the egg and yolk, plus a little of the milk and water mixture into the bowl of your food processor or liquidiser. Start blending, adding the rest of the liquid while it is still running. Switch off and leave for about half an hour.

2. Heat the butter in a small omelette pan with a 6 in (15cm) diameter across the base. If I have to make a large quantity of pancakes, I use two pans at once.

3. Pour the melted butter into the batter and blend for about 5 seconds. Pour into a bowl or jug.

4. Reheat the pan over a medium heat. Have the batter close by and, using a small ladle, pour 1½ fl.oz (40ml) of batter into the pan with one hand, using the other hand to hold the pan and swirl the batter around it, covering it evenly. Cook for 30 seconds, then, using a knife with a rounded end, loosen the pancake and, gently holding the far away edge with both hands, flip it over. This is very hot so you may want to wear rubber gloves. Cook the underside for another 30 seconds, then place on a spotless teatowel and cover. Repeat this process with the remaining batter, adding a little more butter to the pan if necessary. The first side will be golden brown whereas the second side will be much paler – don't worry as this side will be inside the finished pancake anyway. At this stage, the pancakes can wait for a day if wrapped carefully in the teatowel and placed in a plastic bag.

5. *The filling.* Heat ½ oz (15g) of the butter in a frying pan and when hot, add the onion and garlic. Cook over a moderate heat until they become translucent, stirring occasionally.

6. Turn up the heat, add the strips of chicken and stir until they are just cooked through, yet still moist and tender. Remove from the heat.

7. Heat the remaining butter in a pan (a very large one if using fresh spinach), add the spinach, cover with a lid and cook until tender. Frozen will take about 10 minutes, whereas fresh will take about 5 minutes. Empty into a colander or large sieve and shake off the excess liquid.

8. Using a saucer (not your best china), press down on to the spinach so that as much liquid is eliminated as possible.

9. Fit the mincer attachment on to your Kenwood or similar and pass first the chicken mixture and then the spinach through the smallest holed cutter, allowing it to fall into a bowl.

10. Add the cream and 1½ teaspoons salt to the minced mixture and mix in well with a wooden spoon.

11. To fill the pancakes, carefully peel the top pancake from the pile. Lay it, the browner and better side downwards, on a work surface or board. Using a tablespoon, lay a heaped spoonful of filling on it, just below the centre. Fold the pancake nearest you up and over the filling, then fold first one side then the other on top. Finally roll the enclosed filling over so that the far edge of pancake ends up underneath. Try to keep it in as neat and compact a shape as possible.

12.   Lightly butter an ovenproof dish or tray and lay the filled pancakes on it, side by side. It does not matter if they touch. Cover with tin foil.

13.   *The sauce.* Place the dry white wine in a pan, bring to the boil, then boil until it has reduced to 4 tablespoons. Pour out into a small container. Pour the cream into the pan, bring to the boil and allow to simmer until it begins to thicken. Be very careful that it does not boil over – place the pan half on, half off the burner and whisk now and then. When it is thick enough to lightly coat the back of a spoon, add the reduced wine and a little salt. Set aside until required.

14.   *To serve.* Preheat the oven to 350°F (180°C) Gas 4, and bake the filled pancakes for 25-30 minutes. Light the grill so that it is very hot.

15.   Remove the pancakes from the oven and place one or two, depending on whether for a starter or main course, on heat-resistant plates. (I use 5½ in/14cm white porcelain dishes by Apilco, but there are other makes of similar dishes.)

16.   Cover with 2 or 3 tablespoons sauce, sprinkle with the freshly grated Parmesan and brown under the grill until bubbly and golden coloured.

If you do not have suitable dishes, you could pour the sauce over the pancakes in the dish in which they were reheated. Grill until golden, then carefully serve the pancakes on to heated plates, spooning some sauce over them. The appearance won't be so good though!

Saucisson de Pigeon
Pigeon Sausage

Something must have triggered my memory. I am not sure what it was. It may have been a sliced veal and pistachio sausage served with a Pecorino and oil sauce at La Chuisa in Montefollonico, maybe not. But what I was reminded of was David's mother's meat roll. I had not tasted it for years, but suddenly I remembered how good it had been. When we came back from our trip, I was given the recipe, and it was incredibly simple. (Writing a cookery book would not take long if the recipes were all like that one!) Of course, I could not resist making changes, and instead of using minced beef, I used pigeon breast, and I also cooked the mixture in sausage skins which worked very well.

The meat roll or the sausages can be served freshly made while still hot, or left to become cold and sliced thinly. Either way is delicious. A freshly made Pesto Sauce makes an interesting accompaniment.

4 servings

8 oz (225g) fresh pigeon breasts, marinated for a few hours in
1 tablespoon olive oil
4 oz (100g) unsmoked back bacon, rinded (or smoked bacon
if you prefer)
1 oz (25g) fresh white breadcrumbs, made from a day-old loaf
1 egg, size 2, beaten lightly
½ teaspoon salt
dry collagen casings, if making sausages
1 quantity Pesto Sauce (see page 65)

1. Remove all the shot from the pigeon breasts.
2. Pass the breasts and the bacon through a mincer, using the finest holed attachment. If you do not have a mincer, but a processor, blend the meats together to form a smooth paste. The character of the finished dish will be much smoother in this case. Place the minced meat in a bowl.

3. Add the breadcrumbs, the beaten egg and the salt, then mix together with your hand or with a wooden spoon, until thoroughly blended.

4. At this stage, a sausage-making attachment for a Kenwood, or whatever, would simplify matters, but failing that, a piping bag fitted with a plain ½ in (1cm) nozzle will do the trick. Fit the nozzle into the piping bag, spoon the pigeon mixture into it, close the top and shake it down to get rid of any air pockets. Twist the unfilled portion of the bag so that you can exert pressure on it without making a horrible mess.

5. With one hand, fit the sausage casing over the end of the nozzle, and hold on really well while pressing the piping bag to fill the casing. Stop now and again to gently ease the mixture evenly down the 'skin'. This amount of stuffing should fill two 12 in (60cm) lengths. Once you have filled the first length, and you have ensured that it is evenly and firmly packed, tie a knot at both ends. Cut the sausage off, and start on the other one.

6. Place the sausages in simmering water (curling them round to fit the pan), and boil gently for 25 minutes.

7. Meanwhile make the Pesto Sauce as described on the page opposite.

8. Remove the sausages, allow to cool slightly, then gently tear off the skin. Cut at an angle into slices ¼ in (5mm) thick, then arrange these, overlapping, in a semi-circle on warmed serving plates. Spoon a little sauce in the centre and serve immediately. Alternatively, allow them to become cold before slicing.

If you would rather cook the mixture as a pudding or meat roll, simply pack it into a lightly buttered basin or jar of approximately 18 fl.oz (500ml) capacity. Cut a generous piece of foil and make a pleat across the centre which will allow the filling to swell during cooking. Place the basin or jar in a pan filled with enough simmering water to come nearly half-way up the side. Cover with a tight-fitting lid and steam by simmering for 1½ hours. Check that the water does not boil dry, and top up with more boiling water if necessary.

Remove, turn out and cut in wedges. Arrange these overlapping on warm serving plates and add a puddle of Pesto Sauce. If allowed to become cold in the basin before turning out, very much thinner slices can be cut.

Sauce Pesto

Genoese Basil Sauce

Now that fresh herbs are so readily available, it should be possible to make your own pesto sauce. If fresh basil is unavailable, however, jars of commercially prepared pesto are relatively easy to find. Food processors have taken the hard work out of making this wonderful Italian sauce which would traditionally have been made by pounding the ingredients together in a mortar and pestle.

Use fresh Parmesan in this and any other recipe which asks for Parmesan cheese.

6 servings

2 oz (50g) fresh basil leaves
1 medium garlic clove, peeled
1½ oz (40g) pine kernels
1½ oz (40g) Parmesan cheese, freshly grated
¼ teaspoon salt
3 fl.oz (85ml) good olive oil

1. Place all the ingredients except the oil in your food processor fitted with the cutting blade. Process until a purée is formed.
2. Continue to blend while adding the oil in a thin stream. Stop the processor, lift off the lid, and scrape down the mixture from the sides of the bowl. Blend again so that all the ingredients are evenly mixed.
3. Scrape out into a jam jar and cover until required. It will keep for several weeks if refrigerated. The colour may change a little but it will still taste sensational. A little goes a long way and can be used to liven up pasta, risotto and vegetables, etc.

Suprème de Volaille Farci, Salade de Cresson

Stuffed Chicken Breast with Watercress Salad

Chicken breast, stuffed with a mousseline of chicken, hazelnuts and Calvados, is cooked, then sliced and arranged on a mound of watercress dressed in a hazelnut vinaigrette. The flavours marry together well, and it makes a lovely cold starter to a meal where fish is being served as the main course. Make sure that the ingredients for the mousseline are very cold, otherwise the mixture will be too soft.

6 servings

4 boned chicken breasts, approx. 4 oz (100g) each
seasoning

Mousseline
5 oz (150g) chicken breast meat
1 egg, size 2
5 fl.oz (150ml) double cream, chilled
6 teaspoons coarsely ground hazelnuts (see page 72)
1 dessertspoon Calvados

Watercress salad
2 tablespoons hazelnut oil
2 tablespoons olive oil
1 tablespoon white wine vinegar
½ teaspoon caster sugar
2-3 bunches watercress, bright green and strong, rinsed and picked over, thick stems removed

1. Preheat the oven to 350°F (180°C) Gas 4.
2. Prepare the mousseline first. Remove any little bits of bone and fat from the breast. Chop the flesh roughly and drop into the bowl of your

food processor, fitted with the cutting blade. Process until fairly smooth, add the egg and continue until smooth. Add half the cream in a stream, add ½ teaspoon salt, then the rest of the cream. Stop processing as soon as it has been added. Remove the lid, scrape down the sides of the bowl, add the hazelnuts and the Calvados, and process until just mixed. Place the bowl in the refrigerator, and chill for 30 minutes.

3.   Remove any bits of bone and fat from the four breasts, and place them, cut side down, on your chopping board (remember that it is best to keep a board especially for raw meat). Make a cut in each one, along the plumpest side, just above the natural division where the fillet is attached. Open out along this slit and season very lightly with salt.

4.   Fit a piping bag with a ⅜-½ in (9-10mm) nozzle, fill with the chilled mousseline and pipe a generous amount of it along the chicken breast. Fold back into position, partly covering the mousseline.

5.   Transfer the breasts carefully to a lightly buttered baking dish or tray, leaving a little gap between each one. Cover with tin foil and bake for 20 minutes on the middle shelf of the preheated oven.

6.   Remove, and wrap each one in cling film straightaway, in order to keep them as moist as possible. Cool, then refrigerate.

7.   Make the watercress dressing by combining the oils, vinegar, ¼ teaspoon salt and the sugar in a jam jar. Shake vigorously to combine the ingredients. The dressing has a higher proportion of nut oil than usual as you want its flavour to dominate.

8.   Place the prepared watercress in a bowl, and just before serving, pour the well-shaken dressing over it. Toss together gently and place a mound in the centre of each plate.

9.   Unwrap the chicken, trim off the outer ends, then slice each one at an angle, into six evenly thick pieces, giving four per person. Arrange them, overlapping slightly, around the mound of watercress. Serve immediately.

Mousseline de Volaille au Roquefort

Mousseline of Chicken with Roquefort

Meat mousselines tend to be slightly heavier than those made with fish, so these chicken mousselines are lightened by using natural yogurt as well as double cream. The Roquefort filling is enhanced by serving an apple-flavoured hollandaise with it.

6 servings

10 oz (275g) chicken breast, boned and trimmed
3 heaped tablespoons natural low-fat yogurt
2 eggs, size 2
9 fl.oz (275ml) double cream, chilled
1 teaspoon salt

Roquefort butter filling
1 oz (25g) unsalted butter
2 oz (50g) Roquefort cheese

Apple hollandaise
10 oz (275g) Granny Smith apples
2 teaspoons demerara sugar
½ teaspoon powdered cinnamon
⅓ oz (9g) unsalted butter
1-2 tablespoons Calvados
1 quantity Sauce Hollandaise (see page 73)

Garnish
fresh chervil or sweet cicely, and apple slices

1.   Cut the chicken into medium-sized pieces, and place in your food processor fitted with the cutting blade, along with the yogurt. Blend for about 30 seconds, then add the eggs. Continue to blend until smooth. Empty out into a bowl, cover and chill for at least 2 hours.
2.   Make the filling by softening the butter, then mash it into the Roquefort using a fork or knife. It should be thoroughly mixed but it does not need to be too smooth.

3. Place a sheet of cling film on your work surface, form the Roquefort butter into a square or rectangle ½ in (1cm) deep on it, wrap it up, then chill until required, by which time it should be hard.

4. Remove the chicken mixture from the refrigerator and gradually add the chilled cream using an electric hand-held beater. Add the salt once half the cream has been added. Use a rubber bowl scraper to make sure that any mixture up the sides of the bowl is incorporated. At this stage the mousseline will be softer than the sole mousseline, but it will firm up in the refrigerator. Chill again for at least 2 hours.

5. Meanwhile make the apple purée for the hollandaise. Preheat the oven to 350°F (180°C) Gas 4. Brush an ovenproof dish with a little extra butter. Peel, core and thinly slice the apples into the dish. Sprinkle with the sugar and cinnamon and dot with the butter. Cover loosely with tin foil and bake until tender, about 30 minutes.

6. Remove, uncover and, while still hot, flame the apples, by heating the Calvados in a ladle, lighting it with a match and pouring it over. Stir the flaming Calvados through them.

7. Liquidise until smooth, then rub through a sieve into a bowl.

8. Raise oven temperature to 375°F (190°C) Gas 5. Lightly brush six ramekins (4 fl.oz/120ml capacity) with extra butter. Sit these in an ovenproof dish (see note 7, page 70).

9. Cut the Roquefort butter into six cubes. Spoon the mousseline mixture into a nylon piping bag, fitted with a ½ in (1cm) plain nozzle.

10. Half-fill each ramekin, place a cube of Roquefort butter in the centre, then cover with the remaining mousseline, spiralling from the outside into the centre.

11. Place the dish of ramekins on the front of the middle shelf, pour in enough boiling water to come half-way up the sides of the ramekins, and slide the dish carefully into the oven.

12. Bake for 25 minutes until set.

13. Meanwhile make the Sauce Hollandaise, adding the apple purée at the end of the process.

14. Run a round-ended knife around the mousseline, turn out on to your hand, preferably rubber-gloved, and invert on to a warm serving plate. Repeat with the others, then coat each one with 2 tablespoons of the apple hollandaise. (Make sure that this is smooth by giving it a short blend before using it.) Decorate with a sprig of fresh herb such as chervil or sweet cicely and place some finely sliced Granny Smith to one side. Serve immediately.

Mousseline de Sole et de Saumon Fumé

Sole and Smoked Salmon Mousseline

I am very grateful to the late Michael Smith for including his recipe for Sole Creams in his book, *Fine English Cookery*. This, and my other mousseline recipes, are adaptations of that recipe.

Use sole which you have skinned yourself, or which has had the skin cut off by your fishmonger. Some sole which seems to have been skinned may still have a thin but very tough membrane left if the skin has been torn rather than cut off. When the sole is processed, these membranes form stringy ribbons through it.

6 servings

Sole mousseline
7½ oz (215g) lemon sole, skinned weight
7½ fl.oz (225 ml) double cream, chilled
1½ eggs, size 2
¾ teaspoon salt

Smoked salmon mousseline
2½ oz (65g) smoked salmon, finely sliced
a little milk
2½ fl.oz (65ml) double cream, chilled
½ egg, size 2
¼ teaspoon salt

To serve and garnish
1 quantity Sauce Hollandaise (see page 73)
fresh dill or fennel fronds

1. To start with, soak the smoked salmon in a little milk in a bowl. Chill both quantities of cream until needed. If the cream is not cold, the mixtures will not stiffen and will not give such good results.

2. Roughly cut up the skinned sole. Blend in your food processor fitted with the cutting blade. Add the eggs and blend until smooth. Empty out into a bowl, cover and chill in the coldest part of your refrigerator for at least 2 hours.

3. Lift the smoked salmon out of the milk and squeeze to remove excess milk. This process removes some of the salt and oil in the salmon. Blend, adding the half egg, then transfer to a small bowl. Cover and refrigerate. There is no need to wash the processor bowl and blade between these two processes.

4. Using an electric hand-held mixer, gradually add the chilled cream to the sole mixture. Once half of the cream has been added, add the salt which will help to stiffen the mousseline. From time to time, scrape the mixture down from the sides of the bowl using a rubber spatula, to ensure an even mix. Cover and refrigerate again, for at least 2 hours.

5. Repeat this process with the smoked salmon mixture.

6. Preheat the oven to 375°F (190°C) Gas 5.

7. Brush six ramekins (4 fl.oz/120ml capacity) with a little butter. Sit these inside a roasting tin, pyrex dish or suitable ovenproof container – it has to be sufficiently deep to be able to hold enough water to come half-way up the sides of the ramekins.

8. Fill a nylon piping bag fitted with a ½ in (1cm) nozzle with the sole mixture. Pipe it into the ramekins, 3 oz (75g) in each one.

9. Place the salmon mixture into the same bag and insert the tip of the nozzle into the centre of the sole mousseline. Holding it steady, pipe one-sixth into the centre of each one, making it puff up a little.

10. Place the dish of ramekins on the front of the middle shelf, fill with boiling water to come half-way up the sides of them, and slide the dish into the oven.

11. Bake for 25 minutes until slightly risen and barely golden on top. When pressed gently they should feel firm, but not rubbery. Remove and allow to rest for a few minutes.

12. Towards the end of their cooking, make the Sauce Hollandaise.

13. Holding a ramekin in your left hand, run a round-bladed knife around the edge of the mousseline. Turn it out on to your right hand, then carefully invert it on to a warmed serving plate. Repeat with the others. This step is much easier if you wear rubber gloves!

14. Spoon some hollandaise over the top, decorate with a sprig of fresh dill or fennel, and serve immediately.

Mousseline de Sole aux Noisettes à l'Orange

Mousseline of Sole with Hazelnuts and Orange

This is made using the same method as the sole and smoked salmon mousseline, but rather than two different mixtures being made, a proportion of the sole mixture is combined with grated orange rind and ground hazelnuts and used as the filling.

6 servings

10 oz (275g) lemon sole, skinned weight
2 eggs, size 2
10 fl.oz (300ml) double cream, chilled
1 teaspoon salt
finely grated rind of ½ orange
6 teaspoons ground hazelnuts (grind whole hazelnuts, complete with skins, in food processor until fine. Do not over-process or they will become oily)

To serve and garnish
1 quantity Sauce Hollandaise (see opposite)
dill, fennel or parsley

1.   Make the mousseline as described in the previous recipe, using the sole, eggs, cream and salt.
2.   Remove one-quarter of the mixture and place in another bowl. Add to this smaller quantity the finely grated orange rind and the ground hazelnuts, mixing them in lightly but thoroughly.
3.   Chill for an hour or two. Preheat the oven to 375°F (190°C) Gas 5.
4.   Pipe and cook the mousselines as described in the previous recipe.
5.   Meanwhile, make the Sauce Hollandaise.
6.   Turn out the mousselines as described in the previous recipe.
7.   Spoon some hollandaise over the top of each and decorate with a sprig of fresh dill, fennel or parsley. Serve immediately.

Sauce Hollandaise

Hollandaise Sauce

This method of making hollandaise is so easy in comparison to the traditional method. Make it shortly before serving so that you do not have to reheat it. It will keep warm for about 15 minutes if kept covered. Anyone who has John Tovey's cookery books will be familiar with this recipe. If your food processor is a large one, you may have to increase the quantity, but do not *decrease* it.

6-8 servings

3 egg yolks, size 2
1 teaspoon caster sugar
1 tablespoon white wine vinegar
2 tablespoons lemon juice
6 oz (175g) unsalted butter

1. Place the yolks and sugar in a food processor fitted with the metal cutting blade. Cover with the lid.
2. Heat the vinegar and lemon juice in a small pan. Heat the butter in another small pan.
3. When the lemon juice mixture has started to boil, start blending the yolks. After a few seconds gradually pour in the lemon juice. Once this has been added, pour in the bubbling butter. It should be very hot in order to cook the egg yolks. Switch off and keep covered until needed.

Unless your pans have good pouring spouts at one side, transfer the hot liquids to a jug, otherwise you may end up dribbling more outside the processor than inside it!
4. Before using the sauce, blend again as it will have thickened as the butter cools down. It will be lumpy unless you do this. If it is too thick, add a tablespoon or two of warm water.

Gâteau de Smokies, Sauce Vierge

Arbroath Smokies Mousse with Virgin Olive Oil Sauce

Over many years we have had a great deal of pleasure dining at the Peat Inn. We have often talked together with the Wilsons until 3am, catching up on gossip relating to the restaurant and hotel business. Every time that I make this recipe I think of them, as it is based on one of David Wilson's most publicised dishes, a little flan of Arbroath smokies. I have varied the cooking time and method, and have changed the sauce and presentation, so it is quite different from his lovely version. Choose smokies which are large and moist. Some can be rather dry and dull, so avoid them if you can. I serve the 'gâteau' with the Sauce Vierge which complements the strong taste of the fish.

When buying crème fraîche for this dish, check on its fat content. True crème fraîche should have a fat content of 40 per cent, equivalent to whipping cream, but there is a certain brand which is only 18 per cent, the equivalent to single or soured cream. Although undoubtedly much lower in calories and also much healthier, the lower fat variety produces a drier, less delicate result in my recipe. If this is the only type available to you, mix it with double cream so that the average works out at 40 per cent, i.e. 5 fl.oz (150ml) double cream to 2 fl.oz (50ml) 18 per cent crème fraîche (or soured cream).

6 servings

2-3 large smokies, to give 10 oz (275g) flesh once skinned and boned
3 eggs, size 2
7 fl.oz (200ml) crème fraîche (see above)
juice of ½ large lemon
½ teaspoon salt
a little melted butter

To serve and garnish
1 quantity Sauce Vierge (see page 76)
fresh dill or fennel fronds

74

1.   Preheat oven to 325°F (160°C) Gas 3.

2.   Lay the smokies on an ovenproof tray or dish, place in the heated oven and leave for 10 minutes. This makes it easier to remove the skin.

3.   Remove, and separate the flesh from the skin and bones, placing the flesh in a bowl as you do so. Check very carefully as some of the bones are difficult to see.

4.   Weigh out 10 oz (275g) flesh and place in the bowl of your food processor fitted with the cutting blade. Blend until fairly smooth, then break in the eggs. Continue to blend until very smooth, then add the crème fraîche and lemon juice, and finally the salt. Stop processing once the salt has been mixed in.

5.   Transfer back to the bowl, using a spatula to remove every drop.

6.   Brush six individual tins (5 fl.oz/150ml in capacity) with melted butter. Cut out rounds of Bakewell paper to fit the bases, place inside and brush with melted butter also.

7.   Divide the smokies mixture evenly between the tins, then sit them inside a dish or tray which is deep enough to hold water to come half-way up the sides of them. Place the tray in the front of the middle shelf, pour in enough boiling water, then slide into the oven.

8.   Bake for 35-40 minutes, by which time the gâteaux will be set but still moist.

9.   Meanwhile, make the Sauce Vierge. Towards the end of the 35-40 minutes, warm the sauce by sitting the pan in a larger one containing simmering water.

10.   Remove the gâteaux and let them rest for a minute or two. Run a round-ended knife round between the gâteau and the tin, dry the base of the tin by dabbing it on a cloth and turn out on to warmed plates, placing slightly to the top of the plate.

11.   Spoon a tablespoon of the sauce, avoiding the garlic, to the other side. Decorate the gâteau with a frond of dill or fennel and serve immediately.

As a main course for fish-eating vegetarians, I often serve the gâteau in the centre of a plate, surrounded by a circle of overlapping sliced, *al dente* new potatoes, coated with the sauce. If made with cold gâteaux, place the dishes (ovenproof ones, of course) into a very hot oven for 10-15 minutes, to heat thoroughly. During this time the potatoes absorb the basil-flavoured oil and become slightly crisp on the edges. Serve piping hot, decorated with dill or fennel fronds.

Sauce Vierge
Virgin Olive Oil Sauce

Choose an interesting virgin olive oil for this. Delicatessens should have a wide range, all with their own character and flavour. The only way to find your favourite is by trial and error which, I am afraid, will be rather expensive. Two that we like at the moment are *Badia a Coltibuono* and one from Peck, a highly respected food shop in Milan. We are very fortunate in having a marvellous Italian food, wine and kitchen bits and pieces shop in Edinburgh called Valvona and Crolla. It is a real gem, and the owners and staff are so nice.

6 servings

2 fl.oz (50ml) virgin olive oil
4 large leaves fresh basil, finely chopped
a pinch of salt
1 small garlic clove, with skin left on
1 large firm red beef tomato or 2 smaller ones

1.   Warm the olive oil in a small pan over a low heat. Remove from the heat and add the basil, salt, and the whole unpeeled clove of garlic. Let these flavours develop by leaving the pan aside for at least an hour.
2.   Meanwhile prepare the tomato(es). Cut down from the stalk end, then cut each half in two or three depending on size. Cut out the seeds and core, then place the pieces skin side down. Flatten with one hand while cutting the flesh away from the skin with a small sharp knife. Cut each piece into strips ¼ in (6mm) wide, then cut across diagonally to form diamond shapes (or cut into ¼ in/6mm squares).
3.   Add these to the oil shortly before serving. Place the small pan in a larger, shallower one containing a little simmering water. Heat together for about 10 minutes. Remove the garlic and serve a tablespoon of sauce with the appropriate dish.

Crèpes Parmentières
Potato Pancakes with Smoked Salmon and Caviar

On our annual trips around France, we always find it difficult to resist going to Georges Blanc's three-star restaurant at Vonnas. Every time we visit, there are many changes to look at, but as the environment becomes more and more like Disneyland, at least the food remains unchanged. One dish which I had enjoyed as far back as 1985 is fortunately still on his menu: it is a delicious combination of smoked salmon, caviar, potato pancakes and a lemon sauce, a luxury version of his very famous Crèpes Vonnassiennes.

6 servings

Potato pancakes
8 oz (225g) potatoes, peeled weight
seasoning
2 tablespoons milk
1½ tablespoons plain flour
1½ eggs, size 2
2 egg whites, size 2
1½ tablespoons double cream
½ oz (15g) unsalted butter

Filling
8 oz (225g) piece smoked salmon
1 oz (25g) caviar

Lemon cream sauce
5 fl.oz (150ml) crème fraîche or whipping cream
finely grated rind of 1 lemon

Garnish
fresh dill

1.   To make the pancakes, cut the potatoes into even-sized pieces, then boil in salted water until tender. Drain well, then rub through a sieve into a bowl.

2.   Using a wooden spoon, gently beat in the milk, then the flour, then the eggs and egg whites, then finally the cream. Cover and allow this batter to stand for at least half an hour.

3.   Place the smoked salmon on your chopping board and slice it, at an angle, into slices ⅛ in (3mm) thick. Cut these slices into pieces approximately 1½ in (4cm) square. Place on a plate and cover until required.

4.   For the sauce, simply heat the cream with the lemon rind, allowing it to simmer gently until slightly thickened. Do not salt it as the contrast between it and the salty caviar and smoked salmon is intentional.

5.   Open the caviar. (Sounds silly, but I find the jars quite difficult to open. You need to work quickly when making the pancakes so have everything ready.)

6.   Melt a quarter of the butter in a medium-sized non-stick frying pan over a medium heat. When hot, place tablespoons of the batter side by side, leaving room for them to spread. You will probably be able to cook four at one time. As soon as you have spooned out the fourth, it is time to place a ½ teaspoon of caviar in the middle of each pancake, then top the caviar with a slice of smoked salmon. When this has been completed, it will be time to turn the pancakes over, using a palette knife or spatula. As it only takes seconds for the underneath to cook, transfer them on to a plate straightaway. Keep warm in a low oven while making the other pancakes. Add more butter to the pan and repeat the process.

7.   Make sure that the sauce is warm enough, beat it with a balloon whisk to make it slightly frothy, then divide between the warmed serving plates. Arrange three pancakes overlapping on the sauce, decorate with fresh dill and serve immediately.

Les Tricornes de Saumon Fumé

Smoked Salmon Pastry Puffs

These little pastry triangles are filled with the same smoked salmon mousseline as I use in the Mousseline de Sole et Saumon Fumé (see page 70). I like to serve them with a bright green fresh basil and spinach sauce, which contrasts well with their flavour and colour.

Filo, which is pastry in very thin sheets, can either be home made or commercially prepared, but for convenience I will describe making the triangles with the bought variety. It is generally sold frozen, and is readily available at delicatessens and some supermarkets. Allow it to defrost completely before attempting to unroll it, otherwise it will split. Remove the required number of sheets, seal the extra ones securely and re-freeze them. Filo dries up rapidly, so unless you work very quickly, cover the sheets not being used with a clean teatowel.

6 servings

4 sheets filo pastry, approx. 20×11 in (50×28cm)
2 oz (50g) unsalted butter

Mousseline
5 oz (150g) smoked salmon, thinly sliced
a little milk
1 egg, size 2
5 fl.oz (150ml) double cream, chilled
¼ teaspoon salt

Spinach and basil sauce
1 lb (450g) fresh spinach, washed, thick stalks removed,
or 8 oz (225g) frozen spinach, defrosted
1½ oz (40g) fresh basil leaves, any large stalks removed
5 fl.oz (150ml) chicken stock
7½ fl.oz (225ml) double cream
seasoning

1.   Make the mousseline mixture in exactly the same way as described on page 70-1.

2.   Lay the sheets of filo on top of each other on a work surface and, using a ruler as a guide, divide into three strips, approximately 6½ in (16cm) wide by 11 in (28cm) long. Stack these together and cover with a teatowel.

3.   Melt the butter in a small pan.

4.   Lay two or three strips of filo out on your work surface. Using a wide pastry or paint brush (I use a 3 in/7.5cm wide paint brush), brush the right-hand half of each strip with butter. Fold in half so that the butter is covered. Brush this top surface with more butter. Your strip will now be just over 3 in (7.5cm) wide by 11 in (28cm) long.

5.   Using two teaspoons, place a heaped teaspoon of mousseline mixture on the left-hand side of the strip, left of centre and 1½ in (4 cm) up from the bottom.

6.   Cross the bottom right-hand corner diagonally over the filling. Lift the left-hand corner up and over, holding the new right-hand corner down lightly. Fold the new left-hand corner diagonally across, then repeat the process of folding up and over then across until you run out of filo and a triangle is formed.

7.   Turn them so that the final corner of pastry is underneath; press this in place. Brush with more melted butter. Place on a lightly buttered baking tray and repeat the process with the other strips of filo to make twelve triangles in all.

8.   Allow to chill for at least an hour before using, and preheat the oven to 400°F (200°C) Gas 6.

9.   To make the sauce, bring a pan of water to the boil, drop in the spinach and cook for 4-5 minutes. Add the basil and continue to boil for a minute.

10.   Remove from the heat, pour into a colander or sieve, then run cold water through the spinach, to cool it down quickly. This ensures that the colour is set and will remain as bright a green as possible. When completely cold, squeeze out the excess water.

11.   Place the chicken stock in a pan, bring to the boil and reduce until 4 tablespoons remain. Add the cream, move the pan half on, half off the burner to prevent the cream from boiling over, and allow it to simmer until it begins to thicken.

SOLE TISSEE A L'AIGRE DOUX

SAUMON CROQUANTE A LA SAUGE

12. Combine the spinach and basil with the creamy liquid in a liquidiser and blend until a very smooth consistency is reached. Pour back into the pan, and taste for seasoning.

13. Bake the salmon pastries in the preheated oven for 15 minutes, by which time they will be golden brown and crisp. Be sure that they are not too close to each other on the baking tray as they puff up a little, and you do not want them to touch each other. Use two trays if necessary.

14. Make sure that the sauce is hot enough, but avoid boiling it as this would impair the colour. If it is too thick, add a little water.

15. Ladle some sauce into the middle of each heated serving plate. Carefully tilt the plate, using a circular movement, so that the sauce spreads evenly within the inner rim of the plate.

16. Sit one salmon pastry on top of the sauce, then rest the other one against it, at an angle. Serve immediately, being careful that they do not move about on the sauce.

Feuilleté d'Oeufs Brouillés au Saumon Fumé

Scrambled Egg and Smoked Salmon Pastry

Serve this as part of a very special breakfast, or as a light meal. I love the combination of scrambled egg and smoked salmon (as long as the eggs are soft and creamy in texture), and here they are sandwiched between two thin layers of crisp flaky pastry.

6 servings

10 oz (275g) flaky pastry (see page 199)
9 eggs, size 2
1 garlic clove, unpeeled
seasoning
4 oz (100g) smoked salmon, sliced
½ oz (15g) unsalted butter

Garnish
2½ fl.oz (65ml) double or whipping cream
6 teaspoons Keta (salmon roe)
fresh dill or flat parsley

1. Lightly flour your work surface and roll the pastry to a thickness of ⅛ in (3mm). Using a large plain cutter, 3½-4 in (9-10cm) in diameter, stamp out six rounds. Do not twist the cutter as this will alter the shape of the rounds during cooking. Sprinkle a baking tray with a little cold water and shake off the excess.
2. Turn the pastry rounds upside down on to the tray leaving a little space between each one. Place in the refrigerator to rest for at least half an hour.
3. Preheat the oven to 400°F (200°C) Gas 6.
4. Break the eggs into a bowl and beat together with a large fork. It is not necessary to beat too hard, just enough to mix thoroughly. Stick

the unpeeled garlic on to the prongs of the fork and leave in the eggs for 15 minutes. This will be long enough to subtly flavour the eggs. Season with salt and freshly ground black pepper.

5. Cut the smoked salmon into strips or pieces. Lightly whip the garnish cream and keep chilled.

6. Remove the pastry rounds from the refrigerator, dip a pastry brush into the beaten eggs and use this to paint the top surface of the pastry. Do not let it dribble down the sides as this will prevent even rising. Using a pointed knife, lightly mark the tops with three or four lines in one direction then three or four at an angle to form diamonds.

7. Bake in the preheated oven for 15 minutes until golden brown and crisp.

8. Meanwhile, melt the butter over a fairly high heat, add the eggs when hot, then turn the heat down. Cook the eggs very gently, stirring frequently with a wooden spoon. They should remain creamy without being too runny and should not be in the least bit dry. If you do happen to over-cook them, rescue them by adding another lightly beaten egg and stir in, off the heat. While the eggs are still soft, add the smoked salmon and stir in. Remove from the heat.

9. Remove the pastry rounds from the oven, and loosen with a palette knife or fish slice. Cut each one in two horizontally, using a serrated knife. Place the bottom on each warmed serving plate, divide the scrambled eggs between them and cover with the top round.

10. Using a piping bag fitted with a large star nozzle, pipe a swirl of cream on the plate to one side of the pastry. Top with a teaspoon of salmon roe and decorate with a little fresh dill or flat parsley. Serve immediately. The cream will start to melt on the warm plate but it does not really matter. To avoid this, you could pipe the cream on to a large thin slice of lemon.

Feuilletés de Saumon
Salmon Pastries

Roughly ten years ago, *feuilletés* of one sort or another were all the rage in France and in Britain. As with most fashions, it now seems rather infra-dig to serve them, as if they are relics of the past. But there is no reason for this, as a dish which was delicious and attractive in the past should be every bit as good now. Naturally, nutritional awareness may make some dishes less popular nowadays, but that is a different matter.

The most wonderful *feuilleté* that I remember was one that we had at L'Oasis at La Napoule on the Côte d'Azur. Sadly, the restaurant is now closed, but the memory of the dish lingers on. Thin slices of salmon were sandwiched between even thinner layers of pastry and served with a delicious creamy sauce. The presentation was so perfect, the flavours and textures gave so much pleasure that I wished it would never end. Well! Having said all that, here is, I am afraid, a much simpler version, but I hope it too gives pleasure.

6 servings

12 oz (350g) flaky pastry (see page 199)
1¾ lb (800g) middle cut fresh salmon, boned (see page 88)
1 egg yolk
seasoning

Champagne sauce
7½ fl.oz (225ml) champagne (drink the rest of the bottle with the dish)
5 fl.oz (150ml) chicken stock
up to 10 fl.oz (300ml) double cream

Garnish
3oz (75g) shallot or onion, peeled and chopped
fresh chervil or flat parsley

1. Lightly flour your work surface, then roll out the pastry into a large rectangle, just over ⅛ in (3mm) thick and measuring just over 5×15 in (13×38cm). Lift it up occasionally to check that it is not

sticking otherwise it becomes very stretched and will twist out of shape as it cooks.

2. Using a long sharp knife, trim the edges. Do not drag the pastry as you cut it, rather use a clean downward cutting action. Cut the remaining rectangle into six smaller ones, 5×2½ in (13×6cm).

3. Sprinkle a large baking tray with cold water and shake off the excess. Lay the pastry rectangles upside down on the tray, leaving a little gap between each one. Place in the refrigerator to rest for at least half an hour.

4. Preheat oven to 425°F (220°C) Gas 7.

5. Cut the salmon into slices ⅜ in (9mm) thick and remove the skin. Place on a lightly buttered baking tray in one layer, but they can touch each other without any problem if necessary. Cover with cling film until required.

6. Place the champagne in a pan, bring to the boil and reduce by fast boiling until only 2 tablespoons remain. Add the stock, bring back to the boil and reduce by half. Add most of the cream, and simmer, whisking it occasionally with a balloon whisk. Reduce until it forms a smooth, shiny sauce which will coat the back of a spoon. If it thickens too much, add the rest of the cream. Keep to one side while cooking the pastry and salmon.

7. Brush the top of the pastry rectangles with the egg yolk (thinned down with a drop or two of cold water). Take care not to let any dribble down the side of the pastry. Make four or five diagonal light cuts in one direction, and the same in the other to mark a diamond pattern on the surface.

8. Bake on the middle shelf of the preheated oven for 12-15 minutes until golden brown on top and risen. They will not be high like vol-au-vents, so don't worry if they look too flat.

9. During the last 5 minutes, cook the salmon (which you have seasoned lightly with salt and sprinkled with cold water – no need to cover) by placing it alongside or on the shelf below the pastry. Reheat the sauce and taste for seasoning.

10. Loosen the pastry with a spatula or fish slice, cut each one in half horizontally using a serrated knife, and place the base on heated serving plates. Divide the salmon between them, coat with a little sauce, letting some of it spill on to the plate. Sprinkle with chopped shallot or onion, some chervil or parsley, place the lid of pastry back on, and serve immediately.

Saumon Fumé avec Rubans de Légumes à la Coriandre

Home-Smoked Salmon with Vegetable Strips and Coriander

Not smoked salmon as you know it, but chunks of warm salmon with a sweet and smoky flavour. Home smokers come in a variety of sizes, but the smallest is big enough for this dish which will serve four to six people as a starter. The soft salmon contrasts well with the colourful, crisp strips of vegetables. As with the Saumon Croquant (opposite), remember to under-cook the salmon in order to keep it moist. Follow the instructions for your smoker. I tried without success to keep it lit outside, but I eventually discovered that it fitted perfectly over my gas hob in the kitchen. If you do try this, an extractor hood over the hob is essential!

4-6 servings

2 large carrots
2 large leeks
2 medium courgettes, rinsed and dried
16-24 mangetouts, rinsed and dried
3 fresh salmon steaks, each 1½ in (4cm) thick, from the middle cut
Maldon sea salt
1 oz (25g) unsalted butter
1 tablespoon coriander seeds, crushed
1 tablespoon fresh tarragon leaves

Garnish
flat parsley or tarragon

1. Prepare the vegetables as in the previous recipe.
2. Light the smoker, place the salmon steaks on the grid and cover with the lid. Allow to smoke for 20 minutes. Keep your eye on it to check that the burner (if you are using it) remains lit.
3. Meanwhile light the oven as high as it will go.

86

4. After 20 minutes the salmon will be half cooked, the outside being pale pink and the flesh nearest the bone rather translucent still. Remove the steaks and place on a chopping board.

5. Pull off the skin, then, using a knife, work the flesh away from the bone. Cut the resulting pieces into chunks, roughly ¾ in (2cm) square. Place on a buttered baking tray, and sprinkle liberally with lightly crushed sea salt. While the vegetables are cooking, place the salmon into the very hot oven for 5 minutes. This should be long enough to complete the cooking process without *over*-cooking.

6. Melt half the butter in a large frying pan over a medium heat. When sizzling, add the carrots and the leeks, and cook for 5 minutes, stirring all the time. When cooked, but still firm, add the courgettes, the mangetouts and the crushed coriander seeds. Season with a little salt. Cook until warmed through but still crisp and firm. Remove from the heat and add the remaining butter and the tarragon leaves (chop or leave whole).

7. Arrange the vegetables (reheated if necessary) in the centre of your warmed plates, making sure that everyone gets some of every vegetable. Place the chunks of salmon in the centre and decorate nonchalantly with sprigs of tarragon or flat parsley.

Saumon Croquant à la Sauge, Sauce Vierge
Crisp Salmon with Deep-Fried Sage and Virgin Olive Oil Sauce

I love this dish. I love the contrast of crisp dark skin and the pink, lightly cooked salmon, and I love the dressed salad leaves, the olive oil sauce, the crisply fried sage leaves . . .

In 1985, on our annual trip around France, we stopped for two nights at one of our favourite restaurants, Centenaire at Les Eysies-de-Tayac in the Dordogne. It was here that I first tasted fillet of salmon which had been cooked from the skin side only, producing a wonderful contrast between crisp skin and moist flesh. It was a revelation, as up until then any salmon that I had tasted had been cooked through, making it really rather dull. Since then, apart from cooking it this way myself, variations on this method of cooking salmon have cropped up all over the place and it has become very fashionable. The important thing to remember is that by under-cooking salmon slightly, its marvellous taste and texture are enhanced.

6 servings

2 lb (900g) middle cut salmon (fresh of course)
4 oz (100g) each of fresh spinach, *lollo rosso* and oak leaf, rinsed,
dried and any wilted leaves discarded
6 large leaves fresh basil
2 tablespoons French Dressing (see page 150)
6 tablespoons Sauce Vierge (see page 76)
30-36 large leaves fresh sage
oil for deep-frying (e.g. Flora)
2 teaspoons hazelnut oil
Maldon sea salt

1.   Bone the salmon into two flat fillets, with skin on one side of each piece. To do this, place the piece of salmon on its side, insert a thin sharp knife along the central bone, and work it up towards its back. Keep your knife as close to the bones as possible. Cut through the skin, having cut off any fins that are in the way (use scissors for this). Hold this loose flesh in your left hand, assuming that you are right-handed, while cutting the flesh from the bones in the other direction, towards the belly of the fish. Use scissors to cut along the fatty edge as you do not want to include this part. Turn the fish over and repeat the process. You will now have two slabs of salmon with skin on one side of each piece. Run your fingers over the flesh to check for bones and remove any with tweezers (sterilised by boiling for 5 minutes).
2.   Place the fillets skin side down on a chopping board and cut each one into three strips, giving you six even-sized rectangles of salmon with skin on one side of each one. Place on a plate, cover and keep cool until required.
3.   Finely shred equal quantities of the spinach, *lollo rosso* and oak

leaf, along with the fresh basil. Place in a bowl which is large enough for the leaves to be tossed together with the dressing.

4. Make the Sauce Vierge and the French Dressing. Preheat the oven to 350°F (180°C) Gas 4. Place the pan of Sauce Vierge in simmering water and heat gently.

5. Start off by frying the sage leaves, as deep-frying is potentially dangerous and you will need all your concentration to cook the salmon and to complete the other processes. The fried leaves can be reheated quickly just before serving. Heat the oil in a large pan. Test for temperature by dropping in a little piece of stale white bread. It will become golden in 30 seconds when the oil is hot enough. Alternatively, use a thermometer and heat to 350°F (180°C). Carefully drop in the sage and fry for about 30 seconds. Remove with a slotted spoon and drain on kitchen roll.

6. Heat the hazelnut oil in a large non-stick frying pan over a moderate to high temperature. (If you have an extractor fan over your cooker, set it to the highest setting!) When the oil is hot, add the salmon pieces, skin side down, side by side. From this moment they will take 6-8 minutes to cook depending on the thickness of the salmon. Do not guess the timing – look at the clock or set a timer. Season lightly with salt.

7. Allow the salmon to cook for 1 minute, then, using tongs, carefully turn each piece on to its side, then on to its front, then the other side and back on to the skin. This will seal each surface. Continue to cook for another 2 minutes, turn on to the opposite side for another minute, then turn over to cook on its skin for the final cooking time. The skin should be dark brown and very crisp. If it has not browned, turn the heat up and colour it quickly without over-cooking the fish.

8. Remove the salmon from the pan. Place on a baking tray or plate, skin side up. Keep warm in the oven until ready to serve, but work quickly as you do not want to over-cook the salmon. Reheat the sage leaves in the oven.

9. Toss the shredded salad leaves with the 2 tablespoons French Dressing (shake thoroughly before using).

10. Place a mound of these leaves on one side of warm serving plates. Position the salmon, skin side up, in the centre of the plates, then pour a tablespoon of Sauce Vierge to the other side. Sprinkle the skin with lightly crushed sea salt, then top with the leaves of fried sage, laying them out side by side on the skin. Serve immediately.

Saumon Grillé

Barbecued Salmon

At home we have a covered balcony attached to our dining room. This means that we can barbecue 'out of doors', then bring the food into the dining room, which is far more comfortable, especially if it is raining, or, as has been the case a few times, snowing!

One of my very favourite foods is barbecued salmon. Fortunately, David is a dab hand at this, managing to achieve the essential combination of blackened crisp skin and meltingly, lightly cooked flesh. Cooked too long it becomes dull and dry, but if the timing is right it is wonderful. Eaten just as it is with a few new potatoes or fresh vegetables, it makes a lovely, healthy and simple meal, but if you want to dress it up then a Sauce Vierge or a Sauce Chanterelle make delicious accompaniments.

Please try eating the skin with the salmon as it is an important part of the dish. I find it so frustrating when it is left, untouched, on the plate, as whoever has left it has missed out on an interesting taste sensation.

Wire, fish-shaped holders are useful for this dish.

4 servings

2 lb (900g) middle cut fresh salmon
Maldon sea salt
Sauce Vierge (see page 76) or Sauce Chanterelle (see opposite)

1. Set and light your barbecue 30-40 minutes before you wish to use it. Place the grid as close to the coals as possible. Check now and again to ensure that it is still lit.

2. Cut the salmon flesh away from the central bone, giving two pieces of boneless salmon, with skin on one side of each piece. (See the recipe for Saumon Croquant, page 87, for more details.) Run your fingers over the flesh to check for any hidden bones and remove these with sterilised tweezers. Cut each piece in two. The thickness of the salmon will determine its dimension but the pieces should be approximately 2½×5in (6×13cm). The cooking time will also be determined by the depth of the fish.

3. Season the flesh side with a little salt, then lay each piece inside a fish-shaped wire holder. Close together and fix securely.

4. When the coals are white hot, lay the holders on the grid, skin side down. Cook for a minute, then turn over so that the flesh side is facing down. Continue to cook for another minute before turning over again. Complete the cooking time from this skin side which should take another 2 minutes (4 minutes altogether). By this time the skin will be black and the flesh will be ever so slightly under-cooked in the centre.

5. Remove from the grid, open the racks, carefully pushing the skin away from the wires with your finger to avoid tearing it.

6. Place the salmon, skin side uppermost, on warmed serving plates, and sprinkle with lightly crushed sea salt. Spoon some Sauce Vierge or Sauce Chanterelle to one side if desired, and serve immediately.

Sauce Chanterelle
Chanterelle Sauce

One of Scotland's most delicious natural products must be the chanterelle mushrooms which grow wild in many parts of the country. In the north-west they grow so prolifically that they are picked and sent to London and Paris where they fetch a handsome price. Naturally the weather has an influence on their growth and quantity, but in general the Scottish climate seems to suit them. We are lucky enough, in our part of the country, to be able to get locally picked wild chanterelles in the late summer for a few weeks. It is a short season, so I tend to use them as much as I can, knowing I will have to wait another year before using them again. (Imported chanterelles are available at other times of the year, but their quality, flavour and colour just cannot compare.) Unfortunately they do not dry or freeze very well, so we have to be content with that very short season. Perhaps they would not be so special if they were available all year round!

This can accompany any meat or fish, but is *wonderful* with the barbecued salmon.

4 servings

6 oz (175g) fresh chanterelle mushrooms, wiped clean,
dirty end of stalk removed
½ oz (15g) butter
6 fl.oz (175ml) dry champagne
5 fl.oz (150ml) chicken stock
8 fl.oz (250ml) double cream
seasoning

1. Break any very large chanterelles into smaller pieces. Leave most whole if possible.
2. Melt the butter in a frying pan. When hot, add the chanterelles, and sauté for a few minutes. Remove from the heat.
3. Place the champagne in a small pan, bring to the boil and reduce to a few tablespoons. Add the stock, bring back to the boil and again reduce until syrupy and only a few tablespoons remain. Add the cream, place the pan half on, half off the heat, and simmer until it will coat the back of a spoon lightly.
4. Remove from the heat, add the chanterelles, and allow the flavours to infuse for at least half an hour.
5. Reheat when needed, taste for seasoning, adding a little salt if necessary.

Filet de Sole Creswick
Grilled Sole with Cream and Parmesan

This was developed for two of our oldest and dearest customers. As they became older and less interested in eating meat, this dish became a favourite of theirs. So simple to make, so quick and so delicious, especially if you have some bread to mop up the sauce!

Other white fish such as haddock can be used, but alter the cooking time according to the thickness of the fish. It should be just cooked, so that it retains its moisture and flavour. A thick piece of haddock would take approximately 8 minutes. Test it by separating the flakes of cooked fish in the centre, with a knife. If it is easy to do, the fish is ready, but if it puts up some resistance, cook for a little longer.

6 servings

1½ lb (675g) lemon sole, skinned
juice of 1 lemon
seasoning
5-6 fl.oz (150-175ml) double cream
3 oz (75g) fresh Parmesan cheese, grated

1.   Preheat the grill.
2.   Divide the sole between six heat-resistant dishes. I use shallow round or oval white porcelain ones which look very pretty. The sole should be in one layer.
3.   Sprinkle the lemon juice over the sole, season with a little salt and freshly ground black pepper, then pour approximately 1½ tablespoons of cream over each portion. Divide the cheese between them, sprinkling it evenly over the top.
4.   Place under the grill (you may have to do this in two loads depending on the size of your grill), and grill for 4-6 minutes, depending on the depth of the fish: 4 minutes will be long enough for a small piece of sole of about ⅜ in (9mm) depth. The cheese and cream should have formed a lovely, bubbling, golden brown topping.
5.   Remove, being careful not to burn yourself, and sit the dishes on underplates. Serve, just as it is, immediately. A basket of warmed bread as an accompaniment will, I suspect, be irresistible.

Sole Tissée à l'Aigre Doux

Sole Plait with Deep-Fried Beansprouts and 'Sweet-Sour' Sauce

We all have our favourite party pieces, dishes which we serve at every dinner party, until all our friends have had them. Then out comes the next one and so on. This sole plait is my party piece at the moment. It is so attractive and tasty, and the various stages can be prepared in advance, leaving, I must admit, a rather frenzied 10 minutes of work at the last moment.

Although an elegant parody of good old British fish and chips, it is a recipe which has been inspired by various dishes tasted in France. At Taillevent, a wonderful three-star restaurant in Paris, where we go every year on my birthday, we once had a delicious dish of turbot served on an *aigre-doux* sauce. This was a wickedly sweet yet sharp sauce which looked and tasted rather like melted toffee!

Deep-fried vegetables, whether as strips or thin slices, have been used in many great restaurants to add contrast in texture to an otherwise soft dish. Instead of beansprouts as here, you could use 12 oz (350g) of unpeeled courgettes, cut into strips $\frac{1}{10} \times \frac{1}{10} \times 4$ in (2×2mm×10cm). Lay these out on a tray lined with kitchen roll, and allow to dry out for a few hours, preferably overnight (do not worry if the quantity seems to shrink dramatically). This will prevent the oil from bubbling over due to excess moisture in the courgettes. This happened to me once at home, resulting in an inch of oil floating on top of my cooker! In fact, the drier they are, the quicker they will fry.

4 servings

8 medium-sized pieces of lemon sole, skinned, which will weigh
approx. 1½ lb (675g)
12 oz (350g) fresh spinach
oil for deep frying (sunflower or groundnut)
8 oz (225g) beansprouts
seasoning

Sweet-sour sauce
1½ tablespoons caster sugar
3 tablespoons good sherry vinegar
5 tablespoons Noilly Prat
5 fl.oz (150ml) chicken or fish stock
4 tablespoons double cream
½ oz (15g) unsalted butter

1.   Cut the sole lengthwise into ½ in (1cm) strips. Lay these side by side and trim off the narrower flatter end so that they measure 4 in (10cm) in length. You will need nine strips per person.

2.   Lay five strips side by side on a work surface. Take another strip and lay it across the top end. Flip the second and fourth strips over this, then place another strip a little further down. Lifting from the other end lay strips one, three and five over this second piece. Repeat with the other two pieces, creating a plaited effect. Press the side edges together to make a neat square. Using a fish slice, carefully lift it on to a lightly buttered baking tray. Repeat with the other three plaits. Cover with cling film and refrigerate until needed.

3.   Preheat the oven to 450°F (240°C) Gas 9, or as high as it will go.

4.   Start the sauce by melting the sugar in a small heavy pan. Cook over a medium heat until the sugar turns a golden brown. Take care that it does not become too dark as this will give the sauce a bitter flavour, and remember that caramel will carry on getting darker unless a liquid is added to stop it.

5.   Once golden, add the vinegar and reduce by boiling for a minute. Add the Noilly Prat and reduce the mixture by half. Add the chicken stock and once again bring to the boil and reduce by half. Add the cream and simmer until the correct sauce-like consistency is reached.

Because this sauce is thickened by evaporation, the time required depends on the size of the pan and the intensity of heat used. When the sauce will lightly coat the back of a spoon add the butter and put aside until needed, while you prepare the spinach and beansprouts.

6.   Rinse the spinach and remove any large tough stalks. Place in a large pan, season with a little salt and cover with a lid. No extra water is needed.

7.   Heat the oil in a large pan. It should be very hot as the moisture in

the beansprouts will lower the temperature immediately. Carefully lower the beansprouts into the pan and cook until they become a deep golden brown. Remove with a draining spoon and lay on a kitchen-roll-lined tray. Sprinkle with a little salt and leave to one side.

8.   Place the spinach on a medium to high heat and cook until it has fallen and is lightly cooked – about 5 minutes. Drain immediately through a sieve, pressing down with a saucer to remove excess moisture, place back in the pan and snip into small pieces with scissors. Cover with a lid.

9.   Meanwhile, remove the sole from the refrigerator, remove the cling film and sprinkle with a little salt and cold water (the water prevents it from drying out). Place in the very hot oven and cook for 5 minutes – not a second longer or the sole will become over-cooked and dull . . .

10.   Reheat the sauce, and taste. It may need a little seasoning, depending on your stock. Heat plates. Place the beansprouts in the oven for a minute.

11.   Divide the spinach between the plates, placing it in the centre. Spoon the sauce around the spinach, then, using a fish slice, lay a sole plait on top of the spinach. Top with a mound of fried beansprouts and serve immediately.

MOUSSELINE DE SOLE ET DE SAUMON FUME

SUPREME DE PIGEON AUX LENTILLES ET MORILLES

THE THIRD COURSE

MEAT

Until the spring of 1984, I had to rely on a very old cooker which we had inherited when we bought the restaurant. As it would not heat above 350°F (180°C) Gas 4, my repertoire had to take this into account. I could not therefore make dishes which needed to be cooked at a very high temperature. Looking back on it now, I do not really know how I managed for so long with a six-burner, single oven (not a good one at that!), small grill (which heated more on one side than the other) cooker.

Eventually we made some alterations to the kitchen and installed a brand new, two-oven, six-burner, large grill and hotplate cooker. To our horror though, it was faulty and although it would heat up to 500°F (260°C), the coolest it would go was 325°F (160°C) Gas 3 – which ruled out crème brûlée for a start! After countless visits by repair men at inconvenient times, we ordered another make from Glasgow, told the first supplier that theirs would be out on the pavement waiting collection, and installed the new one the very next day. To think that we were preparing for and serving a full restaurant that evening! Fortunately the new cooker was and still is perfect. I love it. Having a second oven is such a wonderful addition to my kitchen equipment, and like life before the food processor, I do not know how I coped without it.

I now tend to cook lean tender cuts of meat quickly in a very hot oven. I marinate them in a mixture of olive and hazelnut oils which means that the meat does not become dry. I prefer this type of marinating to a wine and vegetable marinade as the flavour of the meat is not altered with the oils, whereas often meat tastes more of the wine

marinade than of itself. Obviously there are cuts of meat which do require long, slow cooking to make them tender, and these can be delicious too.

At La Potinière, the third courses are always presented to each table
on a china platter which is laid down on the table. Whoever is voted
'mother' serves the rest of the table which does allow small eaters the
option of how much food they would like on their plate. A certain food
critic who seemed to think that it was bad manners to leave any food,
didn't seem to think that it was bad manners to then give us an unpleasant write-up because he had not been hungry in the first
place!

In the recipes for the meat courses, I serve them on to individual
plates as it is easier to arrange food attractively this way, but if you prefer to arrange it on to one large pretty plate and present this to your
guests, go ahead.

Those of you who know our restaurant are aware that the accompaniments to the meat courses are normally Gratin Dauphinois and a
salad. I do not serve vegetables as such, and one reason is that I prefer to
make them part of other dishes. In fact I use a great deal of vegetables in
my soups, some starters and as part of some meat courses. The recipes I
do use are included at the end of this section.

The meat course opens the door to the whole spectrum of wine,
from palest gold to deepest purple. Steamed chicken, perhaps,
suggests a light young Chardonnay, and steak and kidney pudding a full-bodied Syrah; but in between the possible combinations are
infinite.

The most versatile grape for white or red meats is the Pinot Noir. If
the great wines of Bordeaux are the gods of the wine world, then the
great wines of Burgundy are its heroes. Pinot Noir is, for me, the most
exciting and seductive grape, and it fascinates me that one variety can
produce such a myriad of styles and flavours. It is temperamental and
the greatest challenge to wine-makers, but, perhaps because of this, it is
more likely than any other grape to reflect an individual maker's hand.
Of all the classic types it has the least chance of success outwith its
native soil, and it is only very recently that a handful of 'foreign' win-
eries, such as Calera, Sanford and Au Bon Climat in California, and the
amazing Ca del Bosco in Lombardy, have successfully expressed what
for me is its true but elusive character.

I always decant red wines. If carefully done it cannot harm the wine, will often help awaken it, and is an excuse to employ one of my ever-growing collection of decanters. I do not, however, believe in letting a wine 'breathe' for several hours before serving. With the exception of Italian wines from traditional grape varieties (which always seem to need time and air no matter how mature), I feel that if a wine requires to be opened a long time before it can be drunk with pleasure, then it should probably not be drunk, but left in the bottle for a few more years. Anyway, I should much prefer to watch and wait for a wine to develop in the glass than risk missing any of its nuances by opening it too early.

Poulet à l'Estragon
Tarragon Chicken

Chicken roasted with tarragon may not sound very interesting, but the flavours combine so well that the result is really delicious. By piping a lemon and tarragon-flavoured butter between the skin and the flesh, the chicken is both tenderised by the lemon juice and kept moist by the butter. The cooking juices, along with the highly concentrated sediment, skimmed of all fat, make a very intense, delicious sauce if mixed with a little cream.

If using dried tarragon, choose one with a bright green colour and a fresh smell. Some dried tarragon is too finely chopped and smells more like tea.

This dish sums up all the pleasure and purpose of simple yet elegant cuisine: prime ingredients, straightforward but sensitive cooking, delicious results. In the early eighties, with so much stylised food around in restaurants, we often gained the impression that some of our customers were disappointed to see such an apparently plain dish on the menu. We did not abandon it, however, because we felt that cooking like this should be cherished lest it disappear forever. How reassuring it was that on our first visit to the great

Girardet's restaurant in Switzerland, the main dish which he prepared for us turned out to be Poulet à l'Estragon.

It is a superb dish to accompany a superb bottle, perhaps a stylish burgundy from Tollot Beaut or Armand Rousseau.

4 servings

1 fresh chicken, 3½ lb (1.6kg) dressed weight
4 oz (100g) unsalted butter (this sounds a great deal, but most of it will be removed later on)
2 tablespoons chopped fresh tarragon, or 1 tablespoon dried tarragon
1 tablespoon lemon juice
1 teaspoon salt
5 fl.oz (150ml) double cream

Garnish
fresh tarragon

1.   Remove the lump of fat which is often left attached inside the cavity.
2.   Starting at the neck end, loosen the skin by lifting up the flap of skin and work your fingers under the skin. Start at one breast, then the leg, then repeat at the other side. If you have longish nails, or if you do not really like the feel of doing this, wear rubber gloves. It is important not to break the skin.
3.   If the butter is soft, place in a bowl, add the tarragon, lemon juice and salt, and beat together until smooth. If it is hard, place 3 oz (75g) in your food processor fitted with the cutting blade. Melt the remainder and, when hot, add to the processor. Blend until the butter becomes smooth and creamy. Add the tarragon, lemon juice and salt and blend until well mixed.
4.   Fit a ⅜ in (9mm) plain nozzle in a piping bag and fill with the butter mixture. Lift up the loose skin, insert the nozzle under the skin, and squeeze a quarter of the butter over the thigh and drumstick, then another quarter over the breast. Repeat on the other side. Tuck the loose neck skin underneath and pin down in position with the wings.

Smooth the butter stuffing evenly over the chicken with your hands, then tie securely with string. Cut a length of string 2 feet (60cm) long, place the centre of it under the neck end, between the chicken and the wings. Position the legs together, pull the ends of the string fairly tightly and secure by tying in front of the scaly appendages to the drumsticks.

5. Place in a plastic bag or cover with cling film, then refrigerate overnight.

6. Next day, remove the chicken and let it sit at room temperature for half an hour. Preheat the oven to 400°F (200°C) Gas 6.

7. Uncover and place the chicken on its side in a lightly buttered baking tray or roasting tin. It has to be deep enough to hold the buttery juices which will melt out of the chicken.

8. Roast on the middle shelf for 30 minutes, remove carefully and, using rubber gloves, turn it over on to its other side. After another 20 minutes, remove once more and turn it again so that the breast is uppermost. Baste the breast with some of the melted butter. Continue to cook for another 15 minutes, by which time it should be a lovely golden brown colour.

9. Remove from the oven, again using rubber gloves, and tilt the chicken so that any juices inside are added to the cooking juices. Pour these into a bowl, scraping any dark, sticky sediment into it also, and allow to settle for a few minutes before spooning off the fat. Blot with a piece of kitchen roll to soak up any remaining fat.

10. Meanwhile, cut the string and, using a sharp knife, cut off the legs. If these are still slightly pink near the bone, put back into the oven on the baking tray, skin side up, for another 10 minutes. During this time, the skin should also become crisper.

11. Cut the breasts away from the ribcage, keeping each of them in one piece. Trim off the wings at the joint nearest to the breast. Cover with foil and keep warm while the legs are continuing to cook.

12. Pour the cooking juices into a pan, add the cream and simmer until it thickens enough to lightly coat the back of a spoon. Taste for seasoning but it is very unlikely that you will need to add any more salt.

13. Remove the chicken legs, place on a chopping board and cut in two at the knee joint. Cut the breast in two at a slight angle.

14. Place a piece of leg and a piece of breast on each warmed serving plate. Spoon the sauce over and around the chicken, then sprinkle with chopped fresh tarragon. Serve immediately.

Poulet Persillé

Parslied Chicken

After the influences of Elizabeth David, Margaret Costa, Jane Grigson, Robert Carrier and the 'Galloping Gourmet', along came Michel Guérard. Although it was his *Cuisine Minceur* that first brought him international attention, it was his book *Cuisine Gourmand* which really reflected his wonderful style. This is my version of one of his recipes: it combines the simplicity of a roast chicken with the intense flavours of the stuffing and sauce, all of which are typical of his approach to food at his magical restaurant and hotel. Start it the day before, to allow the flavours to develop.

4 servings

1 fresh chicken, 3 lb (1.4kg) dressed weight
1 tablespoon olive oil
seasoning

Stuffing
1¾ oz (45g) Boursin garlic and herb cheese
1¾ oz (45g) unsalted butter
5 tablespoons chopped parsley
1 tablespoon lemon juice
1 oz (25g) onion, peeled and roughly chopped
1¾ oz (45g) streaky bacon, rinded and roughly chopped
2 teaspoons chopped fresh tarragon, or 1 teaspoon dried tarragon
1 tablespoon chopped fresh chives
1¾ oz (45g) button mushrooms, wiped clean

Sauce
½ oz (15g) unsalted butter
1 oz (25g) onion, peeled and chopped
2 tablespoons sherry vinegar
5 fl.oz (150ml) double cream
1 large, firm red tomato, skinned, de-seeded and cut into
¼ in (6mm) dice

Garnish
fresh herbs such as chervil, tarragon

1.   Make the stuffing first. Place the Boursin in the bowl of your processor fitted with the cutting blade. Gently warm the butter in a small pan and add, along with 2 tablespoons of the parsley, to the Boursin. Blend until smooth, then add the lemon juice in a slow stream, and 1 teaspoon salt. Empty into a bowl.

2.   Place the onion, the streaky bacon, the remaining parsley, the tarragon and the chives in the processor (no need to rinse it) and blend until fairly smooth. Add the green butter mixture and blend until just mixed. Empty into the bowl.

3.   Place the mushrooms in the processor and blend until chopped into small pieces. Be careful not to overdo this as it should not turn into a soft purée, but should remain dry. Add these to the other stuffing ingredients and mix together with a spoon.

4.   Loosen the skin and 'stuff' the chicken as described in the recipe for Poulet à l'Estragon (see page 99). Tie with string, making sure that the stuffing is evenly distributed over the breasts, thighs and drumsticks. Cover with cling film or place in a plastic bag. Refrigerate overnight.

5.   The next day allow the chicken to sit at room temperature for half an hour. Preheat oven to 450°F (230°C) Gas 8.

6.   Place the chicken, breast uppermost, in a roasting tray. Dribble the olive oil over the skin and rub in gently with your hands.

7.   Roast on the middle shelf for an hour, basting occasionally with the escaping fat. Cooking the chicken upright rather than on its side prevents the skin from sticking to the roasting tray and tearing. Because of this, the breast will cook faster than the legs and they will need to be removed at this stage.

8.   Remove the tin from the oven, lift the chicken out, tilting it first so that any juices inside it pour into the tin. Sit it on a plate and carefully, using a small sharp knife, cut each breast off in one piece. Place on an ovenproof plate and cover with foil.

9.   Pour all the cooking juices into a bowl, scraping any dark sediment from the roasting tin and adding these to the juices. Allow to settle.

10.   Remove the legs by cutting close to the body of the chicken and cut through the bone at the joint connecting the thigh to the body. Place these, skin side uppermost, back in the roasting tin and roast for another 15 minutes, by which time the skin will be crisp and dark.

11.   Meanwhile, make the sauce. Melt the butter in a small pan, add the chopped onion and cook until light golden, stirring frequently. Add the sherry vinegar, bring to the boil and reduce until it has virtually evaporated.

12.   De-grease the chicken cooking juices as on page 101, and add them to the pan along with the cream.

13.   Simmer until the sauce is thick enough to lightly coat the back of a spoon. Add a few turns of freshly ground black pepper. Salt will be unnecessary.

14.   Place the breasts back in the oven for the final 5 minutes of the legs' cooking time.

15.   Place the tomato dice in another small pan. Sieve the sauce into the pan, pressing down on the onions to extract as much flavour as possible. Keep warm but do not let the tomatoes soften.

16.   Remove the chicken, cut across each breast and cut each leg in half.

17.   Place one piece of breast and either a thigh or a drumstick on each warmed serving plate, then spoon the sauce over or around the chicken. Decorate with fresh chervil or tarragon and serve immediately.

Poulet Français
Chicken with Mushroom and Pernod Sauce

This is made in the same way as the Poulet à l'Estragon, using either marjoram or tarragon in the lemon butter. The sauce is made from the cooking juices, cream and Pernod-flamed mushrooms. Sliced button mushrooms can be used, but a variety of wild ones make the sauce even more delicious. Chanterelles, cèpes, trompettes de mort and morels all have wonderful flavours and can be used separately or as a *mélange*.

4 servings

1 fresh chicken, 3½ lb (1.6kg) dressed weight
4 oz (100g) unsalted butter
2 tablespoons fresh chopped marjoram or tarragon, or
1 tablespoon dried
1 tablespoon fresh lemon juice
1 teaspoon salt

Mushroom sauce
6 oz (175g) fresh mushrooms, wiped clean
½ oz (15g) butter
2 fl.oz (50ml) Pernod
5 fl.oz (150ml) double cream

1. Prepare and cook the chicken as described on page 100, using the butter, herb, lemon juice and salt in the 'stuffing'.
2. While the chicken is cooking, start the sauce. Slice the button mushrooms thinly. If using chanterelles, trim off the earthy tip and break any large ones into smaller pieces, leaving any small ones whole. If using cèpes, slice these thickly.
3. Melt the butter in a frying pan and, when hot, add the mushrooms. Stir fry for 2-3 minutes. If using gas, turn up the heat, pour the measured Pernod into the frying pan, shake it over the flame and allow it to ignite. If using electricity, pour the Pernod into a ladle, heat it over a hotplate, light with a match, then pour over the mushrooms while still burning. Set aside until the chicken is ready.
4. Prepare the cooking juices and their tasty sediment as described in Poulet à l'Estragon. Add these, degreased, to the mushrooms. Heat, then add the cream. Simmer until a light sauce consistency is reached. Taste for seasoning, but it is unlikely that you will need any.
5. Cut up the chicken as described on page 100, and arrange a piece of leg and a piece of breast on warmed serving plates. Spoon the sauce over the pieces and serve immediately.

Suprême de Volaille Epicé aux Abricots Sauvages

Spiced Breast of Chicken with Wild Apricots

Wild apricots from Hunza, near Afghanistan, are cooked in white wine and served as part of this dish. These delicious little apricots inspired this recipe, which combines chicken breast, freshly ground spices, apricots and mint, and is based on a Middle Eastern combination of tastes. Choose unsulphured dried apricots with which to make the purée, and remember to warn your guests that the little Hunzas contain a large stone! I like to grind the whole spices in an electric coffee mill kept solely for this purpose.

6 servings

6 fresh chicken breasts, boned and skinned, each weighing 4-5 oz (100-150g), trimmed of any pieces of bone or fat
8 oz (225g) unsulphured dried apricots
dry white wine
3 strips lemon peel, approximately ½ x 2½ in (1 x 6cm)
30 Hunza apricots (available from health-food shops)
unsalted butter
seasoning

Spicy sauce
1 medium leek, dark part removed
1 medium garlic clove, peeled and crushed
1 heaped teaspoon each of coriander seeds, cumin seeds, fennel seeds and cardamom pods
5 fl.oz (150ml) dry cider
5 fl.oz (150ml) chicken stock
5 fl.oz (150ml) double cream

Garnish
6 large leaves fresh mint

1. The night before, place the dried apricots (*not* the Hunzas) in a bowl and rinse in cold water. Make sure that the bowl is big enough to allow the apricots to swell to double their original size. Pour off the rinsing water, cover with plenty of cold water and allow to soak over-night.

2. The next day, pour off the water and place the apricots in a sauce-pan. Add 5 fl.oz (150ml) of the wine, enough cold water to cover the apricots, and the strips of lemon peel.

3. Place over a medium heat, bring to the boil, then simmer gently for about an hour or until most of the liquid has evaporated and the apricots have a sticky, cooked look to them. Stir occasionally to make sure that the mixture does not stick to the base of the pan.

4. Meanwhile, preheat the oven to 350°F (180°C) Gas 4. Rinse and drain the Hunza apricots, and place in an ovenproof dish. Add enough white wine to cover, and cover the dish with tin foil. Bake on the middle shelf of the preheated oven for 40 minutes.

5. After rinsing any grit from the leek, chop it into small pieces. Melt ½ oz (15g) of the butter in a small pan and when hot add the leek and crushed garlic. Cook gently until softened.

6. Place the spices in an electric grinder and blend until reduced to very fine powder. Add to the leek and garlic, and cook for 2-3 minutes to release the flavours of the spices.

7. Add the cider, bring to the boil, and then reduce by two-thirds.

8. Add the chicken stock and reduce this by half.

9. Remove the Hunza apricots from the oven, lift up a corner of the tin foil and pour any remaining wine into the spicy sauce. Re-cover the Hunzas and keep warm.

10. Raise the oven temperature to 475°F (240°C) Gas 9, or as high as it will go.

11. Blend the soft dried apricots to a purée in your food processor fitted with the cutting blade. Stop processing before they become too soft. The purée should be fairly chunky and thick. Put back in the pan and keep warm.

12. Season the cut side of the chicken breasts with a little salt and freshly ground black pepper. Place them, seasoned side down, on a lightly buttered baking tray. Brush some melted butter over each one. Bake in the hot oven for 9 minutes.

13. Meanwhile, sieve the sauce into another pan, pressing down on the leek and spice mixture. Add the cream, bring to a rapid boil and

reduce until it is thick enough to lightly coat a spoon. Taste for seasoning and add salt if necessary.

14.   Remove the breasts from the oven. Place a generous spoonful of apricot purée on each warmed serving plate. Slice the chicken breasts across at an angle, into slices ½ in (1cm) thick. Place them on top of the purée, overlapping each other. Spoon some sauce over each one and decorate the plate with a little cluster of the Hunza apricots. Sprinkle the chicken breast with chopped mint. (You can make zig-zag shapes by folding large leaves of mint into W's and then finely cutting at an angle.) Serve immediately.

Suprême de Volaille au Confit d'Oignons, Sauce Moutarde

Chicken Breast with Onion Confit and Mustard Sauce

If you have made a batch of the Confit d'Oignons in advance, this is a very quick, easy dish to prepare. The confit, due to its high sugar content, will last for weeks and can be used for a number of dishes. It is extremely tasty and provides a contrast to the chicken and mustard flavours in this dish. Pigeon breast, duck breast and lamb fillet are just some of the other meats which you could use in this recipe.

6 servings

6 fresh, skinned chicken breasts, weighing 4-5 oz (100-150g) each, trimmed of any small pieces of bone and fat
seasoning
½ oz (15g) unsalted butter

Mustard Sauce
5 fl.oz (150ml) Chambrey vermouth
5 fl.oz (150ml) chicken stock
7½ fl.oz (225ml) double cream
2 teaspoons Moutarde de Meaux
seasoning

To serve and garnish
6 generous tablespoons Confit d'Oignons (see page 148)
fresh parsley

1.   Preheat oven to 475°F (240°C) Gas 9, or as high as possible.
2.   For the sauce, place the wine in a small pan, bring to the boil, then simmer until reduced to 2 tablespoons. Add the stock, bring back to the boil, then simmer until reduced by half. Add the cream and simmer until a light coating consistency is achieved. Set aside.
3.   Meanwhile, lightly season the chicken breasts on the cut side with salt. Place them, salted side down, on a lightly buttered baking tray. Melt the ½ oz (15g) butter and use this to brush over the breasts. Season with a little more salt.
4.   Bake the chicken breasts on the middle shelf of the preheated oven for 9 minutes.
5.   Gently reheat the onion confit, being careful not to allow it to scorch, stirring frequently with a wooden spoon.
6.   Reheat the sauce, whisk in the mustard, then taste for seasoning. Add a little salt and freshly ground black pepper if necessary.
7.   Remove the breasts from the oven. Place a good tablespoon of the onion confit on each warmed serving plate, slice the chicken in slices ¼ in (6mm) thick and place these, overlapping, on top of it. Spoon the sauce over or around the chicken and sprinkle with finely chopped parsley. Serve immediately.

Suprême de Dinde aux Pruneaux

Turkey Breast with Prunes

We are lucky enough to have a turkey farm near us. They sell all sorts of turkey products, but it is the small hen turkey breasts that we like. On a good day, we can buy whole breasts which weigh only 6 or 7 oz (175-200g). Treated with care, they are tasty and moist and can be used instead of chicken breasts.

I originally made this dish with the more traditional pork fillet from an Elizabeth David recipe, but have gradually changed to turkey, which we prefer. It is a very festive dish and would be perfect at Christmas or Thanksgiving if you did not want to cook a whole turkey.

6 servings

6 small hen turkey breasts, weighing 6 or 7 oz (175-200g) each
1 dessertspoon each hazelnut and olive oils
12 extra large Californian or Agen prunes
7 fl.oz (200ml) dry Vouvray wine
seasoning

Cream sauce with cranberries
6 fl.oz (175ml) dry cider
5 fl.oz (150ml) chicken stock
10 fl.oz (300ml) double cream
2 oz (50g) cranberries, fresh or frozen, defrosted

Garnish
fresh salad burnet leaves

1. Remove any thin membrane which may cover the turkey breasts. Place the breasts in a bowl, mix in the oils, then cover with cling film. Leave overnight if possible, refrigerated.
2. When you are ready to cook, preheat the oven to 350°F (180°C) Gas 4.

3.   Place the prunes in an ovenproof bowl, pour the Vouvray over, then cover with tin foil. Bake in the preheated oven, on the middle shelf, for 2 hours.

4.   To make the sauce, pour the cider into a pan, bring it to the boil and reduce until about 3 tablespoons remain. Add the chicken stock, and continue to simmer until reduced by half. Add half of the cream and simmer until it begins to thicken. Pour in a little more cream and cook until it has reached a light coating consistency.

5.   Remove the prunes. Turn the oven up to 475°F (240°C) Gas 9, or as high as possible.

6.   Lift back a corner of the tin foil, and pour the cooking liquid from the prunes into the sauce. Keep the prunes warm.

7.   Place the turkey breasts on a lightly buttered baking tray, and sprinkle with a little salt. Once the oven has become very hot, bake on the middle shelf for 14 minutes.

8.   Meanwhile, check the sauce for seasoning and consistency, adding a little salt if necessary. It should be quite sweet, and a pale toffee colour. Reheat, adding the rest of the cream if it is too thick. If too thin, reduce by boiling a little longer.

9.   Add the cranberries at the last moment. Do not allow the sauce to boil at this stage as the cranberries would burst and spoil.

10.   Remove the breasts when ready, place on a chopping board and slice at an angle into slices ¼ in (6mm) thick. Arrange these on your warmed serving plates, in a curve, overlapping each other.

11.   Spoon the sauce over the turkey and arrange the prunes next to it.

12.   If you can get salad burnet, decorate a few cranberries with a couple of leaves of this herb – very holly berryish!
Serve immediately.

Suprême de Pigeons aux Lentilles et Morilles

Pigeon Breast with Lentils and Morel Sauce

The first time that I ate wood pigeon was at David and Patricia Wilson's restaurant, the Peat Inn. It was sensational! Both the texture and flavour were wonderful, and the sweetish sauce was just delicious. The important thing to remember when cooking pigeon is that by lightly cooking it, the flesh remains tender and moist, but by over-cooking it, even by a few minutes only, it becomes tough, dry and grey. The wood pigeons that we serve are wild and are shot in the countryside around us. I serve only the breasts, the rest makes stock for sauces.

Chicken breasts could be substituted, in which case use chicken stock for the sauce, and cook the breasts as described on page 107.

6 servings

6 fresh wood pigeons
1 dessertspoon each hazelnut and olive oils
4 oz (100g) brown lentils, soaked in warm water for an hour,
flavoured with a slice of onion
2½ fl.oz (65ml) strong pigeon stock
1 tablespoon chopped fresh tarragon, or 1 teaspoon dried tarragon
1 oz (25g) unsalted butter
seasoning

Morel sauce
5 fl.oz (150ml) dry white wine
5 fl.oz (150ml) strong pigeon stock
5 fl.oz (150ml) double cream
½ oz (15g) dried morels, soaked in warm water for an hour

1. Using a small sharp knife, carefully cut away each breast, keeping your knife as close to the rib cage as possible. Pull off the skin and then place the breasts in a bowl. Pour the oils over them and mix well so that every surface is coated. Cover and set aside in a cool place. I normally prepare them the evening before and refrigerate them overnight. The next day, allow them to come to room temperature before cooking.

2.   Prepare the sauce by placing the wine in a small to medium pan, bringing to the boil, and simmering until reduced by half.

3.   Add the stock and once again bring to the boil and simmer until reduced by half. Add the cream, move the pan half on, half off the burner or hot plate, and allow to simmer until a smooth sauce-like consistency is reached.

4.   Squeeze most of the water out of the morels and add them to the sauce. Set aside until needed, during which time the flavour of the morels will penetrate the sauce.

5.   Preheat the oven to 450°F (230°C) Gas 8.

6.   Pour the lentils through a sieve, and place in a pan along with the slice of onion. Cover with cold water, bring to the boil and simmer for 2 minutes. Pour through a sieve, remove the onion, and return to the pan. Add the stock, the tarragon and half of the butter. Season with a little salt and freshly ground black pepper.

7.   Melt the remaining butter in a large frying pan and, when hot, add the breasts. Season lightly with salt, then turn over using tongs. Once they have been browned on both sides, place on a lightly buttered baking tray. You may have to brown them in two batches, depending on the size of your frying pan.

8.   Place on the middle shelf in the preheated oven for 7 or 8 minutes, depending on their size.

9.   During this time, reheat the lentils and simmer for about 5 minutes by which time they should be softened, but still whole and not in any way mushy. Add a little water if the lentils are too dry, and stir with a wooden spoon to make sure that they are not sticking. Check for temperature and seasoning and adjust if necessary.

10.   Reheat the sauce gently. Taste for seasoning, but I normally find that the flavour is intense enough without needing to add any salt.

11.   Remove the pigeons and allow to rest in a warm place for at least 5 minutes, which ensures that they will be evenly rosy inside.

12.   To serve, place a spoonful of lentils on each heated serving plate. Spoon the sauce around the lentils, making sure that everyone gets their share of the morels. Place the breasts on a chopping board and cut across, at an angle, into four slices. Arrange eight of these on each mound of lentils, and serve immediately.

Suprême de Pigeons aux Choux, Sauce Pommard

Pigeon Breast with Cabbage and Red Wine Sauce

Finely sliced cabbage, flavoured with garlic and juniper berries, provides a tasty bed for the slices of pigeon breasts. The sweetness of the sauce rounds off the dish perfectly. One very memorable dish that I ate at L'Auberge de l'Ille at Illhaeusern in Alsace was a combination of pigeon, *foie gras* and cabbage, wrapped in pastry. The result was wonderful and it was certainly the highlight of that visit.

6 servings

6 fresh wood pigeons, prepared as in the previous recipe
1 dessertspoon each hazelnut and olive oils
seasoning
unsalted butter

Cabbage
12 oz (350g) Dutch cabbage, weighed after the outer leaves and core
have been removed
1 small garlic clove, peeled
8 juniper berries
2 tablespoons double cream
2 tablespoons chopped flat parsley

Red wine sauce
8 fl.oz (250ml) red wine (the better the wine, the better the sauce.
We use a Pommard)
1 teaspoon redcurrant jelly
8 fl.oz (250ml) strong pigeon stock

1. Marinate the pigeon breasts for a few hours or overnight in the mixed oils in the refrigerator. Allow to return to room temperature if they have been refrigerated.

2. Preheat oven to 450°F (230°C) Gas 8.

3. Finely shred the cabbage using a sharp knife, or by slicing in your food processor.

4. Place the garlic and juniper berries in a mortar. Add ½ teaspoon salt and pound to a purée using the pestle. Alternatively, mash them together carefully on your chopping board using a large knife.

5. For the sauce, place the red wine and redcurrant jelly in a pan, bring to the boil and simmer until reduced by two-thirds. Add the stock, bring back to the boil, and simmer until reduced by half.

6. Meanwhile, melt ½ oz (15g) butter in a large frying pan. When hot, add the breasts, sprinkle with a little salt, then turn over to brown on the other side, using tongs. Transfer on to a lightly buttered baking tray. Bake for 7-8 minutes, depending on size, on the middle shelf of the preheated oven.

7. During this time, melt another ½ oz (15g) butter in a large saucepan. When hot, but not browned, add the garlic and juniper mixture. Stir with a wooden spoon and cook for a minute to release the wonderful smell and flavour of these aromatics.

8. Add the cabbage, and cook over a brisk heat for 5 minutes, stirring frequently. Add the cream and continue to cook if the cabbage is still too firm. It should remain *al dente*. Season with salt and freshly ground black pepper. Keep warm.

9. Remove the pigeons from the oven and allow to rest for 5-10 minutes in a warm place, to ensure an even rosy hue.

10. Meanwhile check the consistency and flavour of the sauce. Add ½ oz (15g) butter and simmer until a light sauce-like consistency is reached. You will only have just over 6 tablespoons.

11. Stir the parsley into the cabbage. Place a spoonful of cabbage on to each warmed serving plate.

12. Place the pigeon breasts on your chopping board and, using a sharp knife, slice each one into four. Arrange the slices (two breasts per person) on top of the cabbage.

13. Spoon the sauce over and around the pigeon breasts, then serve immediately.

Lasagne de Pigeon
Pigeon Lasagne

This is not lasagne as you would normally imagine it, but instead consists of a layer of leeks and mushrooms, and a layer of finely sliced pigeon breast, sandwiched between thin square sheets of pasta and served with a wild mushroom sauce. To give the dish more impact visually, the top layer of pasta has a leaf of flat parsley incorporated into it while being rolled out, which makes it very unusual and pretty. If you have your own pasta rollers, do have a go, as it is not as difficult as it sounds.

4 servings

6 pigeon breasts
1 tablespoon hazelnut oil
1 quantity pasta dough (see page 48)
a small bunch of large-leaved flat parsley
¾ oz (20g) unsalted butter
4 oz (100g) white part of leek, rinsed and finely chopped
8 oz (225g) button mushrooms, wiped clean and sliced
2 tablespoons double cream
seasoning
olive oil

Morel sauce
5 fl.oz (150ml) dry white wine
5 fl.oz (150ml) pigeon stock
5 fl.oz (150ml) double cream
8-12 medium-sized dried morels, soaked in warm water for 1 hour

1. Prepare and marinate the pigeon breasts in the oil as described on page 112. Cover and refrigerate overnight.
2. Next day, prepare a batch of pasta dough, rest and roll out as described, and when you reach stage 4, keep back one-third of it. Roll the other two-thirds out to as thin a stage as possible without it tearing.

Cut into eight 3 in (7.5cm) squares and lay out to dry on a well-floured surface or tray.

3. Roll out the remaining dough to one stage thicker than the squares. Pick out four of the most perfect leaves of flat parsley and press these in two rows of two on half of the dough. They should be roughly 1 in (2.5cm) apart and ½ in (1.2cm) in from the outside edge of the dough.

4. Fold the plain half of pasta over the parslied half, lightly pressing the two layers together.

5. Feed this through the rollers, at the same setting. The dough will stretch, as will the leaves of parsley. Cut the dough in two vertically between the two rows of parsley.

6. Turn these two strips so that the next time they are rolled the parsley will be stretched in the other direction.

7. Change the position of the rollers to the thinnest setting, that is, to the same thickness as the plain squares. Run the pieces of parslied dough through, cut each piece in two, then trim them so that you now have four 3 in (7.5cm) squares of parslied pasta. Place these on a well-floured surface or tray to dry.

8. Preheat the oven to 450°F (230°C) Gas 8. Allow the pigeon breasts to sit at room temperature for an hour before cooking them.

9. Prepare the sauce by bringing the white wine to the boil in a pan, and reduce until 2 tablespoons remain. Add the stock, bring back to the boil and reduce by half. Add the cream and simmer, being careful that it does not boil over, until a light smooth sauce is formed which will lightly coat the back of a spoon.

10. Squeeze most of the moisture out of the soaking morels and add them to the sauce. Set aside to allow the flavour of the morels to permeate the sauce.

11. Melt ½ oz (15g) of the butter in a pan and, when hot, add the leeks. Cook for 3-4 minutes, stirring frequently, then add the mushrooms. Continue to cook, adding the cream and a little salt after a couple of minutes. The mixture should be creamy but not too wet, so evaporate off any excess moisture if necessary. Taste for seasoning, adding more salt if necessary. Set aside until needed.

12. Place a large pan of cold water over a high heat and bring to the boil.

13. Meanwhile, heat the remaining butter in a frying pan and, when hot, brown the pigeon breasts on one side, season lightly with salt, then turn over with tongs to brown the other side.

14. Lay them on a lightly buttered baking tray and place on the middle shelf of the preheated oven for 8 minutes, while cooking the pasta.

15. When the water comes to the boil, add a tablespoon of salt, and a teaspoon of olive oil (to prevent the pasta from sticking together), then drop in the pasta squares. Run a wooden spoon through the water to make sure that none of the squares have stuck to the bottom. Bring back to the boil as quickly as possible, and cook for 3 minutes or until the pasta has reached the *al dente* stage (firm yet soft enough to bite into easily). Carefully lift out with a draining spoon and lay on a clean teatowel to dry.

16. Chop the remaining parsley and add to the leek and mushroom mixture. Reheat it, and reheat the sauce.

17. Remove the pigeon breasts after the 8 minutes, and allow to rest in a warm place for 5 minutes, during which time they will become evenly rosy and tender. Cut into four or five slices lengthwise.

18. Lay one square of plain pasta in the centre of each warmed serving plate. Divide the leek mixture between them, spreading it over the pasta. Lay another square on top, then arrange the strips of pigeon in a star shape over this. Spoon the sauce over the pigeon, allowing it to spill down on to the plate, being careful to divide the morels evenly between them. Finally top with the square of parslied pasta and serve immediately.

Suprême de Faisan à la Normande

Pheasant Breast with Apples and Chestnuts

Pheasant breasts can become very dry, so I prefer to cook them this way as opposed to roasting the birds whole. I have combined chestnuts with the more traditional apple and cider sauce to make a delicious winter dish. Stages 1 to 6 should be done the day before serving this dish.

6 servings

3 fresh hen pheasants, hung but not high, drawn and plucked
1 dessertspoon each hazelnut and olive oils
unsalted butter
1 large carrot, celery stick, a leek and an onion for the pheasant
stock, cut into large dice
seasoning

Chestnuts
20 dried chestnuts
3 fl.oz (75ml) dry cider
5 fl.oz (150ml) strong pheasant stock (see method)
2 teaspoons caster sugar

Sauce
9 fl.oz (275ml) dry cider
5 fl.oz (150ml) strong pheasant stock
8 fl.oz (250ml) double cream

Apples
4 large Cox's Pippin apples
2 teaspoons powdered cinnamon
2 teaspoons soft brown sugar
1 fl.oz (25ml) Calvados

Garnish
flat parsley

1.   Using a sharp knife, remove the breasts from the pheasants. Remove the skin and place them in a bowl, cover with the oils, mix well, cover and leave to marinate overnight.

2.   Preheat the oven to 450°F (230°C) Gas 8. When hot, roast the carcasses (having removed the legs to use in another recipe) for approximately 20 minutes until browned.

3.   Melt ½ oz (15g) of the butter in a large pan, add the diced vegetable when hot, and cook until they take on a nice golden colour. Do not allow them to burn as this will give the stock a bitter flavour.

4.   Add the browned bones, top up with enough cold water to cover the bones, bring to the boil, then simmer, half covered, for at least 4 hours.

5.   Pour through a colander into another pan and allow to boil rapidly until reduced to just over 10 fl.oz (300ml). Pour into a bowl, allow to cool, then refrigerate so that you can remove all the fat which will rise and set on the surface.

6.   Soak the chestnuts overnight in a bowl containing plenty of cold water.

7.   Next day, remove the pheasant breasts from the refrigerator and allow to stand at room temperature for at least an hour. Preheat oven to 375°F (190°C) Gas 5, or as high as possible.

8.   Drain the chestnuts, place in a pan with the cider, degreased pheasant stock, the sugar, ½ oz (15g) of the butter and ½ teaspoon salt. Add cold water until the chestnuts are covered.

9.   Bring to the boil, then simmer for about 30-40 minutes until they are tender but not mushy. Test one of the least good-looking ones. The liquid should be slightly syrupy.

10.   While they are cooking, put the cider for the sauce in a pan, bring to the boil, and reduce until only 2 tablespoons remain. Add the stock, bring back to the boil and reduce by half. Add the cream and simmer until a light smooth creamy sauce is achieved.

11.   While the chestnuts and the sauce are simmering, prepare the apples. Peel and core them, then slice roughly into slices ¼ in (6mm) thick. Place in an ovenproof dish, dot with ½ oz (15g) of the butter, sprinkle with the cinnamon and sugar, then cover with tin foil. Place in the centre of the preheated oven and bake for 30 minutes or until translucent and tender.

Remove from the oven.

12.   Heat the Calvados in a ladle until it ignites, pour over the apples and stir in carefully to ensure that all the apples are 'inflamed'. Cover with foil and set aside until required.

13. Raise oven temperature to 475°C (240°F) Gas 9, or as high as possible.

14. Melt another ½ oz (15g) butter in a frying pan, and when hot, place the pheasant breasts beside each other, cut side uppermost. Season with a little salt, then turn over using tongs. Cook just long enough to seal all the surfaces of the breasts, then place on a lightly buttered baking tray.

15. Bake in the centre of the preheated oven for 7 minutes until lightly cooked.

16. Reheat the chestnuts and the sauce. Check for seasoning, adding a little salt to both if necessary. Reheat the apples in the hot oven for a few minutes while the pheasant breasts are cooking.

17. Remove the breasts. Place a spoonful of apple in the centre of each warmed serving plate. Slice each breast into slices ⅜ in (9mm) thick and arrange over the apples. Spoon some of the sauce over the pheasant and decorate with a cluster of chestnuts. The cooking liquid from the chestnuts can be quickly reheated, thickened by adding an extra knob of butter and spooned over them. Garnish with a leaf or two of flat parsley.

Magret de Canette à la Japonaise
Duck Breast Teriyaki

I use the breasts of small Barbary or Gressingham ducks for this dish. They are dark, tender and flavourful, like a cross between wild duck and the traditional domestic farm variety. Marks and Spencers often stock Barbary ducks, but their supply is fairly erratic.

This recipe has been influenced by many things, but it definitely has oriental overtones. It is made up of many components, so it is important to be organised when serving it.

6 servings

6 small breasts of Barbary or Gressingham duck
1 tablespoon hazelnut oil
seasoning

Vegetables
6 oz (175g) Dutch cabbage, trimmed weight
6 oz (175g) Chinese leaves, trimmed weight
½ oz (15g) unsalted butter
1 oz (25g) sesame seeds
1 tablespoon double cream
a handful of fresh mint

Sauce and glaze
2 fl.oz (50ml) dry sherry
2 fl.oz (50ml) chicken stock
2 fl.oz (50ml) soy sauce (choose one which is additive free)
1 tablespoon caster sugar
2 teaspoons cornflour or arrowroot
7½ fl.oz (225ml) double cream

Garnish
3 spring onions, root and outer skin removed

1.   Lay the breasts, skin side down, on your chopping board and, using a sharp knife, remove the skin. Use the same method as if skinning a piece of fish by making a cut at one end between the flesh and the fat. Hold on to the fatty skin while moving the knife, which is held perpendicular to the board, with a sawing motion along the length of the breast. As you do this, you will cut the skin and fat away in one piece. Repeat with the others, then place the breasts in a bowl, mix with the hazelnut oil, cover with cling film and refrigerate overnight.
2.   The skin and fat will have to be cut into ¼ in (6mm) cubes. This is easier when it is cold and firm, so cover and refrigerate for a while. When firm, cut into dice, cover and refrigerate again until needed.
3.   Next day, let the duck sit at room temperature for an hour or so before cooking it.
4.   Preheat the oven to 375°F (190°C) Gas 5. When hot, place the fat cubes on a baking tray, and place on the middle shelf for approximately

30 minutes until golden brown and crisp. Stir now and again, as some will stick to the tray. A great deal of melted fat will be produced so be careful when handling the tray as it will be very hot.

5.   When they are ready, remove from the tray with a slotted spoon so that the fat runs off them. Place on a double sheet of kitchen roll on an ovenproof tray or plate. Raise oven to 475°F (240°C) Gas 9, or as high as possible.

6.   While the fat is in the oven, prepare the other parts of the dish. Cut the vegetable leaves into very fine shreds by hand, or in your food processor fitted with a slicing blade.

7.   Place the sherry, stock, soy and sugar in a small pan and bring to the boil. Slake the arrowroot or cornflour in a small container by stirring a little water into it. When smooth and liquid, add some of the hot soy liquid, then pour back into the pan, stirring all the time. Bring back to the boil, then simmer gently while completing the preparation.

8.   In another small pan, bring the cream for the sauce to the boil, then simmer until it thickens slightly. Stir now and again to check that it does not stick to the base of the pan.

9.   Chop the mint for the vegetables finely. Place the garnish spring onions on your chopping board and cut them at an angle into 1/8 in (3mm) thick slices.

10.   Transfer the duck breasts to a lightly buttered baking tray, leaving some space between each one. Season with a little salt, then place on the middle shelf of the preheated oven. Bake for 9 minutes, remove and allow to rest in a warm place for 5-10 minutes.

11.   Meanwhile, melt the butter in a large pan, and when just beginning to turn brown, add the sesame seeds. Stir round with a wooden spoon until they take on a golden colour. Add the cabbage and Chinese leaves, stir together, and cook quickly for 3-4 minutes. Add the cream, a teaspoon of salt and the mint. Turn the heat down and cook gently.

12.   Add *half* the soy mixture to the pan of cream and whisk in until blended.

13.   Reheat the cubes of crispy skin in the hot oven.

14.   To serve, place a tablespoon of the minty vegetables in the centre of each warmed serving plate. Spoon some creamy sauce around it. Cut each duck breast into slices ½ in (1cm) thick, and lay, overlapping, on the cabbage. Brush the meat with the soy glaze, scatter the crispy fat cubes and some sliced spring onion over. Serve immediately.

Whew! Do I really make and serve this for 30 people at a time? I feel exhausted just reading it!

Filet d'Agneau, avec Sauce aux Herbes et Petits Pithiviers de Poireaux

Fillet of Lamb with Herb Sauce and Little Leek Pies

Every now and again we serve lamb fillet in the restaurant. I have struggled up the road from the butcher's carrying about 30 lb (13.5kg) of racks of lamb, removed the fillets and ended up with only 7½ lb (3.4kg) of meat! The meaty bones are used to make wonderful stock and the fat is thrown out. It's quite an effort and it is expensive, but the tender, lean fillets are worth it.

Allow an eight-bone rack between two people. To remove the fillets, ask the butcher to cut off the bone running along the length of the rack, at the very base, without actually cutting any of the meat which forms the fillet. The fillet is surrounded by a membrane, which, if pulled and eased from the layer of fat, will come away quite easily. Use a sharp knife to cut the meat away from the bones, being careful not to waste any. You will now have a long thin piece of lamb fillet, with a layer of membrane still along one side. Cut this away carefully with a sharp knife, again being careful not to cut off any of the precious lamb, and you will now have a completely fat-, bone- and membrane-free piece of meat. Place the fillets in a bowl or plastic container, pour over a dessertspoon of hazelnut oil per two fillets, mix to coat evenly, cover and refrigerate overnight.

Cut down between the ribs of the remaining bones, brown in a very hot oven, add to lightly browned diced carrots, onion, leek and celery. Top up with cold water, enough to cover the bones, bring to the boil, then simmer very gently for 3 or 4 hours, half covered. Pour the stock through a colander into another pan and boil rapidly until well reduced. Pour into a bowl, allow to cool, then refrigerate. When cold, remove the layer of fat and use as required.

The pink of the meat, the bright green of the sauce and the golden colour of the crisp, tasty little *pithiviers* add up to a very pretty plateful, if carefully arranged. Use whatever herbs are available, just fresh mint for example, but a mixture is more interesting.

Bone out the lamb and make the stock the day before serving it.

6 servings

3 racks of lamb, with 8 ribs in each
1½ dessertspoons hazelnut oil
6 small leek *pithiviers*, made with 8 oz (225g) flaky pastry and
1 quantity leek purée (see page 139)
½ oz (15g) unsalted butter
seasoning
1 egg yolk

Herb sauce
5 fl.oz (150ml) lamb stock, all fat removed
7½ fl.oz (225ml) double cream
1 oz (25g) fresh herbs, weighed once any large stalks have been
removed (chervil, parsley, mint, tarragon, sweet cicely etc)

1.   Prepare and marinate the lamb in the oil, and make the stock for the sauce as described on the previous page.
2.   Next day, remove the lamb from the refrigerator and allow it to sit at room temperature for at least an hour before cooking it.
3.   Make the leek *pithiviers* as instructed on page 140 and refrigerate until required.
4.   Preheat the oven to 475°F (240°C) Gas 9, or as high as possible.
5.   Place the lamb stock in a pan, bring to the boil and let it reduce a little before adding the cream. Bring back to the boil and let the sauce reduce until it thickens slightly.
6.   Meanwhile bring a pan of lightly salted water to the boil, throw in the herbs, make sure that they are all submerged, then boil for a minute. Pour immediately through a sieve into the sink, then run lots of cold water over them, to set the colour.
7.   Squeeze the herbs dry, and place them in your liquidiser. The sauce will be much smoother made in this as opposed to in a food processor.

8.   Pour the hot sauce over the herbs and blend until very smooth. Return to the pan and whisk in a little salt. Do not reheat until needed, as over-heating will spoil the colour.

9.   Weigh each fillet of lamb. Place them, spaced apart, on a lightly buttered baking tray. Sprinkle with salt, then dot with butter or brush it over them if it has been melted.

10.   Mix a few drops of cold water with the egg yolk, then brush this over the tops of the leek *pithiviers*. Be careful that the egg wash does not dribble down over the edges of the pastry as this would result in uneven rising. Mark their tops as instructed in the recipe.

11.   Bake the lamb and the *pithiviers* side by side on the middle shelf, but failing this, if you do not have space, on the shelves above and below the centre. The lamb will take 1 minute per ounce (25g) plus 2 minutes extra – 9 minutes for a 7 oz (200g) fillet of lamb, for example. Remove when done, turn down the oven to 400°F (200°C) Gas 6 to finish off the *pithiviers*. They will take another 5 minutes roughly, or cook until they are golden, crisp and risen.

12.   When you remove the fillets, turn them over in the browned butter to give them a good colour. Leave to rest in a warm place for 5-10 minutes.

13.   Reheat the sauce, check the seasoning, consistency and temperature. If it is too thick, add a little water. Do not let it boil for more than a minute or two in order to preserve its colour.

14.   Place the fillets on a chopping board, trim off the small ends, then slice, at an angle, each one into eight pieces, approximately ½ in (1cm) thick.

15.   Pour some sauce on to the heated serving plates, enough to cover the base. Gently swirl the plate so that it covers the surface perfectly smoothly.

16.   Arrange four slices of lamb in a slight curve, overlapping, on the top half of the plate. Place a leek *pithiviers* on the bottom half, and serve immediately.

Alternatively, a red wine and lamb stock reduction can be served instead of the herby sauce. In this case, reduce by fast boiling, 5 fl.oz (150ml) of red wine with 2 teaspoons of redcurrant jelly, until only 3 tablespoons remain. Add 10 fl.oz (300 ml) strong lamb stock, bring to the boil and reduce until it begins to look syrupy. Shake in ½ tablespoon double cream and ½ oz (15g) butter. Season to taste with salt.

Noisettes d'Agneau des Tournelles aux Pâtes Fraîches

Lamb with Noilly Prat Sauce and Fresh Pasta

Change the herb and the alcohol, substitute a little cream for the butter, and you have endless possibilities for this dish. Fillets of lamb are cut into pieces an inch (2.5cm) thick, pan-fried and served with a sauce made by deglazing the pan with alcohol, adding lamb stock, herbs and a little butter. For this version I use a mixture of Noilly Prat and sherry flavoured with tarragon, but you could use other spirits such as brandy or whisky, and any herb, to make a different version. Lamb cooked in this way is moist, tasty, very tender and quick to make.

6 servings

3 fillets of lamb, 7-9 oz (200-250g) each (see page 124 for
more details)
1 dessertspoon hazelnut oil
seasoning
fresh tarragon, chopped
1-1½ oz (25-40g) unsalted butter
fresh pasta made from 6 oz (175g) strong plain flour, etc (see
page 49)
2½ fl.oz (65ml) double cream
1 oz (25g) fresh Parmesan cheese, finely grated

Noilly Prat sauce
2½ fl.oz (65ml) Noilly Prat
2½ fl.oz (65ml) medium dry sherry
10 fl.oz (300ml) strong lamb stock (see page 124)

Garnish
flat parsley or fresh coriander leaves

127

1.   Prepare the lamb as described on page 124, and make the lamb stock for the sauce. Marinate the fillets in the hazelnut oil, cover and refrigerate overnight. Allow the stock to cool and refrigerate.

2.   Next day, cut each fillet into six pieces, approximately 1 in (2.5cm) thick. Sit them, cut side up, on a tray or large plate, flatten them ever so slightly to give them a better shape, then sprinkle them with a little freshly ground black pepper and chopped tarragon. Cover with cling film and allow the flavours to develop at room temperature for an hour or two if possible.

3.   Make the pasta dough, cover with cling film and allow to rest in the refrigerator.

4.   Roll out as described, leaving it to dry for half an hour after the final rolling before cutting it into spaghetti, using the appropriate cutter. As mentioned, I like to cut it seconds before cooking it, so try to time it accordingly.

5.   To start cooking the dish, bring a large pan of cold water to the boil.

6.   Meanwhile, melt ¼ oz (10g) of the butter in a frying pan, and when it stops sizzling, but before it starts to brown, place half of the noisettes in the pan, cut sides down. Sprinkle with a little salt. Using tongs, turn over after a minute and brown the lamb on the other side. Turn again, and when the beads of blood appear on the surface, turn over once more. To achieve pink but not rare meat, they will need roughly 4 minutes altogether, but the heat of the pan will determine just how long they will take. When pressed with a finger, they should feel springy and neither hard nor too soft. If still soft, give them a little longer.

7.   Remove from the pan and place on a tray or ovenproof plate. Keep warm in a low oven while repeating with another ¼ oz (10g) of butter and the remaining lamb.

8.   Once the final noisettes have been cooked and removed, add the Noilly Prat and the sherry to the pan. The pan should be hot, so they will bubble fiercely and reduce quite quickly. Scrape up any dark sediment left in the pan.

9.   Reduce until only a few tablespoons remain, then add the lamb stock. Bring back to the boil and simmer until the stock starts to look syrupy.

10.   While the sauce is cooking, season the boiling water with a tablespoon of salt, run the pasta through the spaghetti cutters and drop into

NOISETTES DE CHEVREUIL DES TOURNELLES AVEC PATES FRAICHES

FILET D'AGNEAU AVEC SAUCE AUX HERBES ET PETIT PITHIVIER DE POIREAUX

the boiling water. Once it comes back to the boil (watch that it doesn't boil over), cook for 3 minutes, then drain through a sieve or colander.

11.　Return to the pan, add the cream and cheese, and stir over a gentle heat until the cheese melts and a sauce is formed.

12.　Add the remaining butter, cut into small pieces, to the lamb stock sauce which should thicken the sauce slightly. If it is not thick enough, carry on reducing it, but what you are trying to achieve is a light sauce which will just coat the back of a spoon. Taste for seasoning.

13.　Place three noisettes on each warmed serving plate. Form a little mound of pasta by twisting it on a fork in the bowl of a spoon. Sit it upright on the plate, spoon the sauce over or around the lamb, decorate the pasta with sprigs of flat parsley or coriander and serve immediately.

If you prefer, you could substitute 5 fl.oz (150ml) double cream for the butter in the sauce, which would result in a paler, creamy sauce (and more of it).

Venison fillet, cut into noisettes, can be cooked in the same way and served with the same sauce and pasta. Alternatively, the red wine and redcurrant sauce mentioned on page 114 is delicious served with venison. 4 mins each side

Filet d'Agneau 'Baumanière'

Fillet of Lamb with Kidney and Mushrooms

Many, many years ago, we dined at L'Oustaù de Baumanière in Les Baux-de-Provence. This was one of the first three-rosette restaurants we went to. There we ate a very famous dish which was a leg of baby lamb, stuffed with kidneys, mushrooms and truffles, then surrounded with puff pastry. I have to admit that we had to look for the stuffing and I think that we eventually found one little piece of kidney. Before we went there, I had actually made the dish, as its recipe is featured in a lovely book, *Secrets of the Great French Restaurants,* edited by Louisette Bertholle. Because I had the recipe, and therefore knew what to expect, it was rather a disappointing experience.

My version of it, using fillet of lamb, ensures that everyone gets a share of the stuffing! I do not use the wrapping of pastry, as personally I don't think that they are compatible. It is difficult to cook the pastry long enough without over-cooking the meat, so I miss it out.

6 servings

3 racks of lamb, with 8 ribs in each
1½ dessertspoons hazelnut oil
1½ oz (40g) unsalted butter
seasoning

'Stuffing'
4 lamb's kidneys
8 oz (225g) mushrooms (closed cap or open, it does not matter which)

Sauce
5 fl.oz (150ml) dry Madeira
dried or fresh rosemary
10 fl.oz (300ml) lamb stock (see page 124)
1 tablespoon double cream

130

1. Prepare the lamb as described on page 124 and marinate it overnight in the hazelnut oil. Make the stock for the sauce with the bones and root vegetables as described on page 124. Allow to chill, then refrigerate.

2. The next day, remove the lamb and let it sit at room temperature for at least an hour.

3. Preheat the oven to 475°F (240°C) Gas 9, or as high as it will go.

4. Place the kidneys in a bowl, and cover with boiling water. After 2 minutes, pour off and run plenty of cold water over the kidneys.

5. Remove the outer membrane from the kidneys. Cut the meat away from the core, then cut into ¼ in (6mm) dice.

6. Wipe the mushrooms clean. Cut off the stalk, then cut these into the same size of dice.

7. Melt ½ oz (15g) of the butter in a small frying pan, and add the kidneys when it starts to sizzle. Stir around until sealed on all sides. Add the mushrooms, season, stir together and cook gently for 5 minutes.

8. Weigh each fillet of lamb. Place them on a lightly buttered baking tray, a little apart. Sprinkle with salt, and either dot with little pieces of butter, ½ oz (15g) altogether, or brush with melted butter.

9. Bake on the middle shelf for 1 minute per ounce (25g) plus 2 minutes. If your fillets are 7 oz (200g), they will take 9 minutes to cook, which will give a rosy result.

10. While the lamb is cooking, place the Madeira and a sprig of rosemary in a fairly wide pan. Bring to the boil, reduce until only 2 tablespoons remain, then add the stock and continue to reduce. When it begins to look syrupy, add the remaining butter. You will have only about 6 tablespoons left.

11. After the calculated cooking time, remove the fillets, and roll them over in the slightly browned butter to give them a nice colour. Leave to rest in a warm place for 5-10 minutes so that they will relax.

12. During this time, make sure that the mushroom and kidney mixture is hot. It should not be too moist, so turn up the heat and let any liquid from the mushrooms evaporate until the mixture is quite dry.

13. Bring the sauce to the boil, check for seasoning, and add a little salt if necessary. Add the tablespoon of cream.

14. Using a sharp knife, trim off the small end of the fillet, then cut, at an angle, into eight slices, approximately ¼ in (6mm) thick.

15. Spoon a sixth of the mushroom mixture in a little mound on each heated serving plate. Lay four slices of lamb on top, overlapping slightly. Spoon a little sauce around the meat. Serve immediately.

Filet de Boeuf, Sauce Madère

Fillet of Beef with Madeira Sauce

During my early college days, when I became obsessed with food and cooking, we bought a *Time-Life* publication called *Classic French Cooking*. I can vividly remember being totally enraptured by it, being transported into the world of three-star restaurants. At that stage we had no idea that we would ever visit one, let alone all of them, and some many times! As the title suggests, the recipes in the book are very classical and therefore rather old-fashioned as opposed to the new style of cooking, but there are certain techniques and ideas which are relevant to any style.

I think that it must have been this book and its wonderful photograph of a fillet of beef which changed my attitude to cooking meat. We were both brought up on thoroughly cooked meat, but at some time around then, we realised that the only way to eat it was, as far as we were concerned, rare. There is such a difference in taste, texture and appearance. We don't, in fact, eat all that much red meat, but we certainly wouldn't bother at all if it was dry and over-cooked. I have based my recipe for fillet of beef on the one in *Classic French Cooking,* but I have increased the cooking time as their recipe would produce an almost raw result, more appealing to the French, I suspect.

6 servings

2½ lb (1.1kg) piece of fillet, cut from the wide end of the whole fillet
2 tablespoons hazelnut oil
1½ oz (40g) unsalted butter
seasoning

Madeira sauce
5 fl.oz (150ml) dry Madeira
10 fl.oz (300ml) beef or chicken stock
7½ fl.oz (225ml) double cream
a small black truffle, fresh preferably, or tinned

Garnish
fresh herbs such as flat parsley, tarragon or chervil

1. The fillet will be surrounded by at least a thin membrane and possibly by some fat also. Remove all traces of both, using a sharp knife. Tie the meat with string at 2 in (5cm) intervals.
2. Rub with the oil, cover and refrigerate overnight.
3. Next day, remove and allow to sit at room temperature for at least a couple of hours before cooking it.
4. Preheat the oven to 450°F (230°C) Gas 8. Weigh the fillet.
5. Place the meat in a lightly buttered baking tray, and spread with the butter (if it is hard, cut into little pieces and dot over the meat). Sprinkle 1½ teaspoons salt evenly over it.
6. Place in the middle of the preheated oven, and cook for 1 minute per oz (25g), plus 5 minutes extra. After 20 minutes, turn the oven down to 400°F (200°C) Gas 6.
7. While the meat is cooking, make the sauce. Place the Madeira in a pan, bring to the boil and reduce by fast boiling until 2 tablespoons remain.
8. Add the stock, bring back to the boil, and reduce by half. Add the cream and simmer until a smooth sauce is formed, which will lightly coat the back of a spoon.
9. Finely chop the thinly peeled fresh or tinned truffle. Add to the sauce and allow to infuse. Add the truffle juice if using a tinned truffle. Taste for seasoning, adding salt if necessary.
10. Remove the fillet and allow to rest, covered loosely with foil, in a warm place for 10 minutes which will give the meat time to relax.
11. Using a sharp knife, cut the fillet into ½ in (1cm) slices, removing the string as you reach it. Arrange two slices on each heated serving plate and half coat with some sauce. Decorate with some fresh herbs and serve immediately.

As a variation I sometimes make the fillet into a 'roulade', something which our good friend Betty Allen at Airds Hotel serves. The cooking time and herbs may not be the same as hers, but the concept is. Having trimmed the fillet, make a ½ in (1cm) cut along the top length of it, turn the knife to the horizontal inside the cut, and cut around inside the fillet, ½ in (1cm) from the outside edge, unrolling the meat as you cut. You are aiming to form a flat piece of meat, roughly ½ in (1cm) thick. Sprinkle liberally with a mixture of chopped fresh tarragon and parsley and season with freshly ground black pepper. Roll up tightly to form the original shape and tie with string at 2 in (5cm) intervals. Rub with hazelnut oil and follow instructions for the simpler version.

Boeuf Grillé au Charbon de Bois

Barbecued Steak

Sirloin, cooked on the barcecue as thick steaks, then cut across into slices, showing the contrasting colours of crisp blackened outside against the red meat, is a different and striking way to serve barbecued meat. As always, choose meat which has been well hung to ensure that it is tender and has flavour. The difference is very marked as will be apparent to those of you who have eaten steaks at Clive and Ann Davidson's restaurant, Champany Inn, at Linlithgow. There they take enormous care to serve beef that is reared and hung to their requirements, and the result is wonderfully tender, flavourful meat.

When the meat itself is moist and full of flavour, a sauce is not always necessary, and for this reason I serve these slices of sirloin with the puréed potatoes with olive oil and cream, which double as a vegetable and as a sauce due to their rich creamy texture. The combination makes a refined and sensual dish made up of rustic flavours. Carefully presented, it looks dramatic with the black, red and white colours contrasting with each other.

6 servings

4 sirloin steaks, 2 in (5cm) thick, most of the excess fat removed, but
leaving a thin layer
2 tablespoons hazelnut oil
seasoning
1 quantity Purée de Pommes de Terre à l'Huile d'Olive (see
page 144)
virgin olive oil (optional)

1. Place the trimmed steaks on a plate or flat dish, rub with the hazelnut oil and season with freshly ground black pepper. Cover with cling film and allow the flavours to develop for at least a few hours, but preferably overnight, refrigerated in that case.

2. Before cooking, remove and allow to sit at room temperature for a couple of hours. Set and light the barbecue half an hour in advance. Check it now and again to make sure that it is lit. When ready, the coals will be white and very hot. The grid should be approximately 3 in (7.5cm) from the coals.

3. Make the creamy potatoes and set aside while cooking the steaks.

4. Using tongs, place the steaks on the grid, season with salt, and cook for 1 minute. Turn over, and cook for another minute. Turn again, giving them 5 minutes longer on each side. It is difficult to state exactly how long they will need, as the heat of the coals will determine this, but you will learn from experience how to tell by feel. If you press gently with your tongs or a finger and the meat feels very soft, it will be very rare. If it gives a little resistance but still feels springy, the meat will be rare to medium rare, and if it feels firm, then it will be over-cooked. Please remember that to retain flavour, texture and moisture, meat which is rare to medium rare is a must.

5. Remove the steaks, placing them on a tray or plate, and allow to rest in a warm place for 5 minutes to allow their juices to be evenly distributed.

6. Meanwhile, carefully reheat the potato purée, beating with a wooden spoon as you do so. Cook over a gentle heat, otherwise the olive oil may separate out. Check for seasoning and temperature.

7. Cut the steaks across into slices ½ in (1cm) thick, discarding any large remaining chunks of fat. Divide between the warmed serving plates, arranging the slices side by side but overlapping slightly, to form a gentle curve. Spoon the potato purée to the inside of the curve and serve immediately.

The charm of this dish is its simplicity and all that is needed, if anything, to finish it, is a dribble of virgin olive oil over the potatoes.

135

Porc aux Pruneaux
Braised Pork with Prunes

This dish is unlike most of my meat courses in that it is cooked for a long time in a slow oven, as opposed to fast cooking in a very hot oven. The chops are marinated overnight in a sugar and salt solution which makes them more tender. An optional addition to the marinade is salt-petre which will make the chops pleasantly pink, but in these days of avoiding chemicals and additives you may prefer to omit it. This dish is hearty, tasty, warming and colourful, and is best served in the winter.

6 servings

6 large fresh double-loin pork chops
2½ oz (65g) soft brown or demerara sugar
2½ oz (65g) sea salt
¼ oz (10g) saltpetre (optional)
½ oz (15g) unsalted butter
12 fl.oz (350ml) dry cider
12 extra large prunes, Californian or Agen
10 fl.oz (300 ml) Vouvray wine
7½ fl.oz (225ml) double cream
2 oz (50g) fresh or frozen cranberries

Garnish
salad burnet leaves

1.   Heat 1½ pints (900ml) water with the sugar, salt and optional salt-petre in a pan. Once they have dissolved, bring to the boil. Boil for 2-3 minutes, remove from the heat and pour into a glass or plastic bowl or container. Allow to become completely cold.
2.   Using a sharp knife, trim most of the fat away from the chops and place in the cold marinade. Cover, having made sure that the chops are submerged in the liquid. Refrigerate overnight.
3.   Next day, preheat the oven to 300°F (150°C) Gas 2.
4.   Lift the chops out of the marinade and dry them on both sides using a clean towel or kitchen roll.

5. Melt the butter in a large frying pan, and when hot add the chops. Turn over with tongs after a minute to seal the other side. Transfer to an ovenproof dish which will take the chops in one layer (they can overlap slightly if necessary).

6. Pour the cider into the frying pan, bring to the boil, then pour over the chops. Cover with a layer of cling film, then tin foil. Bake in the preheated oven for 3 hours. Check now and again that they are cooking very gently. If, after say 1½ hours, the liquid is doing more than bubbling very gently, turn the heat down to 250°F (120°C) Gas ½ for the final cooking time.

7. Place the prunes in another glass or ceramic dish, pour the Vouvray over them, and cover with tin foil. Cook alongside the chops for at least 2 hours.

8. Half an hour before serving, remove the dish of chops, lift back the foil and pour out a little of the cooking liquid (approximately 5 fl.oz/150ml) into a bowl. Return the dish to the oven to complete cooking.

9. When the fat rises to the surface of the cooking liquid, spoon it off. Place the degreased liquid in a pan, bring to the boil and reduce a little. Add the cream, bring back to the boil and simmer until it has thickened.

10. Remove the prunes from the oven and pour any remaining wine into the sauce which will add sweetness and colour to it. Keep the prunes warm.

11. Add the cranberries to the sauce and allow them to heat through. Do not boil the sauce at this stage otherwise the cranberries will burst and spoil. It is important, therefore, that the consistency of the sauce is just right before adding them, as you do not want to have to reduce it any more. Taste the sauce for seasoning, but it is very unlikely that it will need any salt.

12. Place a chop on each warmed serving plate, coat with a spoonful or two of sauce and place a couple of prunes to the side. Decorate the cranberries with a leaf of salad burnet on either side of a few of them. Serve immediately.

Bouillon

Stock

The majority of my sauces are dependent on good stock. I do not use it in my soups, as I would rather keep it for sauces. Stock made by simmering vegetables and aromatics in water is useful for adding flavour when thinning down a sauce, but for the wonderful texture and intensity of a reduced sauce, a strong meat stock is essential.

After boning pigeons, pheasants, lamb, etc, I can make a large panful of stock, but by the time it has simmered gently, been strained and boiled rapidly to concentrate it, there is not all that much left. My recipes which require it in their sauces rely on the stock being well reduced and almost jelly like. If your stock is thinner, then you will need more of it and you will need to reduce it for a longer period of time to achieve the correct consistency and intensity of flavour.

If you do not use all the stock you have made, it will last for up to a week in the refrigerator, or it can be frozen. A useful notion is to boil it rapidly to reduce it dramatically, allow it to cool, then fill an ice-cube tray with it. Frozen like this the little cubes are very useful for popping into sauces. Remember, though, that these will be very much more concentrated than the stock in my sauces, and you will therefore not need to reduce it at this stage at all. After reducing the wine, cider or whatever, add the frozen cubes and the cream and simmer until the correct consistency is achieved.

I follow the same pattern when making any type of stock. Place the bones on a baking tray and roast these in a hot oven, 450°F (230°C) Gas 8, until they are nicely browned, about 20 minutes. Meanwhile cook diced onions, celery, carrot and leek in a suitably sized pan in a little butter. Allow these to brown lightly. Add the bones, then pour on enough cold water to cover them. Bring the water to the boil, skim off any scum which will have risen to the surface, then simmer gently, half covered, for 8 hours or longer. If I am making a large quantity I will simmer it overnight. The rate at which you simmer stock is very important. There should be no more than a gentle bubble in order to achieve a clear stock, as rapid boiling will produce a cloudy one. Strain through a colander into another pan, turn up the heat and boil rapidly to evaporate the water and to concentrate the flavour.

Pour into a bowl, allow it to cool, then refrigerate. It is very, very important to keep stock chilled as, if kept in warm conditions, it could be a source of bacterial growth. Always boil stock when using it, rather than just warming it up, and do not keep it longer than a week. If you know that you will not be using it all, then freeze it.

Try to make the stock in advance so that it has time to become cold before using it. The fat will rise to the top and set, enabling you to remove every scrap of it so that your stock is totally fat free. A greasy stock tastes most unpleasant, and can spoil the flavour of what should be a lovely sauce.

Pithiviers de Poireaux
Leek Pies

These little pies are filled with a purée of leeks and are served surrounded by a fresh herb sauce. Large ones can be served as a starter or vegetarian main course (in which case omit the stock in the sauce) or smaller ones as an accompaniment to slices of lamb fillet (see page 124).

4-6 servings

12 oz (350g) flaky pastry (see page 199)
1 egg yolk
seasoning

Leek purée
1 lb (45g) white part of leeks
½ oz (15g) unsalted butter
3 tablespoons double cream
4-6 leaves mint or basil

Herb sauce
2 handfuls mixed fresh herbs (tarragon, parsley, mint, chervil)
5 fl.oz (150ml) chicken stock
7½ fl.oz (225ml) double cream

1.   Clean the leeks by splitting in half and rinsing under cold water. Chop them finely by hand or in a food processor (in which case stop before they become too soft).

2.   Melt the butter in a pan and let it colour ever so slightly, then add the leeks. Stir together, add 1 teaspoon of salt and the cream, then cook for 15 minutes. Stir occasionally to make sure that they are not sticking. By the end of the cooking time, they should have softened and the mixture should be fairly dry. If still rather moist, turn up the heat and, stirring constantly, let the excess moisture evaporate. Taste and if necessary add an extra ½ teaspoon salt.

3.   Turn out on to a plate to cool thoroughly before using.

4.   Lightly flour your work surface. Roll the pastry out to a thickness of just less then ⅛ in (3mm). Using a 4 in (10cm) and a 4½-5 in (12-13cm) cutter, cut out four rounds of each size. You may have to lay the scraps of pastry on top of each other and re-roll to get all eight rounds. (If making smaller *pithiviers* use 3½ and 3¾ in (8 and 9cm cutters.)

5.   Moisten the outer surface of the smaller rounds with a little cold water, place a mound of leek filling in the centre and top with a large leaf of fresh mint or basil. Make sure that there is a ½ in (1cm) border which is completely leek free, as this is essential if the pastry is to stick together without any gaps where the filling would come out during the cooking.

6.   Place the larger rounds over the filling, matching outer edges perfectly. Press together well, without damaging the cut edges. Place an upturned cutter, the same circumference as the mound, over it, while you knock up the cut edges with a sharp knife. The upturned cutter ensures that the finish is neat and even, and you don't have to touch the pastry too much. Knock up the edge by making several cuts into the pastry all the way around. This ensures that the pastry is sealed together and that the pastry will rise evenly.

7.   Make a decorative border by pressing your thumb outwards while pushing the edge of a knife in towards the centre. Repeat, at a thumb's breadth apart, all around the *pithiviers.*

8.   Moisten a baking tray with a little cold water, shake off any excess, and place the *pithiviers* on it, leaving ½ in (1cm) space at least between each one. Allow to rest in the refrigerator for at least an hour.

9.   Preheat oven to 400°F (200°C) Gas 6.

10.   Meanwhile, make the sauce by dropping the herbs into lightly salted boiling water. Bring back to the boil, then drain through a sieve.

Refresh with plenty of cold running water, to set the colour. Drain, squeeze out most of the moisture and place in your liquidiser. (You will get a smoother sauce if liquidised rather than by blending in a food processor.)

11. Place the stock in a pan, bring to the boil and reduce it a little by fast boiling. Add the cream, bring back to the boil and simmer until it has reduced enough to form a light coating consistency.

12. Pour on to the herbs and blend until a smooth sauce is formed. Pour back into the pan, using a rubber bowl scraper to remove every last drop. Rinse out with a very little hot water and add to the sauce. Taste for seasoning, adding a little salt if necessary.

13. Beat the egg yolk with a few drops of cold water, then, using a pastry brush, give each *pithiviers* a light coating of egg wash. Be careful not to let it dribble down the sides as this would seal the edges together, thus preventing even rising.

14. Using a small sharp pointed knife, lightly mark their tops. Do this by marking from the centre, a curved line to one of the scallops around the edge. Repeat, starting from the centre again and curve towards the next scallop, until all the scallops are used up.

15. Bake for 15-20 minutes, until risen, golden brown and crisp.

16. Reheat the sauce carefully. Do not let it boil for more than 2-3 minutes otherwise the colour will spoil. Check taste and consistency.

17. Ladle or spoon some sauce on to each warmed serving plate, and swirl the plate carefully to spread it evenly around. Loosen each *pithiviers* with a fish slice or spatula and sit one in the centre of each plate. Serve immediately.

Gratin Dauphinois

Potato Gratin

When I first made Gratin Dauphinoise, I made it in the traditional manner, layering thinly sliced potato, grated Parmesan cheese and double cream. This was extremely time-consuming as the potato slices had to be rinsed and dried individually, and it was very rich as a great deal of cream was needed. Fortunately, the Troisgros brothers came to my rescue. In their book *La Nouvelle Cuisine,* which features recipes from their restaurant in Roanne, they included a recipe for their version of a potato gratin. Although I have changed the method slightly and have cut down on the cream considerably, I am grateful to them for showing me an alternative way of making this dish. Contrary to how it looks and tastes, it is actually fairly light in comparison to the traditional method, as it is made with both milk and cream, rather than solely with cream.

5 servings

1½ lb (675g) potatoes, peeled weight (large baking potatoes save time)
6 fl.oz (175ml) milk
2 teaspoons salt
1 small garlic clove, peeled and crushed
2½ fl.oz (65ml) double cream
½ oz (15g) fresh Parmesan cheese, grated

1. Preheat oven to 350°F (180°C) Gas 4.
2. Thinly slice the potatoes in a food processor fitted with the slicing blade. Alternatively, use a mandoline or a very sharp knife.
3. Place the potato slices in a wide pan. Add the milk, salt and the crushed garlic. Mix together thoroughly with a large spoon. Cover with a lid, place over a medium heat and bring to the boil. Check now and again, then once boiling, add the cream. Stir it in thoroughly but carefully as you do not want to break up the potato slices.
4. Continue to cook for 3-5 minutes, or until the starch in the

potatoes combines with the milk and cream to produce a thick, creamy mixture.

5.   Transfer the potato slices and their creamy sauce into an ovenproof gratin dish. Sprinkle the grated Parmesan cheese over the top.

6.   Bake in the preheated oven for 45-60 minutes, by which time the potatoes will be tender and the top will be golden brown. At this stage they can be served straightaway as an accompaniment to a main course or they will happily wait a few hours (reheat them for 15 minutes until piping hot).

Alternatively, let them become cold and set. Cover and refrigerate overnight if time permits. Stamp out rounds using a pastry cutter, or cut into small squares or triangles, then place on a lightly buttered baking tray and reheat at 350°F (180°C) Gas 4 for 10-15 minutes. This gives a neater result than serving in spoonfuls.

Do not use a non-stick pan when cooking the potatoes with the milk. It is normal for them to scorch when cooking, and a certain proportion will to an extent stick to the pan and remain there. (Your pan will be difficult to clean, but it helps if you soak it for a while.) If you use a non-stick pan, the browned potato would be stirred throughout the rest of the mixture when you mix in the cream.

Gratin Dauphinois au Citron

Potato Gratin with Lemon

Follow the previous recipe, but in place of the garlic, add the finely grated rind of a lemon. I think that this makes a lovely, fresh alternative to a garlicky version, and it goes particularly well with the Suprême de Dinde aux Pruneaux (see page 110), as the sharpness contrasts well with the sweetness of the sauce.

Purée de Pommes de Terre à l'Huile d'Olive

Mashed Potatoes with Olive Oil

It is funny to see how a fairly simple dish can be hyped up by media and food writers, which transforms it into something exciting and original in the eyes of the public. One such dish is a purée of potato made famous by Joël Robuchon. I agree that these are very special mashed potatoes, but they are not really worth getting into a frenzy over. What makes them so very appealing to some people is that they contain at least 9 oz (250g) butter to 2 lb (900g) potatoes! (*Anyone's* mashed potatoes would be delicious if these proportions were used!)

My potatoes are still very rich, and a little goes a long way, but they are especially good with a piece of simply barbecued steak or chicken. No sauce is needed as the potatoes are creamy enough.

4-6 servings

1 lb (450g) potatoes, peeled weight
4 tablespoons double cream
5-6 tablespoons virgin olive oil
seasoning
flat parsley (optional)

1. Cut the peeled potatoes into even-sized pieces, then boil in lightly salted water until tender. Drain well.
2. Press the potatoes through a sieve or mouli into a bowl.
3. Heat the cream in the same pan, add the potato purée and stir together with a wooden spoon.
4. Gradually add the olive oil, beating well between each addition. Taste for seasoning and add a little salt and freshly ground black pepper if desired. Reheat gently, stirring frequently.
5. Serve as it is, or add some finely chopped fresh parsley just before serving. How much depends on personal taste, and on how green you would like it to be.

(clockwise from front) *SUPREME DE DINDE AUX PRUNEAUX,*
CREME BRULEE, PANFORTE, POUDING DE NOËL

ST CHEVRIER EN SALADE, BRIE, PAINS VARIES, MUFFINS AUX FRAMBOISES, BISCUITS D'AVOINE

Ratatouille

This is a more sophisticated version of the usual ratatouille. The vegetables are cut into very small dice which gives the finished dish a neater effect. Served in small heaps with the Aubergine Terrine on page 54, it complements the flavour of the terrine as well as making the whole dish look very pretty. Apart from this use, serve the ratatouille as a vegetable, as a bed under scrambled eggs (like pipérade) or baked in a ramekin topped with an egg, cream and freshly grated Parmesan. Ratatouille is equally good served hot, warm or cold.

6-8 garnish servings

3½ oz (90g) each, prepared weight, of aubergines, courgettes, red peppers, green peppers and tomatoes
1 teaspoon salt
1 tablespoon olive oil
3½ tablespoons passata (a tomato purée available in cartons which has a consistency half-way between juice and paste)
freshly chopped basil

1. Skin and seed the tomatoes, seed the peppers, then chop all the vegetables – separately – into neat ⅛ in (3mm) dice.
2. Place the courgette and aubergine dice in a sieve and sprinkle with salt. Allow to drain for half an hour.
3. Heat the oil in a non-stick frying pan, add the pepper dice, and cook for 3 minutes, stirring all the time. Shake the water from the sieve and add the aubergines and courgettes. Cook for another 3 minutes, then add the passata and diced tomato. Stir together and cook for a few minutes longer – from start to finish it should take about 10 minutes.
4. Remove from the heat. Serve hot, warm or cold, adding a few leaves of finely chopped fresh basil just before serving.

Ratatouille Grillée

Grilled Ratatouille with Rocket Salad

For a different, more rustic treatment of ratatouille, I like this version. Chunky strips of aubergine, courgette, red and green peppers and leeks are grilled with virgin olive oil. Serve at room temperature with a rocket salad, topped with fine flakes of fresh Parmesan cheese as a starter or light summer main course, or on its own as an accompaniment. Rocket is one of our favourite products from the formal herb garden which we have created at La Potinière.

6 servings

3 leeks with approx. 5 in (13 cm) of white once the green part has been removed
salt
1 firm aubergine, wiped
3 medium, dark, firm courgettes, wiped
3 red peppers, wiped
3 green peppers, wiped
3 tablespoons olive oil
1 small garlic clove, peeled and crushed
1 large handful of freshly picked rocket
2 tablespoons French dressing (see page 150)
1 oz (25g) fresh Parmesan cheese, in one piece

1. Trim the leeks by cutting off the root end and removing the coarser outer layers. Cut along their length to within ½ in (12 mm) of the root end. Rinse under cold water, then tie together in a bundle with string.
2. Bring a pan of water to the boil, add a teaspoon of salt and drop in the leeks. Boil for 5 minutes, then drain and refresh by running cold water over them. Drain well, untie and pat dry with paper towels. Cut each half in two, lengthwise.
3. Cut the stalk off the aubergine, cut in half lengthwise, then cut into strips with a ¼ in (6mm) cross section and 5 in (13cm) long. You do not need to be too precise about this.

4. Trim the ends off the courgettes, cut in half lengthwise, then cut each half in two, again lengthwise, giving four long strips per courgette. If the courgettes are rather large, cut into six or eight pieces instead.

5. Place the aubergines and courgettes in a colander or sieve. Sprinkle with a teaspoon of salt, and drain over a bowl for half an hour. Shake well before using.

6. Preheat the grill.

7. Skin the red peppers by blackening over a gas flame or under a hot grill as described in the recipe for Aubergine Terrine (see page 54), and cut into ¼×5 in (6mm×13cm) strips.

8. Cut the green peppers into ¼ in×5 in (6mm×13cm) strips.

9. Place the strips of vegetable on a baking tray, spread out evenly, and spoon the olive oil over them. Place under the grill and grill for about 10 minutes, or until they are lightly cooked and browned in places (carefully turn the vegetables over half-way through). If necessary cook them in two batches if your grill is not big enough.

10. Transfer to a non-metal dish, add the crushed garlic and gently mix together, taking care not to break up the strips. Season to taste with a little salt if necessary. Allow to cool to room temperature before serving.

11. Pick through the rocket and toss it in a bowl with the well-shaken French dressing.

12. Arrange the grilled ratatouille to one side of each serving plate, and pile a few pieces of rocket to the other side.

13. Cut wafer-thin flakes of Parmesan and scatter them over the ratatouille.

Confit d'Oignons
Onion Confit

This is a highly flavoured, well reduced, tasty mixture of sliced onion, sugar, sherry vinegar and Crème de Cassis. It can be used like chutney, or as a bed for meats such as chicken or duck breast. A little goes a long way as it is so intense. Although you need to caramelise the onions, avoid burning as this will produce a bitter taste.

8 servings

1½ oz (40g) butter
2 lb (900g) onions, peeled and finely sliced
4 oz (100g) demerara sugar
3 tablespoons sherry vinegar
1½ tablespoons Crème de Cassis
2 teaspoons salt

1.   Melt the butter in a medium-sized saucepan and when it starts to turn light brown, add the onions. Stir together and cook gently for 5 minutes, stirring with a wooden spoon now and again.
2.   Add the remaining ingredients, including the salt, stir together, then simmer uncovered for 1½-2 hours. The time required will depend on the size of your pan, the heat and even the onions, as some are more watery than others. Stir occasionally in order to prevent the mixture from sticking and scorching. The finished 'marmalade' should look dark golden and sticky.

Use the onion confit as required while still hot or transfer to a bowl and cover when cold. Due to the high sugar content, this will keep for weeks in the refrigerator. Make sure that it is well sealed as its smell may affect other foods in the refrigerator. Make a larger quantity if you want to have some on hand in the future, to add interest to meat, fish or cheese dishes.

Salade

My salads are made from a variety of ingredients which provide contrasting colours, textures and tastes, and are dressed with a walnut and olive oil French dressing. Prepare your ingredients as near to serving them as possible, and only dress the salad at the last minute.

Use raw vegetables such as fennel to add crunch and to raise the salad's nutritional value. Raw vegetables retain their minerals and vitamins, whereas cooking destroys some of them. Seeds and nuts, such as sunflower seeds and hazelnuts which are very high in certain vitamins and minerals, also provide a contrast in texture. The other ingredients that I normally use are iceberg, lollo rosso, oak leaf and frisée lettuces, raddichio, sugar peas or mangetouts and fine asparagus. Frisée and raddichio are both rather bitter so don't let them dominate.

If you are making a salad for four or six people as opposed to a restaurantful, you will probably find the packs of mixed salad ingredients which are available from good supermarkets useful as you only buy what you need, rather than be left with half of this and half of that. Fresh herbs such as rocket, basil and tarragon are wonderful in salads and can be used separately or together. Finely grated orange rind is interesting too.

6 servings

6-8 oz (175-225g) prepared weight of as wide a variety of lettuces as possible
1 fennel bulb, outer layer removed
4 oz (100g) sugar peas or mangetouts, topped and tailed (keep in the refrigerator so that they will be as crisp as possible)
4 oz (100g) fine asparagus, woody ends broken off
1 tablespoon sunflower seeds
1 tablespoon whole hazelnuts
fresh herbs such as rocket, basil or tarragon
French dressing (see page 150)

1. Examine the leaves carefully, remove outer leaves, rinse and shake dry. Break them into bite-sized pieces and place in a large bowl. Add the fennel, cut into slices, and the remaining salad ingredients.

2. Shake the dressing well and add 3-4 tablespoons to the salad. Toss together gently but thoroughly, so that every ingredient is covered lightly and evenly dispersed throughout. The dressing should coat each leaf without leaving a pool at the bottom of the bowl. Too much dressing will make the salad heavy and limp, so add a little at a time if you are not sure. The drier the leaves the better, so that the dressing clings to the leaves and is not watered down.

As soon as a leaf salad is dressed, it should be served immediately.

Sauce Vinaigrette
French Dressing

A dressing can make or mar a salad. A good one, using interesting oil and a good vinegar, can transform simple salad leaves into something very delicious. There are so many different oils to choose from, and which one you use depends on your taste and their availability. Nut oils such as hazelnut and walnut have a very strong but lovely flavour and, if added to olive oil, make a French dressing more interesting. If using a nut oil as well as olive oil it would be a waste to use virgin olive oil as the flavours would compete.

Makes 1¼ pints (750ml)

15 fl.oz (450ml) olive oil
5 fl.oz (150ml) walnut oil (refrigerate any left over)
5 fl.oz (150ml) white wine vinegar
2 teaspoons salt
2 teaspoons sugar
2 teaspoons Moutarde de Meaux

1. Place all the ingredients in a liquidiser and blend for 30 seconds. Pour into a large screw-topped jar.
2. Shake well before using.

THE FOURTH COURSE

CHEESE
AND
SWEETS

 In the restaurant at lunchtime we offer a choice between the sweet, and Brie served with oatcakes (see page 209) and a wedge of Golden Delicious apple, and at dinner we serve both, the cheese preceding the sweet. We prefer to serve just one cheese in perfect condition, and we serve Brie because we like it, because of our affection for all things French, and because as far as cheese goes, it is one of the less rich ones. It may look smooth and creamy, but at about 50 per cent it is actually lower in fat than the harder cheeses such as Cheddar or richer ones such as Stilton.

When serving any cheese, its flavour and texture are greatly enhanced if it is not too cold. It should never be refrigerated. I prefer Brie to be soft and creamy throughout, without being unpleasantly ripe, whereas David prefers it to be soft under the skin, but with a slightly firmer centre.

At home we occasionally serve a goat's cheese salad (see page 153) as a cheese course or instead of a sweet. I've also included some breads which could accompany cheese.

Many of my childhood memories are linked with food – what we ate on holidays, what my friends' mothers made, when I 'stayed for tea', what we ate at home, which sweets I surreptitiously ate during classes at school. My first attempts at cooking were sweet things such as Empire biscuits and tablet for the school tuck shop. As I became older and more interested in cooking it was the baking side of cooking that I continued with, making cakes and pies and puddings. When I started college, I continued to concentrate on this type of cooking and constantly experimented at home, aided by the generosity of my parents. They were very encouraging, and I never had to consider the cost of the ingredients I was using. Perhaps this is why, to this day, we don't cost any of the dishes we prepare in the restaurant.

Many of the sweets here can be made in advance, which is always a help if you are preparing a meal of several courses. It is best, if possible, to spread the work load so that you do not have too much to do at one time.

I do not like ostentatious looking sweets – you won't find any spun sugar domes here – but made and served with care, the following recipes should look good and taste even better!

The cheese course is traditionally the point in the meal dedicated, by wine drinkers, to the 'special' bottle. It is ideally suited to this purpose since there is no pressure to enjoy the food before it goes cold or spoils, and all one's attention can be focused on the contents of the glass. Furthermore, if cheese is taken before the sweet, it provides an opportunity to finish off the wine from the previous course, or have a little more of it, before changing to a 'dessert' wine.

Yet most of the wines you might plan to drink with sweets would probably be more enjoyable drunk before or after, and would be perfect with cheese. Apart from the very strong and the very sweet, even 'dessert' wines will find a pudding an unequal contest. At least try the first glass with some cheese as therein lie some of the most successful food and wine combinations of all. It would be a great pity, for example, to save all the Sauternes for the Creme Brulee and never experience it with Roquefort. But although fine sweet wines are singularly compatible with various cheeses, dry white wines also make some very suitable partners, and more often than red. Try, for example, Savennières with a fresh goat's cheese, a *vin jaune* from the Jura with a ripe Camembert, or Gewurztraminer with Munster.

Saint Chevrier avec Huile de Truffe et Salade de Roquette

Goat Cheese and Truffle Oil with Rocket Salad

Truffles are unique. If you have never tasted them, they are difficult to describe to you as their smell is unlike anything else. It is their smell rather than their flavour that is so overpowering and mysterious. We have experienced both French and Italian truffles many times on our travels, and very different they are too. It is the white Italian ones, which are at their peak in October, that are the most striking. Very fine slivers over pasta or risottos, or even just over toasted bread sprinkled with virgin olive oil, will transform these dishes into something very special (and something very expensive, unfortunately).

An alternative to using the truffle itself is to use an olive oil which has been infused with it, so that the perfume and some of the flavour is absorbed. One dish that we think works well is this one, slices of Saint Chevrier, a goat cheese, marinated in a little truffle oil and served with a rocket salad. Rocket, a herb which is very easy to grow, also has an intriguing taste, but they complement each other well. Serve this on individual plates as a starter, or as a cheese course, serving it on one large pretty platter along with a bowl of the salad. A sweetish bread such as a sultana soda bread, toasted, makes a wonderful accompaniment.

6 servings

12 oz (350g) Saint Chevrier cheese
3 tablespoons truffle oil
3 oz (75g) mixed leaves such as oak leaf, frisée and lambs lettuce,
rinsed and dried
2 oz (50g) rocket leaves
4 oz (100g) sugar snap peas
4 oz (100g) thin asparagus
2-3 tablespoons French dressing (see page 150)

1.   Cut the cheese into six slices. This will be easier if it has been in the refrigerator. Arrange the slices on a plate and dribble the truffle oil over them. Cover with cling film and allow the flavours to develop for at least 2 hours. The truffle taste will be much stronger if you leave them marinating overnight in the refrigerator.

2.   Pick over the salad and the rocket leaves, discarding any wilted ones. Top and tail the sugar snap peas. Break off the woody end of the asparagus by bending them near the base. Where they snap will be the spot where the woodiness starts. Place all of these ingredients in an attractive salad bowl. Cover if not using straightaway.

3.   Make the French dressing.

4.   When ready to serve, shake the dressing well and dress the salad with 2-3 tablespoons of it, then toss with a wooden salad spoon and fork.

5.   If serving as a starter, arrange some salad on each plate, then place a slice of cheese next to it, dribbling any excess oil over it. If serving as a cheese course serve the cheese on the platter, with the salad served from the salad bowl. Your guests can help themselves to as much or as little as they still have room for. Serve with toasted slices of Sultana Soda Bread (see page 202).

Parfait au Caramel
Caramel Parfait

I think that our friend David Wilson's eyes nearly popped out when he saw how small this was, but after tasting it, understood why. It is so rich and intense, rather like eating a large soft toffee. Make it when you have got peace and quiet in the kitchen as you need to concentrate on various stages.

9 servings

10 oz (275g) caster sugar
1 large soft vanilla pod, cut open lengthwise to release the seeds
1 pint (600ml) double cream
8 egg yolks, size 2

To serve and decorate
2½ fl.oz (65ml) double cream
2 teaspoons crushed praline (see page 171)
or chopped browned almonds

1.   Place the sugar and vanilla pod in a frying pan. Heat over a medium heat until the sugar melts and becomes a deep golden brown. Stir now and again to ensure that the sugar melts and browns evenly.
2.   At the same time, heat the cream in a *large* pan.
3.   Add the caramel to the hot cream as soon as the caramel is the correct colour. Remember that it will carry on getting darker, even if taken off the heat, until it is added to the cream. Wear rubber gloves for this, as the caramel and cream react violently and will splutter and foam up, hence the reason for the large pan.
4.   Stir gently until they mix completely, returning it to the heat if the caramel does not dissolve into the cream.
5.   Place the egg yolks in a bowl which will fit inside a pan of simmering water. Beat gently, then pour the hot caramel cream on to them, stirring as you do so.
6.   Place the bowl in the pan of simmering water (the water should come half-way up the custard). Whisk constantly as the custard cooks. When it is thick enough to coat the back of a spoon, pour it through a sieve into another bowl.
7.   Whisk occasionally as it cools, and when it is cold, cover with cling film and refrigerate until very cold and thick.
8.   Transfer to a good pouring jug, using a rubber bowl scraper to get every drop. Pour into nine small white *pot-au-crème* dishes, place on a tray, then place in the freezer until firm.
9.   Remove from the freezer shortly before serving. They should be firm, but soft enough to push your spoon into them. Fill a piping bag fitted with a large star nozzle with the lightly whipped cream. Pipe a swirl in the centre of each pudding and sprinkle with the praline or chopped nuts. Serve immediately.

Velour d'Abricot
Iced Apricot Cream

Here is the dessert which has evoked more moans of pleasure than any other. It is velvety smooth, creamy and sweet. Although it is fairly straightforward, I don't think that you should attempt it if you are not practised at making a real egg custard. It would be such a waste of time and money if the custard curdled, but if you do want to have a go, read the recipe on custard making (see page 188) for some advice.

If you have not had the foresight to make your own apricot preserve from fresh apricots, use a manufactured one such as Tiptree with a high fruit content and no preservatives or colourings. Surprisingly, the flavours of apricot brandies vary enormously. Try to find one which tastes of the fruit rather than of almonds.

8-10 servings

16 fl.oz (475ml) double cream
2 thin strips lemon rind, approx. ½×2 in (1×5cm) (avoid cutting the pith)
8 egg yolks, size 2
1¾ oz (45g) caster sugar
12 oz (350g) apricot preserve
8-10 teaspoons apricot brandy

1.   Bring the cream and lemon rind to just under boiling point in a pan over a moderate heat.
2.   Meanwhile beat the egg yolks and sugar together with a balloon whisk in a bowl which will sit inside a pan of simmering water. I use a stainless steel one which is part of a Kenwood. It is quite steep sided and fits neatly into a large pan.
3.   When the cream is very hot, pour it on to the yolks, whisking as you do so.
4.   Sit the bowl in the pan of simmering water (which should reach two-thirds of the way up the custard) and, whisking constantly, cook the custard until it is thick enough to coat the back of a spoon fairly

thickly. It will be more stable than a custard made with milk, so you can afford to let it cook that little bit longer. However, as soon as it reaches this stage, remove the bowl and pour the custard through a sieve into another bowl. While you cook the custard, use a rubber spatula to make sure that the custard nearest the bowl (which will cook quickest) is mixed with the rest.

5. Whisk the custard now and again as it cools. It should be very smooth, and as it cools it will thicken. When cold, cover with cling film and refrigerate until very cold.

6. Place the preserve in the bowl of your food processor fitted with the cutting blade. Blend for a minute until smooth. Add the cold custard, scraping every morsel from the bowl into the processor. Blend again until well mixed.

7. Sit a fine-meshed sieve over the bowl (the same, no need to wash it), and pour the apricot custard through it, again scraping out every last drop. Use a wooden spoon to rub it through the sieve, pressing fairly hard so that only a few apricot skins remain in the sieve.

8. Transfer the custard to a good pouring jug such as a measuring jug, and pour into eight to ten small white porcelain *pot-au-crème* dishes. (Leave enough space at the top to allow apricot brandy to be floated on, without spilling down the sides as you transport them to the table.)

9. Freeze for at least 4 hours, by which time they will be set and firm.

10. Remove from the freezer for up to 10 minutes before serving. If they have only had the 4 hours, then 3 or 4 minutes will be long enough, but if they have been frozen overnight, 10 minutes will be required to allow them to reach the right consistency. They should be firm but soft enough to push your spoon into.

11. Top with a teaspoon of apricot brandy and serve immediately.

Parfait au Chocolat
Chocolate Parfait

Serve this in little white china *pot-au-crème* dishes topped with Tia Maria. It is simple to make providing that you have either a liquidiser or a food processor. The texture is a cross between an ice cream and a mousse, and it makes a lovely filling for the Gâteau St Jean on page 160. It is set by freezing and it will keep well in the freezer, so you can make it ahead if necessary.

6-8 servings

4½ oz (120g) Bournville plain chocolate (the 2 oz/50g bars are
easier to break up)
2 oz (50g) caster sugar
4 tablespoons cold water
3 egg yolks, size 2
10 fl.oz (300ml) double cream, very cold
Tia Maria

1. Make sure that your liquidiser or food processor bowl is spotlessly clean, with no lingering onion smells. (I keep a separate bowl for sweet dishes.) Break the chocolate into it.
2. Place the sugar and water in a small pan. Place on a medium heat and allow the sugar to dissolve. Bring to the boil and boil rapidly for about 4 minutes. The exact length of time depends on the size of your pan and the intensity of the heat used, but you are aiming to have 4 tablespoons of sugar syrup left. Measure it out into a cup or small bowl to check, and if there is still too much liquid, return to the pan and carry on boiling. If you have less than 4 tablespoons, too much water has evaporated, so add enough hot water to make it up.
3. Without wasting any time, while the syrup is very hot, pour it into the chocolate. If you don't add it quickly enough the chocolate will remain gritty. Cover with the lid and blend for about 15 seconds, then drop in the egg yolks with the motor running.

4. Continue to blend until the mixture lightens in colour slightly and becomes thick and smooth. Stop after a short time, remove the lid and scrape down the sides of the bowl and the lid with a rubber spatula. Cover again and continue to blend.

5. Meanwhile, whip the cream lightly until it will form a soft trail when lifted by the whisk or electric beaters. If you over-beat the cream, small lumps of cream will freeze throughout the parfait which will spoil its smooth texture.

6. Using the rubber spatula, scrape out every last drop of the chocolate mixture on to the cream. Using a balloon whisk, gently amalgamate the two, until you have a smooth chocolate mixture, without any streaks of cream.

7. Transfer this into a good pouring jug (a measuring jug is ideal), and carefully pour it into the small pots. I fill eight little pots, but you may wish to serve larger portions. It is quite useful to make one more than you need, so that when it comes to serving, you can test the spare one to see if it has defrosted enough. If the surface is not smooth, bang the pots gently on your work surface and this should level it off.

8. Sit the pots on a tray and place in the freezer for at least 4 hours.

9. Remove from the freezer shortly before you wish to serve. How long depends on how long they have been frozen. If only for the 4 hours, 2 or 3 minutes will be long enough, but if they have been in the freezer overnight or longer, then they will need 10 minutes to come to the right consistency. They should be firm, but soft enough to be able to push your spoon into.

10. Top each one with a teaspoon of Tia Maria and serve immediately.

Gâteau St Jean

Chocolate Ice Cream Cake

I invented this in the summer of 1986 and first served it on Midsummer's Eve to a group who came for dinner on that evening every year. As Midsummer's Day is *La Saint Jean* in France, it seemed appropriate to call it Gâteau St Jean. It is made by sandwiching the Parfait au Chocolat mixture between two layers of the lightest of chocolate sponges, setting it in the freezer, then serving it cut into wedges on a Crème Anglaise. Make the sponge in a tin which is slightly larger in diameter than the deep tin in which you will be assembling the dessert, as the sponge will shrink away from the sides of the tin as it cools. It is safer to cut down a larger one, than to risk using one that is too small as the filling will leak out the bottom.

8-12 servings

3 eggs, size 2
2 oz (50g) caster sugar
1 oz (25g) cocoa powder, plus extra for dusting
1½ quantities Parfait au Chocolat (see page 158)
2 quantities Crème Anglaise (see page 188)

1.   Make the sponge first. Preheat the oven to 350°F (180°C) Gas 4. Lightly brush the base and sides of a 7½-8 in (19-20cm) sandwich tin with melted butter. If you have one of that size with a loose bottom, so much the better. Cut out a round of Bakewell or greaseproof paper to fit the base exactly, fit it in and butter that also.
2.   Separate the eggs, placing the yolks in one bowl, and the whites in another. Both bowls should be medium-sized to allow the contents to expand in volume.
3.   Start whisking the yolks in a free-standing mixer or using an electric hand-held one, and gradually add the sugar. When the mixture is thick and pale, sieve in the cocoa. Gently mix the two together.
4.   Wash the beaters thoroughly and dry them. Whisk the egg whites until stiff, but stop before they become dry.

5. Add a quarter of the whites to the chocolate mixture and fold in fairly roughly, then empty the remaining whites on top and fold these in gently and carefully with a large metal spoon. You may need to use a spatula to loosen all of the chocolate mixture from the sides of the bowl.

6. When thoroughly mixed, pour into the sandwich tin, level the top, and bake on the middle shelf of the preheated oven for 18 minutes. By this time it will have risen and be slightly springy to a gentle touch.

7. Remove and allow to cool before turning out. It will shrink during this time, but that is normal, so do not worry. Because the sponge contains no flour, it is extremely light and fragile, and turning it out can be tricky. The top surface will spoil if you touch it, so you have to remove it from the tin without doing so. This is why a tin with a removable base is better, but not essential. I insert a palette knife down the side and under the outside edge of the Bakewell paper, lift it so that I can get a hold on the paper and pull the cake out gently on to my other hand. Peel back the paper while sliding it on to your cooling tray.

8. When cold, trim it with scissors or a sharp knife so that it will fit exactly into a deep cake tin with a removable base (6½ in/16cm in diameter, 3¼ in/8cm in height). Very carefully cut in two horizontally using a serrated bread knife. Lower the bottom half into the tin, and if there are any gaps, patch with scraps of sponge.

9. Make up the recipe for the Parfait au Chocolat, making 1½ times the recipe. Once the cream has been mixed in, pour it into the tin, on top of the sponge.

10. Transfer it to the freezer and freeze until it begins to set but is still slightly soft. Remove, carefully drop the remaining sponge layer on top, then return to the freezer and freeze overnight.

11. Make up a double quantity of Crème Anglaise and allow to cool. Cover and refrigerate.

12. Remove the gâteau one hour before you wish to serve it, and allow it to soften at room temperature. If it is very hot in your kitchen transfer it to your refrigerator for some of that time.

13. Sieve cocoa powder over the top of the gâteau, sit the tin on a salt drum or similar, pull down the sides of the tin, then transfer the gâteau, on its metal base, to a flat plate or board.

14. Ladle some custard on to your serving plates, and swirl it around to cover the plate evenly. Cut the gâteau into wedges, slide out using a palette knife and sit upright on top of the custard. Serve immediately.

Larmes de Chocolat Agenaise
Chocolate Tears

These teardrops are springing up all over the place! I first made them in 1988 on our return from France, where we met them at Michel Trama's restaurant, L'Aubergade at Puymirol. He is amongst the the best cooks in France, and will surely gain a third Michelin star soon for his imaginative, perfectly executed and delicious food. His cookery book *La Cuisine en Liberté* includes the original recipe. Michel's son-in-law, who runs the front of house, kindly gave me some of the plastic strip required to make them, but strips cut from sheets of celluloid from artists' supply shops will do. I substitute my own filling and I have changed the sauce, adding prune juice as a little homage to the origins of the dish.

8-10 servings

6 oz (175g) Menier plain chocolate

Mousse
6 oz (175g) Bournville plain chocolate
9 fl.oz (275ml) double cream, chilled
2 eggs, size 2, separated
1 tablespoon caster sugar
1 tablespoon cocoa powder

Sauce
10 fl.oz (300ml) Banyuls wine
5 fl.oz (150ml) unsweetened prune juice
2 level teaspoons arrowroot

1. Line a tray with a sheet of Bakewell paper.
2. Break the Menier chocolate into a bowl and melt over a pan of gently simmering water. Stir now and again and when completely smooth, remove from the pan. Do not over-heat otherwise the chocolate will become dry and dull.
3. Lay a strip of celluloid, 1⅜×10½ in (a scant 4cm×26cm), on a flat surface and, using a palette knife, spread one-eighth of the chocolate

thinly over the entire surface. Without damaging the surface, carefully lift it on to its side and curve into a teardrop shape so that the two ends meet, chocolate sides touching for about an inch of their length. Slide the ends together so that they match each other perfectly. Lift it up and, holding the two edges together, transfer the teardrop on to the Bakewell paper-lined tray. Ease it into a pleasantly curved shape. Repeat with the others, then refrigerate.

4.   For the mousse, break the chocolate into a bowl, and add 2 tablespoons of the double cream. Sit the bowl over a pan of simmering water and let it melt. When smooth, remove the bowl from the heat and let it cool for a minute or two.

5.   Add the egg yolks, placing the whites in a spotlessly clean bowl. Mix the yolks thoroughly into the chocolate, then allow to cool.

6.   Using an electric hand-held mixer or balloon whisk, beat the egg whites until stiff, gradually adding the sugar as you do so. Gently fold these into the chocolate mixture.

7.   Pour the remaining cream into the empty bowl and beat until stiff. Gently but thoroughly fold it into the chocolate mixture.

8.   Remove the teardrops from the refrigerator. Fit a piping bag with a large plain nozzle. Fill with the chocolate mousse, twist the piping bag closed and pipe it into the chocolate shells. Do not grasp the piping bag around the mousse as the heat of your hand would soften it.

9.   Smooth the top of the mousse with a palette knife so that it is level with the chocolate shell. Refrigerate, preferably overnight.

10.   To make the sauce, place the Banyuls in a pan, bring to the boil and let it ignite, by lighting it with a match or by shaking it over a gas flame. Let it burn itself out, then reduce in volume by half.

11.   Add the prune juice and simmer until 7½ fl.oz (210ml) remain.

12.   Place the arrowroot in a small container, add 2 or 3 teaspoons of cold water, and mix until smooth. Pour a little hot liquid on to it, stir together, then pour into the pan. Stirring constantly, bring back to the boil and simmer for a couple of minutes. Pour into a bowl and allow to cool. Cover when cold.

13.   To serve, dust the tops of the teardrops with sieved cocoa powder. Gently prise each one away from the Bakewell paper, then, starting at one corner of the plastic strip, carefully peel it away.

14.   Transfer on to a serving plate. To avoid spoiling it with fingerprints, hold the chocolate with another piece of clean plastic.

15.   Spoon a little sauce beside the inner curve. Serve immediately.

Petit Pot de Chocolat et Orange

Chocolate and Orange Pot

As I am sensitive to sugar, caffeine and alcohol, I have excluded them from my diet. I eat fresh fruit instead of sweets and puddings, and drink decaffeinated coffee and mineral water. I don't feel at all deprived although I am sorry that I cannot share David's enjoyment of wine, as part of the pleasure of drinking wine is to share the experience with someone else. However, I do remember from my pudding-eating days that this one, along with Crème Brûlée, was a favourite. It's the pudding that if given a 'one-day warning' (4 minutes would not be enough time), I would make a batch of this, and eat the lot!

Make them in straight-sided ramekins as I have found that they do not set evenly if made in the little *pot-au-crème* dishes. As part of a large meal, the smaller size is kinder as they are fairly rich.

6-8 servings

6 oz (175g) Bournville plain chocolate
½ oz (15g) unsalted butter
7½ fl.oz (225ml) milk
7½ fl.oz (225ml) double cream
4 egg yolks, size 2
1½ oz (40g) caster sugar
finely grated rind of 1 orange
1 dessertspoon Grand Marnier

To serve and decorate
2½ fl.oz (65ml) double cream
2 slices of pip-less orange, cut into quarters

1. Preheat the oven to 300°F (150°C) Gas 2.
2. Break the chocolate into a bowl or deep plate. Add the butter, then sit the bowl or plate over a pan of simmering water. Allow the chocolate to melt, stirring it now and again. If the water boils, the chocolate

164

will over-heat and become dry and dull. When completely melted, re-move from the pan and stir until smooth.

3. Combine the milk and cream in a pan, and bring to near boiling point.

4. Beat the egg yolks and orange rind in a bowl. Pour the hot milk and cream mixture on to them, stirring as you do so.

5. Gradually whisk this into the chocolate (or vice versa if you have melted the chocolate on a plate). You are aiming for a smooth mixture.

6. Add the sugar and Grand Marnier, mix well to dissolve the sugar, then pour through a muslin-lined sieve into another bowl, pressing down on the orange rind to extract as much flavour as possible.

7. Transfer to a measuring jug or other good pouring jug. Sit six or eight ramekins in a roasting tray, then fill them, pouring carefully as you do not want any drips on the edge of the ramekins. (I use size two ramekins, and fill eight, but you may prefer to use larger ramekins and fill only six).

8. Place on the front of the middle shelf of the preheated oven. Pour enough boiling water into the roasting tin to come half-way up the sides of the ramekins. Slide the tray carefully into the oven and bake for 30 minutes.

9. To test to see if they are set, gently shake the tray containing the ramekins. The chocolate mixture should merely shudder if cooked. If they look too liquid, continue to cook for another 5 minutes.

10. Remove from the oven and allow to cool. When cold, place on a tray and refrigerate, preferably overnight. As with most chocolate desserts, they improve if made a day before serving them.

11. Lightly whip the remaining chilled cream. Fit a large star nozzle into a piping bag, fill with the cream and pipe a large swirl of cream in the centre of each dessert. Decorate with a quarter slice of orange placed to one side of the cream.

Crème Brûlée

Some are baked, some are cooked custards set in the refrigerator, some use all double cream, others single. Every recipe for Crème Brûlée is different, but I think that mine is a version which works well, giving a set, but not too rich, texture. I bake it in ramekins, but you could make one large one, in which case increase the cooking time to approximately one hour, depending on the depth of the dish. Once the custards have been *brûléed*, serve them within 4 hours, otherwise the crisp top will become soft. If you want to prepare the custards the day before, allow them to cool, then refrigerate overnight. *Brûlée* them, allowing time for them to cool again before serving, but serve within the 4 hours.

The custards have to be watched carefully towards the end of the cooking time because, as with all custards, there is a risk of curdling if overcooked. The result should be deliciously thick and smooth. Although she does not normally eat sweet things, our cat, Bouchon, is particularly keen on Crème Brûlée.

7 servings

10 fl.oz (300ml) double cream
10 fl.oz (300ml) milk
½ vanilla pod, cut open to release the seeds
5 egg yolks, size 2
3 oz (75g) caster sugar
½ teaspoon natural vanilla essence
7 heaped teaspoons demerara sugar

1. Preheat oven to 300°F (150°C) Gas 2.
2. Place the cream, milk and vanilla pod in a pan. Heat gently until near boiling point.
3. Meanwhile, lightly beat the egg yolks, sugar and vanilla essence together in a bowl.
4. Gradually pour the hot liquid on to the egg yolks, stirring as you do so. When well mixed, pour through a sieve into another bowl.
5. Sit seven ramekins (5 fl.oz/150ml capacity) in a baking tray or

roasting tin which will hold enough water to come half-way up the sides of the ramekins.

6. Stir the custard gently so that any foam will be incorporated into it. Any that is not, spoon off.

7. Using a ladle, divide the mixture between the ramekins (pour from a good pouring jug if you prefer).

8. Place the tray of ramekins on the front of the middle shelf of the preheated oven. Pour enough boiling water into the tray to come half-way up the sides of the ramekins, then gently slide the tray in.

9. Bake for approximately 40 minutes until set. Check after 35 minutes by pulling out the tray a little and gently shaking a ramekin. If it wobbles very slightly it is set. If it looks too soft, return to the heat, and cook until set. Remove from the oven and allow to cool in the water.

10. When cool, place on a tray and refrigerate. They must be cool before you put them in the fridge, otherwise water will condense on to their surface which will spoil what should be a crisp caramel topping.

11. At least 1½ hours and at most 4 hours before serving, preheat the grill. It has to be very hot in order to melt the sugar as quickly as possible. A gas grill seems to give better results than an electric one.

12. Cover each custard with a heaped teaspoon of demerara sugar, spreading it over evenly. Place as many as will fit under the grill on a metal tray, and grill until the sugar melts and becomes a deep golden brown. Keep checking to gauge their progress, and remember that once it starts caramelising, sugar will change from being perfect to being burnt all too readily. Some may brown quicker than others, depending on your grill, so remove them once ready (use rubber gloves for this).

13. Allow to cool for 5 minutes, then return to the refrigerator. Serve while still crisp. If, for any reason, they are not eaten on the day you have *brûléed* them, the custard will be just as delicious the next day, but the caramel will be soft and runny.

Soufflé Glacé à l'Orange
Iced Orange Soufflé

If I cut down the quantities for this dessert too much, it becomes less successful. It is made by whisking egg yolks and sugar together until thick, adding orange juice and rind, then Cointreau, and finally folding in whipped cream and whisked egg whites. When whisking the yolks and sugar, a greater volume will be achieved (proportionally) when whisking four to six yolks rather than only two. I would recommend therefore that you make the quantity stated, and make two terrines or one terrine plus some individual ramekin-shaped ones.

When making this, I use a free-standing Kenwood in which to whisk the yolks and sugar, and a hand-held electric beater to first whip the cream, then the egg whites. If you do not have this set-up then it will take longer to make, as while the yolks and sugar are merrily whisking in the free-standing mixer, the other two stages can be completed.

16-18 servings altogether

4 eggs, size 2
5 oz (150g) caster sugar
finely grated rind and juice of 2 small oranges
2 tablespoons Cointreau
1 pint (600ml) double cream, chilled
5-6 oz (150-175g) almond ratafia biscuits, crushed to a powder in
your food processor

Caramel sauce
8 oz (225g) caster sugar
strips of orange peel

Decoration
navel oranges (1 medium-sized per 4 people)

1. Make the caramel sauce first so that it has time to cool. In a heavy pan or frying pan, let the caster sugar melt over a moderate heat. Stir now and again to make sure that it melts evenly. When it has turned a deep golden or chestnut colour, add 5 fl.oz (150ml) hot water. Remember that the caramel will continue to darken until the water is added, so

168

have it ready. Be careful as the combination will produce sparks of very hot caramel. Either use a long-handled spoon to stir the hot caramel, or wear rubber gloves. Stir over a moderate heat until the caramel and water mix thoroughly and a smooth sauce is formed. Let it boil for a few minutes until it thickens slightly. The diameter of the pan determines how long this will take, as the wider the pan, the quicker the water will evaporate. Pour into a bowl. It will thicken more as it cools.

2.   While it is cooling, cut some julienne strips of orange peel. Rinse and dry one of your decoration oranges. Using a sharp fine knife, cut very, very thin strips, about ¾ in (2cm) wide, down the length of the orange. Place these on a chopping board and cut into thin strips. Place in a small pan of cold water, bring to the boil and boil for 5 minutes. Pour through a sieve, run plenty of cold water over them to remove their bitter taste, shake dry and add to the cooling caramel sauce.

3.   Separate the eggs, being very careful that no egg yolk, not even a speck, goes into the whites. (This applies any time you are going to be whisking them.) Place the yolks in the bowl of a free-standing mixer, if using one, and the whites in another bowl. Both should be fairly big to allow room for expansion.

4.   Start whisking the yolks, gradually adding the sugar, a tablespoon or so at a time. This ensures as light a mixture as possible. Continue to whisk while adding the orange juice and rind, and carry on until the mixture is very pale and thick, and has increased in volume. Add the Cointreau at the last minute and switch off when mixed in.

5.   If your hands are free, while this is whisking, beat the cream in yet another bowl until it will form soft trails if dropped from lifted beaters. (Be careful when beating the cream that flying cream doesn't go into the bowl of egg whites, as anything fatty spoils their whisking qualities.)

6.   Wash the beaters thoroughly, dry them, then whisk the whites until they will form little peaks when the surface is dabbed with the beaters.

7.   Using a spatula, empty the cream on to the orange mousse mixture, and using a balloon whisk or large metal spoon, fold together.

8.   Add a spoonful or two of the whisked whites, beat in fairly roughly, then very gently fold in the remainder using a large metal spoon. At this stage the mixture should start to thicken. Stop as soon as the ingredients are thoroughly mixed.

9.   Sprinkle 2 tablespoons of crushed ratafias evenly along each base of two loaf tins of 1¾-2 pint (1-1.2 litre) capacity. Ladle the soufflé into

them, being careful not to disturb the crumbs. Gently level the top with the back of a spoon or a palette knife, then sieve the remaining crushed ratafias over the surfaces. Pat down gently, then transfer to your freezer straightaway.

10.   Freeze for at least 4 hours. I generally make mine the day before (or should I say in the wee small hours, as very often I start some preparation for the next day once we have cleared up the restaurant after serving dinner, at about 1am).

11.   Allow the soufflé to soften before serving. How long this takes depends on how long it has been frozen, and the temperature of your kitchen. If it has had 4 hours only, 10 minutes should be long enough, but if it has been frozen overnight or longer, remove it from the freezer 45 minutes before you wish to serve it. I prefer to serve the slices of soufflé when they are rather soft and mousse-like, but you may prefer them to be fairly hard.

12.   While the soufflé is softening, prepare the oranges by cutting away the skin and pith. Using a sharp knife, cut off the top, then using a sawing motion, and turning the orange round in one hand, peel away the skin and pith in one long strip. Alternatively cut off the top and the bottom, sit it on a chopping board, and cut downwards in inch-wide (2.5cm) strips, cutting between the flesh and the pith.

13.   Cut the oranges in half lengthwise, then across into ¼ in (6mm) slices.

14.   Turn the soufflé out onto a flat plate or board, by running a knife round the edge of it, right down to the base of the tin. Turn upside down and if it does not come out immediately, grasp both the tin and the board and give them a sharp jolt.

15.   Trim off the very outside edge, then cut into ½-¾ in (1-2cm) slices, allowing the slices to fall on to a fish slice as you cut them. Transfer on to a serving plate, on the fish slice. Repeat with the other slices.

16.   Place two or three pieces of orange on the plate, to the underside of the slice, coat with a tablespoon of caramel sauce and serve immediately.

Individual soufflés can be made by lining the base of 5 fl.oz (150ml) ramekins with Bakewell or greaseproof paper, then sprinkling the ratafias over the paper before filling with the soufflé mixture. Sieve the remaining crumbs over the top, pat down gently, then freeze. They will need only 5-15 minutes to soften before serving, depending on how long they have been frozen.

Soufflé Glacé Praliné
Iced Coffee Soufflé with Hazelnut Praline

This is made by the same method as the orange version, and is served with a raspberry purée sauce, decorated with little hearts of thinned-down Greek yogurt. I will not give a detailed recipe for this as you can refer to the other one, but here are the changes in ingredients.

16-18 servings altogether

4 eggs, size 2
5 oz (150g) caster sugar
4 tablespoons hot coffee
2 tablespoons Frangelico liqueur
1 pint (600ml) double cream, chilled
5-6 oz (150-175g) almond ratafia biscuits, crushed to a powder

Hazelnut praline
3 oz (75g) whole hazelnuts
3 oz (75g) caster sugar

Raspberry purée sauce
8 oz (225g) raspberries, fresh or frozen and defrosted
1 tablespoon icing sugar
juice of ½ lemon and ½ orange

Decoration
2 tablespoons Greek yogurt

1.   Make the praline first by melting the sugar in a small frying pan. When evenly melted and dark golden, add the whole hazelnuts (I use ones which still have their skins). Stir together over a moderate heat until each hazelnut is coated in caramel. Pour on to a lightly buttered baking tray and allow to cool. When cold, break into the bowl of your food processor fitted with the cutting blade, and process until coarsely ground. Alternatively, beat the praline with a rolling pin to crush it, having covered it first with a clean cloth.

2. Make up the soufflé as in the previous recipe, adding the Frangelico and the crushed praline once the coffee mousse is pale and increased in volume. Switch off once they have been incorporated. Whip and add the cream and egg whites.

3. Line the terrines with crushed ratafias, fill and freeze as described.

4. Place the raspberries and the other sauce ingredients into your processor and blend until smooth. Rub through a sieve into a bowl. Cover until required.

5. To serve, place a tablespoon of sauce to one side of your serving plate, swirl the plate slightly so that it covers half the plate, then place a slice of soufflé with its base lying against the sauce.

6. Thin down the Greek yogurt so that it has the consistency of cream, drop three blobs on the purée and run a skewer through them to form heart shapes. Serve immediately.

Mousse Glacée au Citron
Iced Lemon Mousse

It helps if you have an electric mixer, either hand-held or free-standing, for this dessert, as the egg yolks are beaten with sugar for quite a long time. It is very smooth with a sharp flavour and looks pretty topped with a swirl of cream and fine julienne strips of lemon rind.

8 servings

8 egg yolks, size 2
8 oz (225g) caster sugar
juice of 2 large lemons
10 fl.oz (300ml) double cream, chilled

To serve and decorate
4 thinly pared strips lemon peel, no pith
2½ fl.oz (65ml) double cream, chilled

1.   Place the egg yolks in a bowl large enough to allow them to expand considerably, and, using an electric hand-held mixer or a free-standing Kenwood mixer, start whisking them at high speed. After about a minute, start adding the sugar a little at a time. The egg yolk and sugar mixture will start increasing in volume and will become very pale in colour.

2.   When all the sugar has been added and the mixture is thick, add the lemon juice gradually, while continuing to whisk.

3.   In another bowl, whisk the cream until it will form soft peaks. Avoid over-beating, as little lumps of cream will freeze solid through the dessert, spoiling its texture.

4.   Fold the cream into the lemony mixture, using a large metal spoon. Make sure that they are both thoroughly mixed.

5.   Place the bowl in the freezer or transfer to a container if the bowl will not fit in. Freeze until the mixture is firm but not solid. The time this takes depends on the shape of the container and the temperature of your freezer. Check it after 2 hours to see how it is coming along.

6.   When ready, remove from the freezer, spoon into your food processor fitted with the cutting blade, and blend until smooth. If it is too firm, allow it to soften a little before trying to process it, as too much strain will be put on the motor if it is.

7.   Transfer to a good pouring jug, then pour into eight freezerproof ramekins with a 5 fl.oz (150ml) capacity. Place on a tray, put back into the freezer and freeze until firm.

8.   Cut the lemon peel into very thin strips using a sharp knife. Place in a small pan, cover with cold water, bring to the boil and simmer for 5 minutes. Pour through a sieve, run plenty of cold water over them, then place on a doubled sheet of kitchen roll to dry. Cover with another sheet of kitchen roll to prevent them drying out too much.

9.   Remove the puddings shortly before serving. How long they will need depends on how long you have frozen them. If they are just frozen and no more, they can be served straightaway, but if they have had, say, a night in the freezer, they may need about 10 minutes.

10.   Lightly whip the cream. Fill a piping bag fitted with a large star nozzle, and pipe a swirl of cream in the centre of each one. Sprinkle with fine strips of lemon peel, and serve immediately.

Tortoni
Rum and Macaroon Cream

This is my version of a sweet which we ate on our first ever visit to Houston House which, as David mentions, was a restaurant that had a great deal of influence on our future. The Knights kindly sent me the recipe, of which this is my variation.

6-8 servings

10 fl.oz (300ml) double cream, chilled
2 oz (50g) macaroons, crushed (place in a strong plastic bag and beat with a rolling pin. Do not reduce to too fine a powder)
3 oz (75g) caster sugar
2 tablespoons Bacardi rum
2 egg whites, size 2

Decoration
lightly browned flaked almonds, or crushed praline (see page 171)

1. Place the chilled cream in a large bowl and whisk it, using an electric hand-held mixer or a whisk, until it begins to thicken.
2. Add the macaroons, half of the sugar and the rum, then continue to whisk until the cream will form soft peaks.
3. In a spotless bowl, using spotless beaters or a balloon whisk, whip the egg whites until they are stiff, but not dry. Whisk in 2 teaspoons of the sugar, then fold in the remainder.
4. Empty the whipped whites on to the cream and, using a metal spoon, fold the two together gently but thoroughly.
5. At this stage you can spoon the mixture into ramekins, but I spoon it into a piping bag fitted with a ½ in (1cm) plain nozzle, and pipe it into tall white porcelain goblets (which we brought back from France).
6. Sit the dishes on a tray and place in the freezer for at least 3 hours.
7. Remove from the freezer approximately 5 minutes before serving, but they may need a little longer if they have been frozen overnight. They need to soften a little but should still have a fairly firm texture.
8. Sprinkle with browned flaked almonds or crushed praline. Sit each dish on a saucer or plate and serve immediately.

Citron Surprise
Lemon Surprise Pudding

The surprise aspect of this is the separation which takes place during the cooking, to form a light spongy layer on a soft curd-like base. We use ramekins which are decorated on the outside with twisting strips of lemon peel and, to add to the 'surprise', once the pudding has been eaten, two cheeky lemon pips are found painted on the base.

They have to be served immediately, but they can wait for half an hour or so before cooking.

6 servings

2 oz (50g) unsalted butter, softened
2 eggs, size 2, separated
3½ oz (90g) caster sugar
½ oz (15g) plain flour
finely grated rind and juice of 1 lemon
8 fl.oz (250ml) milk

1.   Place butter, egg yolks, sugar, flour and lemon rind in the food processor fitted with the cutting blade. Blend until smooth, adding the lemon juice, then the milk.
2.   Pour into a bowl and leave for at least an hour.
3.   Preheat oven to 350°F (180°C) Gas 4. Place six ramekins (with a capacity of 5 fl.oz/150ml) in a bain-marie – a container such as a roasting tin or pyrex dish which will take enough water to come half-way up the sides of the ramekins.
4.   Place the egg whites in a spotless bowl (see page 42). Using an electric hand-held beater or balloon whisk, beat until stiff. Fold into the lemon mixture gently but thoroughly with a large metal spoon.
5.   Ladle into the ramekins, place on the front of the middle shelf of the oven, pour enough boiling water into the tin, then slide it in.
6.   Bake undisturbed for 35-40 minutes by which time they will be slightly risen, rounded on top and golden brown.
7.   Remove, sprinkle with extra caster sugar, place on plates or saucers and serve straightaway.

'Cheesecake' au Citron
Lemon Cheesecake

This is a magically light cheesecake, in both texture and fat content, which is different from the normal type. It is more of a lemon soufflé, set between two layers of sponge. If you make it a day ahead, the sponge becomes softer and more moist, which is all to the good, but it is not essential to do so. This, by the way, was one of two desserts which I made for our wedding reception. An hour before the service, while the rest of the family were in a state of fluster and excitement, I was to be found in the kitchen, apron over wedding dress, calmly adding the finishing touches.

6-8 servings

1 sponge cake, baked in an 8 in (20cm) tin (see page 201)

Lemon soufflé
1 sachet powdered gelatine
2 eggs, size 2
3 oz (75g) caster sugar
6 oz (175g) cottage cheese (the lumpy sort)
6 fl.oz (175ml) single cream
juice and finely grated rind of 1 lemon

Decoration
icing sugar

1. The sponge will need to be trimmed to fit the 6½ in (16cm) diameter, 3¼ in (8cm) deep cake tin with a removable base. Sit the base of the tin on the sponge, and use this as a guide. Cut the sponge with scissors or a sharp knife, so that it is slightly larger than the base. Using a serrated bread knife, cut the sponge in half horizontally, lift off the top layer and place the bottom layer on the base, inside the tin. If by any chance there are any gaps, patch with some scraps of sponge. If the fit is not exact, the soufflé mixture, which is very liquid before it sets, will leak.

SOUFFLE GLACE A·L'ORANGE

LES TRICORNES D'AMANDE, FONDANTS A LA MENTHE

2. Melt the gelatine by placing 4 tablespoons of cold water in a teacup or small bowl. Sprinkle the gelatine over the water, stir it in using a teaspoon, then set this inside a pan containing enough water to come halfway up the sides of the container. Bring the water to the boil, turn down and simmer until the gelatine dissolves. Stir it now and again, then check by looking at the back of the teaspoon for any remaining grains of gelatine. The liquid should be clear and grain-free. The temperature of the gelatine mixture should be hot enough to feel hot if you dip your pinkie into it. If it is too cool, it becomes stringy when added to the other ingredients. If it is very hot, remove from the water while making up the soufflé mixture.

3. Separate the eggs, placing the yolks in the goblet of your liquidiser, and the whites in a spotlessly clean bowl (see page 42). Add the sugar and cottage cheese to the liquidiser, cover and blend until smooth. Add the cream (while the motor is still running), then the rind and lemon juice, and finally the hot gelatine.

4. Using a balloon whisk or electric hand-held mixer whisk the egg whites until stiff, but stop before they become dry. Pour the lemon mixture over them and, using a large metal spoon, fold together gently but thoroughly. You may have to be a bit rougher with stubborn lumps of egg white as they may be difficult to incorporate.

5. Pour this into the cake tin, on top of the sponge base, then place in the refrigerator until it just begins to set. Check by shaking the tin gently after half an hour or so.

6. Remove from the refrigerator, carefully lower the top layer of sponge, cut side down, on to the cheesecake, then return it to the refrigerator to set completely. If leaving it overnight, cover with cling film or foil.

7. When ready to serve, sprinkle the top with sieved icing sugar, sit the tin on a salt drum or similar, and gently pull the sides of the tin downward.

8. Place on a flat plate, still on its base, and cut into wedges using a serrated bread knife.

9. Transfer on to serving plates, sitting each wedge upright if possible. Serve immediately.

Tarte au Citron
Lemon Tart

This is my recipe for a modern classic dessert which features on many top restaurant menus. The combination of tastes and textures makes this apparently simple dessert deliciously sensual.

6-8 servings

1×7 in (18cm) sweet shortcrust pastry case, made in a fluted tin with a removable base (see page 197), rested overnight

Filling
5 eggs, size 2
7 oz (200g) caster sugar
finely grated rind of 1 lemon
4 oz (100g) unsalted butter
juice of 3 lemons
juice of 1 orange

To serve and decorate
icing sugar for dusting
5 fl.oz (150ml) double cream chilled (optional)

1.   Preheat the oven to 400°F (200°C) Gas 6. Place a baking tray in it to heat up.
2.   Line the pastry case with a round of tin foil, large enough to come up the sides of the pastry, cover with dried beans to weigh it down, then bake in the preheated oven on the baking tray for 20 minutes. After 15 minutes, remove from the oven, lift off the foil and beans, return to the oven and complete the cooking process. The pastry should be light golden brown and the base should have a cooked rather than translucent look to it. Remove from the oven.
3.   Turn the oven down to 350°F (180°C) Gas 4.
4.   While the pastry is cooking, make the filling. Break the eggs into the bowl of your food processor fitted with the cutting blade. Add the sugar and the lemon rind. Blend together until well mixed, about a minute.

the height of the tin if it is a deeper one. Flip the edges in towards the centre, fit the base into the flan tin, then gently press the sides into position. Any excess pastry should be bent over the edge of the tin, as it will be cut off later. Make sure that the pastry comes at least level with the top of the tin, patching with little scraps of pastry if necessary.

4.   Roll the remaining round of pastry on a lightly floured surface, turning it a quarter turn after each roll, until a circle 1 in (2.5cm) bigger than the top of the tin is made.

5.   Place the walnuts on a chopping board (check that it doesn't smell oniony or garlicky first), and chop the nuts fairly finely. If you use a food processor, the result would be too powdery.

6.   Place the sugar in a heavy pan or frying pan and heat over a moderate heat until it starts to caramelise. Stir now and again to make sure that it melts evenly. When it has become a golden caramel, add the cream. It will spurt a bit, so be careful. Stir until the two have combined smoothly, then add the chopped walnuts. Stir together, then pour into the prepared pastry case.

7.   Working very quickly at this stage, moisten the pastry which is folded over the rim of the tin, and cover the tart with the lid of pastry. Do this by placing your rolling pin on the top end of the pastry round. Holding the top edge of the pastry on to the rolling pin, roll it back towards you so that the lid is wrapped around the rolling pin. Lift up and then unroll it over the tart, making sure that the pastry overlaps slightly all the way round.

8.   Press the two edges firmly together, then cut off any excess by pressing against the top of the tin with your thumb or rolling pin.

9.   Place the tart on to the heated baking tray and bake for 30 minutes, by which time the pastry will be cooked and lightly coloured.

10.   Remove from the oven, sprinkle with extra caster sugar and allow to cool. Serve while still warm, cut into wedges, having pushed the tart, on its base, out of the tin first of all. Remember that it is very sweet, so a little will go a long way. If there is any left over, it keeps well and can be served as a cake with coffee.

If you wish to serve it with cream, lightly whip 5 fl.oz (150ml) double cream, place in a piping bag fitted with a large star nozzle, and pipe a straight line of swirls down one side of the plate. Place a wedge of tart beside it.

Les Tricornes d'Amande
Almond Pastry Puffs

Little filo pastry triangles filled with an almond and rum mixture. The filling is in fact derived from the classic Gâteau Pithiviers which is a puff pastry round encasing this lovely filling. When experimenting with filo pastry, it was David who suggested I try this and his idea worked very well. Served on Crème Anglaise and decorated with browned flaked almonds and little 'hearts' of raspberry purée, it looks very pretty. If you have time, make up this quantity and freeze those you don't need straightaway, in which case less Crème Anglaise will be required.

12 servings

8 sheets filo pastry, approx. 20×11in (50×28cm)
3 oz (75g) unsalted butter, melted

Almond filling
5 oz (150g) ground almonds
5 oz (150g) caster sugar
2½ egg yolks, size 2
1½ oz (40g) unsalted butter, melted
1½ tablespoons dark rum
1½ tablespoons double cream

Raspberry purée
4 oz (100g) raspberries
½ tablespoon icing sugar
1 tablespoon orange juice
1 tablespoon lemon juice

To serve and decorate
2 quantities Crème Anglaise (see page 188)
2 oz (50g) browned flaked almonds

1. Make the Crème Anglaise first so that it has time to become cold. Whisk occasionally as it cools, cover with cling film, then refrigerate.

2.   Place all the almond filling ingredients in the bowl of your food processor fitted with the cutting blade. Process till smooth and well mixed. Transfer to a bowl, cover with cling film, then refrigerate for at least an hour.

3.   Stack the eight sheets of filo pastry together and using a ruler as a guide, cut them into strips, 6¼×11½ in (16×29cm). (If using Pittas filo, this will be three strips wide.) Place on top of each other and cover with a cloth.

4.   Following the method for Les Tricornes de Saumon Fumé (see page 79), make up the almond triangles, using the melted butter and a heaped teaspoon of filling for each one.

5.   Refrigerate until needed, and preheat the oven to 400°F (200°C) Gas 6.

6.   Make the raspberry purée by combining the raspberries, icing sugar and juices in your food processor and blending until smooth. Rub through a sieve into a small bowl.

7.   Arrange the required number of almond triangles on a lightly buttered baking tray, making sure that they are not touching. Bake on the middle shelf of the preheated oven for 15 minutes, by which time they will be crisp and golden brown.

8.   Remove from the oven and dust with a light coating of extra sieved icing sugar.

9.   Spoon a ladleful of Crème Anglaise on to each serving plate. Holding the plate so as to avoid putting fingerprints around the rim, swirl the plate so that the custard spreads in an even circle. Place one triangle on the custard, then lean a second one against it, at right angles.

10.   Using a teaspoon, drop three small blobs of raspberry purée on the custard, to one side of the triangles. Run a skewer through each one, using a quick curved action, to form heart shapes. Scatter a few browned almonds to the other side and serve immediately.

Pouding au Pain
Bread and Butter Pudding

At one of our favourite restaurants in France, Hiély in Avignon, I used to have the same sweet every time we went there (it was only once a year at most!). It was simply called 'Pudding' (pronounced with a French accent of course) and was very like a Cabinet pudding cooked in a loaf tin, turned out when cold and served cut into slices. They used slices of brioche which is very light, buttery bread, mixed with dried fruits. This inspired me to try to make a bread and butter pudding in a terrine and serve it in a similar manner, as the ingredients are roughly the same. A slice of pudding, along with some raspberry purée, makes a very elegant version of this nursery pudding.

8-10 servings

9 fl.oz (275ml) double cream
9 fl.oz (275ml) milk
1 vanilla pod, split lengthwise
3 eggs, size 2
1 egg yolk, size 2
3 oz (75g) caster sugar
3 white rolls
1½ oz (40g) unsalted butter
4 oz (100g) large stoned raisins, soaked in boiling water for
20 minutes

Raspberry purée
8 oz (225g) raspberries, fresh or frozen
1 tablespoon icing sugar
juice of ½ lemon and ½ orange

1.   Preheat the oven to 350°F (180°C) Gas 4.
2.   Place the cream, milk (or you could use 18 fl.oz/550ml single cream instead) and the vanilla pod in a pan, and bring to just under boiling point. Remove from the heat.

184

3. Beat the eggs, the yolk and the sugar together in a bowl, then, whisking all the time, pour the hot liquid over. When well mixed, sieve into another bowl.

4. Thinly slice the rolls vertically and spread with a little butter.

5. Lightly brush a 2 pint (1.2 litre) capacity loaf tin with melted butter. Cut out a strip of Bakewell paper which is the width of the tin and long enough to cover the base, extend up the ends and protrude a little. This will make it easier to turn out.

6. Layer the bread, buttered side up, with the drained raisins, then pour the custard over. Push any floating bits of bread under the custard. Allow to sit for half an hour, before cooking.

7. Place the terrine in an ovenproof dish or tin, and fill with enough boiling water to come half-way up the sides of the terrine. Carefully transfer to the middle shelf of the preheated oven, and bake for approximately 40 minutes. Test by inserting a skewer down into the centre, removing it and, if the pudding is ready, the skewer will be clean.

8. Remove, lift the terrine out of the water and allow to cool.

9. Meanwhile, make the raspberry purée. Place the raspberries, icing sugar and juices in your food processor or liquidiser and blend until smooth. Rub through a sieve into a bowl, pressing down on the purée with a wooden or plastic spoon.

10. To serve the pudding, run a knife round between the tin and the paper, reaching right down to the bottom. Turn out on to a board (you may have to tug on the ends of the paper to ease it out), remove the paper, then cut into slices ¾ in (2cm) thick, using a serrated bread knife and a gentle carving motion.

11. Spoon some raspberry purée on to one side of each serving plate, swirl the plates slightly to spread it over one half, then place a slice of pudding on the other half.

Pouding d'Été
Summer Pudding

Summer pudding, that wonderful combination of soft summer fruits encased in juice-soaked bread, is normally made in a pudding bowl, turned out and served in wedges, but my variation is to make it in a loaf tin and serve it cut in slices. This looks neater than a wedge cut from a pudding shape. It needs to be made at least the day before you wish to serve it.

8 servings

8 oz (225g) strawberries, hulled
8 oz (225g) raspberries, hulled, picked over, and any mouldy ones
discarded
4 oz (100g) blackcurrants, topped and tailed
4 oz (100g) redcurrants, topped and tailed
4 oz (100g) blueberries (if unavailable, use ripe gooseberries)
4 oz (100g) black cherries, stoned and halved
6 oz (175g) caster sugar
1 large white loaf from a home bakery, thinly sliced

Decoration
Greek yogurt and 8 sprigs of redcurrants

1. Halve any large strawberries. Place all the fruit in a large pan and gently mix in the sugar.
2. Place over a low heat and as soon as a fruity juice starts to run, remove. Do not let it boil as this will spoil the fruit.
3. Line the tin with cling film. I use a 2 lb (900g) Le Creuset loaf tin as this gives a pleasant square-shaped slice.
4. Cut the crusts from the bread, using a serrated knife or an electric carving knife. Cut the bread into shapes which will neatly line the tin. Start by placing two or three slices along the central panel of the terrine (along the base and ends), overlapping slightly, then place in the other slices which should fit the sides exactly. There should not be any gaps, and the bread should be the same height as the terrine.

5. Fill the bread-lined tin with the warm fruit. Cut more slices of bread to fit over the top and place these over the fruit. Press down gently and pour any leftover juice over. Cover with cling film.

6. Cut a piece of thick card which will fit inside the terrine. Place this on top and lay a 2 lb (900g) weight on it. I usually use a couple of tins or jars or bags of sugar. Check that the card is pressing down evenly on the surface of the bread, and not on the edges of the tin.

7. Place on a tray to catch any drips of juice and refrigerate for at least 24 hours.

8. Turn out on to a flat board, trim off one of the very end pieces of bread and, using a serrated knife, cut into slices ½ in (1cm) thick. When cutting, press against the fruit with the flat surface of a fish slice to keep it in position and transfer on to a serving plate on the fish slice. Repeat with the other slices.

9. Place some Greek yogurt in a piping bag fitted with a large star nozzle, and pipe a swirl beside it. Top with a little sprig of redcurrants.

Soupe aux Fraises
Strawberry Soup

This was inspired by a dessert served by Edith Remoissenet at her charming restaurant, Au Petit Truc, near Beaune. Make both the sorbet and the custard in advance – the day before if you like, if that is more suitable.

We transferred some wild strawberries, which magically appeared one year in the front 'garden' at the restaurant, to our herb garden. They grow very well there, and in July we pick them and use them in this dish, scattering them over the custard.

4-6 servings

12 oz (350g) strawberries
1 quantity Crème Anglaise (see page 188)
sprigs of fresh herbs such as sweet cicely or mint

Raspberry sorbet
12 oz (350g) raspberries
4½ oz (120g) icing sugar
juice of ½ lemon and ½ orange

1.   To make the sorbet, place the raspberries and the icing sugar in your food processor fitted with the cutting blade. Blend until smooth, adding the fruit juices towards the end. Sieve into a bowl, pressing down on the mixture with a wooden spoon or ladle.

2.   Either a) place in your sorbetière or ice-cream machine and churn until frozen, then transfer to a container and freeze until required, or b) pour into a container and freeze.

3.   Hull the strawberries, choosing ones of roughly the same size. Halve them and set aside.

4.   Approximately 15 minutes before serving the dessert, remove the sorbet from the freezer, allow to soften slightly, then cut up into chunks. Place in your food processor and blend until smooth. Omit this stage if you churned the sorbet as in 2a.

5.   Lay out your serving dishes, using large deepish ones if possible, like flat soup plates. Ladle some custard into each one, then arrange the strawberries, cut side down, on top. Leave a gap in the centre for the sorbet.

6.   Using two dessertspoons, place a spoonful of sorbet in the centre, and top it with a sprig of fresh herb. (Dip the spoons in hot water, shake off the drips, and use these to shape the sorbet into a neat oval shape.) Serve immediately.

Crème Anglaise

Custard Sauce

This is tricky to make due to the fact that egg yolks, if over-heated, will over-cook giving a curdled, scrambled egg appearance and an 'eggy' taste and smell. The knack is to know exactly when to stop cooking the custard. I personally would rather cook a custard in a bain-marie as opposed to over direct heat. This will take a little longer, but is less risky. Finally, please do not start to cook your custard unless you know that you won't be disturbed. It is a quick process which can go wrong if your attention is attracted elsewhere. If you are in on your own – take the phone off the hook! Having said all this, a real egg custard is delicious and well worth making.

4-6 servings

9 fl.oz (275ml) milk
½ vanilla pod (try to buy soft plump pods, as they contain more seeds)
3 egg yolks, size 2
2 oz (50g) caster sugar

1.   Place the milk and the split vanilla pod in a saucepan. Bring to just below boiling point, remove from the heat and allow to infuse for at least 10 minutes.
2.   Meanwhile, place the yolks and the sugar in a bowl which will fit inside a large pan. Whisk together using a balloon whisk.
3.   Pour the hot milk on to the yolk and sugar mixture, whisking as you do so.
4.   Bring a few inches of water to the boil in a large pan. Have another bowl with a sieve fitted over it at the ready, to take the cooked custard.
5.   Place the custard bowl in the water, and whisk with a balloon whisk until the custard starts to thicken. The water should be simmering. Use a rubber spatula now and again to scrape down any custard sticking to the bowl. Now, how to tell if it is cooked – take a spoon, metal or wooden, run it through the custard and lift it out, rounded side uppermost. Run a finger over the surface and if a clean channel is formed, the custard is ready. Do this occasionally so that you can see the change taking place for yourself. The custard will still look very thin, but do not be tempted to continue to cook it, as it will thicken as it cools.
6.   As soon as this stage is reached, pour it through the sieve into the other bowl. Lift out the vanilla pod and pop it into the custard.
7.   Whisk now and again as it cools and, when cold, cover with cling film and chill until needed. Remove, wash and dry the vanilla pod. (Store inside a jar of caster sugar to give you vanilla sugar.)

Pouding de Noël
Christmas Pudding

I have always loved the look of a round Christmas pudding. I remember years ago, in 1975, our first Christmas at La Potinière, trying to invent some way of making one. I formed the pudding by tying two sieves together, which made a fairly good shape, but it was all rather hair-raising! I was delighted, therefore, when some firm started making small, round Christmas pudding moulds and, although we now close for Christmas, I still make a couple every year. The perfect accompaniment, by the way, is Crème Brûlée. The flavours and textures complement each other beautifully.

I have tried different variations of pudding, even an ever-so-healthy one which was sugar-, flour- and fat-free, but this is the favourite. The quantities will fill two round pudding moulds. Make them ahead of time, at least a couple of months, and store in a cool, airy place. When you prepare the ingredients, tick each lightly in pencil to ensure that you have not omitted any, as the list is long.

2 oz (50g) plain flour
1 level teaspoon each of powdered cinnamon, grated nutmeg and ground allspice
2 oz (50g) each of soft light brown sugar and soft dark brown sugar
4 oz (100g) fresh white breadcrumbs
3 oz (75g) cooking apple, washed and grated
2 oz (50g) peeled and finely grated carrot
6 oz (175g) currants
8 oz (225g) sultanas
9 oz (250g) seedless raisins
4 oz (100g) candied peel, cut into ¼ in (6mm) cubes
3 oz (75g) dried apricots, cut into ¼ in (6mm) cubes
3 oz (75g) stoned prunes, cut into ¼ in (6mm) cubes
3 oz (75g) glacé cherries, roughly chopped
4 oz (100g) blanched almonds, finely chopped   *use flaked*
2 teaspoons finely grated orange rind
2 teaspoons finely grated lemon rind
4 oz (100g) unsalted butter
1 level tablespoon treacle (use a hot spoon to measure it)

1 tablespoon orange juice
1 tablespoon lemon juice
1 tablespoon brandy
3 fl.oz (85ml) stout
2 eggs, size 2

To serve
holly and cognac

1. Sieve the flour, spices and sugars into a large bowl. Add the breadcrumbs, grated apple and carrot, dried and candied fruits, nuts and grated orange and lemon rind. Stir together until well mixed.

2. Melt the butter, add to the remaining ingredients in another bowl and beat together. Pour on to the dry ingredients and stir thoroughly. Cover and leave overnight to allow the flavours to develop.

3. Next day, stir again, then divide between the two well-buttered moulds. To do this, divide the mixture in half, and spoon half into the base of one of the tins, rounding it so that it forms a fairly round pudding. As it cooks it will swell, so a gap between the top of the pudding and the tin is important. Place the top part of the mould over the pudding and make sure that it is properly closed. Wrap the mould in cling film to ensure that it is watertight. Repeat with the other pudding and fit them into their stands.

4. Bring one large or two smaller pans containing 3 in (7.5cm) of water to the boil. Lower the puddings into the water, checking that the water does not come more than a third of the way up the mould. Cover the pan with foil, then top with the lid, having checked that the water is bubbling gently. Steam for 6 hours topping up with boiling water if necessary.

5. Remove from the pan and allow to cool. When cold, unwrap, carefully remove the puddings from the moulds and wrap cling film around them. Wash and dry the moulds and return the puddings to them. Store in a cool, airy place until needed.

6. When you want to serve the pudding, remove the cling film, return to the mould and re-steam for 2-3 hours. Remove from the mould and turn out on to an attractive plate. Place a sprig of fresh holly on top (if it is too dry, it will catch light so wet it first). Pour a measure of cognac into a ladle, heat it over a gas flame or electric ring, set light to it with a match and pour it over the pudding. Carry it quickly to the table.

Panforte

Sienese Christmas Cake

A delicious Italian 'cake' which is traditionally served at Christmas. It is a speciality of Siena, where every food shop proudly shows off its particular make. They vary in size, height, colour, taste and texture, but basically are all made from spices and candied fruit.

I like to candy my own fruit peel as this ensures a soft result. Bought candied peel is very often rock hard and therefore difficult to use. I use a Jane Grigson recipe for this, and although the candied fruit goes into the Panforte, it is also wonderful just as it is, as an after-dinner nibble, as is the Panforte cut into little wedges or cubes.

Candied fruit
1 large pink grapefruit
1 large orange
1 large lemon
10 oz (275g) caster sugar

Paneforte
7 oz (200g) candied peel (see above), cut into ⅜ in (9mm) cubes
3½ oz (90g) blanched and skinned almonds
3½ oz (90g) skinned hazelnuts
2 oz (50g) candied fruit, such as papaya (available from health-food shops), cut into ⅜ in (9mm) cubes
2 oz (50g) dried figs, cut into ⅜ in (9mm) cubes
3½ oz (90g) plain flour
3 teaspoons powdered cinnamon
1 teaspoon mixed spice
4 oz (100g) honey
4 oz (100g) caster sugar
icing sugar

1. Prepare the peel at least 2 days before making the Paneforte. Cut a slice off the top and bottom of the citrus fruits. Using a sharp knife cut through the skin and pith, in sections 1 in (2.5cm) apart. Remove these

(clockwise from left) *LARME DE CHOCOLATE AGENAISE, GATEAU ST JEAN, PARFAIT AU CHOCOLAT, PETIT POT DE CHOCOLAT*

TARTE AU CITRON

sections (which will leave you with peeled fruit to use in some other recipe).

2.   Blanch these strips of peel by placing in a pan of cold water and bring to the boil. Boil for 20 minutes, drain and repeat the process once more, by which time they will be tender and will have lost their bitter taste.

3.   Place the sugar and 5 fl.oz (150ml) cold water in a pan, and heat gently until the sugar dissolves, stirring now and again. Add the blanched peel, bring to the boil, then simmer until the peel has absorbed the sugar syrup and looks translucent.

4.   Cover a tray with Bakewell paper and empty the peel on to it. Spread out evenly and leave uncovered in a warm place until dry. They will still be soft and slightly sticky. This drying out process may take two or three days. Cut into ⅜ in (9mm) cubes with scissors.

5.   Preheat the oven to 400°F (200°C) Gas 6. Lay the almonds and hazelnuts on a baking tray and cook until they become a rich brown colour. Remove from the oven and when they are cool enough to handle, chop half of each type of nut, fairly finely, and leave the remainder whole. Lower the oven temperature to 300°F (150°C) Gas 2.

6.   Place the nuts, diced candied peel and fruit in a bowl. Sieve in the flour and spices and mix together thoroughly.

7.   Melt the honey and sugar in a small pan and, once the sugar has dissolved, bring to the boil. Pour on to the dry ingredients and, using a strong wooden spoon (I broke one recently!), combine, making sure that all the ingredients are evenly mixed.

8.   Cut a round of rice paper to fit the base of a 7 in (18cm) cake tin with a removable base. Fit inside the tin, then lightly butter the sides. Pack with the spiced fruit mixture and press down lightly to ensure an even surface.

9.   Bake on the middle shelf of the preheated oven for 35-40 minutes, then remove. Allow to cool slightly and sieve a generous coating of icing sugar over it.

10.   Place the tin on a salt drum or similar and pull down the sides. Remove the cake, on its rice paper, and transfer to a cooling tray.

It will keep for a month or so, stored in an airtight plastic bag, or wrapped in tin foil. When serving, cut into thin wedges using a sharp, strong knife.

Fondants à la Menthe

Peppermint Creams

We should have been more convinced by the much publicised preoccupation of many chefs with 'lighter, healthier cooking' if most of those same chefs did not confront their clients with a deadly assortment of *petits fours* and chocolates at the end of the meal. Food guides are probably to blame since restaurants, rightly or wrongly, believe that they gain points for such gestures. We only offer a single mint, easy to refuse yet fresh tasting and not too harmful if you cannot.

Makes about 3 dozen

1½ egg whites, size 2
1 lb (450g) icing sugar, sieved
1½ teaspoons peppermint essence

1.   Lightly whisk the egg whites in a medium-sized bowl, then gradually stir in the icing sugar and peppermint essence, using a strong wooden spoon.

The first time I made these, I used a hand-held electric mixer with plastic beaters, but unfortunately they snapped in two under the strain, as the mixture becomes very stiff. Start by using a mixer if you wish, but you'll need to finish off with a wooden spoon.

2.   Dust your work surface with extra sieved icing sugar. Empty the paste on to it, and form into an even sort of shape. Dust your rolling pin with sieved icing sugar and roll the paste out to a thickness of approximately ¼ in (6mm).

3.   Using a cutter (1 in/2.5cm round is traditional, but we make heart-shaped ones for St Valentine's Day which are very pretty), stamp out as many as you can. Transfer using a palette knife on to a tray lined with Bakewell paper. Re-roll the scraps and repeat until all the paste has been used.

4.   Allow to dry out in a cool airy place for at least 24 hours.

PASTRY
AND
BAKING

Pastry should be light and crumbly, so it helps if you treat it with lightness and delicacy. No thumping or bashing it or you will get a tough, solid pastry. First time rolled pastry is always the best, but the scraps can be gently combined, re-rolled and used for something else. At teacher-training college we were taught to demonstrate making jam tarts with the scraps, but I really do think there must be something more interesting to make with them than that. Who eats jam tarts anyway?

Good pastry does depend on a few things.

1.   Over-mixing or over-kneading will toughen your dough. Shortcrust pastry made in a food processor can be wonderful, but it is very easy to over-process it and thereby toughen it, so I avoid making it this way unless my butter is very, very hard and I do not have time to soften it.

2.   Although I like the fats to be fairly soft, if they are so soft and warm that they actually oil, this will also toughen and spoil the pastry. If your hands are very hot, cool them down in cold water.

3.   After being handled, pastry likes to rest. Most recipes say to rest the pastry after making it, before rolling out for your chosen recipe. Unless it is very soft, I would rather roll out shortcrust straightaway, line the tin with it, and then refrigerate it for a few hours or overnight, giving it time to relax. If you are gentle with it and don't stretch it as you roll it, this should be successful.

4. For best results, pastry should be cooked in a hot oven. If too cool, the fats melt before the starch bursts, resulting in a soft, greasy pastry. Preheating the oven is very important, therefore, to ensure that the cooking process starts straight away.

Pâte Brisée

Shortcrust Pastry

Some people seem to shy away from making shortcrust pastry, but really, there is no need to fear it. Hopefully, by following this recipe, this feeling will be changed. The instructions for making the pastry and for lining a flan tin sound complicated but they are not really. Seeing something like this being made makes it so much easier to understand, but until I make a video (only joking!), you'll have to try to visualise it for yourself.

Contrary to general notions on pastry making, I like my fats to be fairly soft, and I use a mixture of unsalted butter and block Stork margarine, the butter for flavour and the margarine for shortness.

The recipe for the savoury version includes a little icing sugar as this increases its short, melting properties, and the sweet version contains caster as well as the icing sugar.

This quantity of pastry will be enough for two 7 in (18cm) flan tins or for one covered tart or for eighteen mince pies.

2½ oz (65g) unsalted butter
2½ oz (65g) block Stork margarine
8 oz (225g) plain white flour
1 rounded tablespoon icing sugar (plus 1 tablespoon caster sugar for the sweet version)
1 egg, size 2, lightly beaten

1. Place the butter and margarine in a wide bowl and, using an electric hand-held mixer, beat them together until smooth and soft. If the butter is hard, cut it into small pieces and place in a warm place for a while.

2. Sieve the flour and sugar(s) over the butter and margarine mixture. Add the egg, then with the motor at the slowest setting, gradually mix all the ingredients together. Turn the bowl slowly and move the beaters around the bowl to make sure that all the ingredients are incorporated.
3. When a dough starts to form, stop beating, mixing just long enough for it to form large pieces of dough rather than one smooth ball.
4. Lightly flour your work surface, and empty the dough on to it. Gather it together and knead very gently until it becomes smooth, then, using the palms of both hands, roll it into a thick sausage shape (as if rolling plasticine).
5. Divide in two, turn the pieces on their end and gently press down with the heel of your hand so that you form a thick circle of pastry.

If using it for a covered tart, cut one piece larger than the other, the smaller piece being used for the lid. Cut in half if lining two flan tins.
6. Now as I have said, I like to roll it out straightaway, but if for some reason it is very soft and sticky, cover and refrigerate for 15 minutes until the fats have set a little.

To line a flan tin

1. Lay the removable base of an 7 in (18cm) crinkle-edged flan tin on your work surface. Sprinkle flour over it and the surface. Place the pastry in the centre of the metal base.
2. Lightly flour your rolling pin and roll out the pastry. Hold the pin lightly, and gently roll away from yourself, turning the pastry a quarter turn round (don't turn it over) after each time you roll it. This ensures that it keeps to its circular shape. Lift it up from the base occasionally to check that it is not sticking.
3. Repeat, flouring your rolling pin when necessary, until the pastry is ⅛ in (3mm) thick, and forms a circle which is large enough to cover the base and sides of the tin with a little extra over. For an 7 in (20cm) tin, therefore, it will need to be 1¼ + 8 + 1¼ in (3 + 18 + 3cm), i.e. 9½ in (23cm) in diameter.
4. Flip the outer pastry in towards the centre, transfer it on the base to the rest of the tin, then unfold the pastry in reverse order. It will be pliable, so you will be able to ease it into the corners of the tin and press it into the crinkles of the side. Take care not to press too hard as you must avoid making holes in it.

5. When making an open flan, I like to make the sides as high as possible, so that a deep filling can be accommodated. To do this ease the excess pastry round on to the top edge of the tin, which will force a bulge of a double thickness of pastry to be made. Once you have made this bulge all the way around, press it lightly between thumb and forefinger to make it roughly the same thickness as the rest of the pastry. You will now have a raised edge of about ⅜ in (9mm).

If making a covered tart, merely fold the excess pastry over the edge of the tin and it will be cut off later.

6. To make the raised edge more attractive it can be crimped. Push from the outside, using your index finger, between your thumb and forefinger which are held slightly apart against the inside of the pastry. Repeat all the way around so that you achieve an undulating effect. For Tarte au Soufflé (see page 44), leave the sides plain and straight, as this gives the filling more of a grip, to help it rise.

7. Prick the base lightly with a fork, and place in the refrigerator to set and to relax. Leave for a few hours or preferably overnight. Keep any scraps in case you have to patch any little cracks.

To bake the tart 'blind'

1. Preheat the oven to 400°F (200°C) Gas 6. Place a baking tray on the middle shelf.

2. Cut out a 9 in (23cm) circle of tin foil. Place this against the base and sides of the pastry. Cover with some dried beans or macaroni, enough to give an even layer, then place in the preheated oven, on the baking tray. The beans ensure that the base stays flat. Air can sometimes get trapped between the pastry and the base of the tin, and as it expands when heated, the pastry is pushed up and sets in this position.

3. Bake for 15 minutes. Remove from the oven, lift off the foil and beans, then return the tin to the oven to finish cooking. When ready, after another 5 minutes approximately, the base will be pale golden and will have a glistening, cooked look to it rather than a translucent one.

4. Remove from the oven and use as required having checked it over for any little cracks. Soft, runny fillings such as the one for Tarte au Citron (see page 178) would leak out, so patch with tiny pieces of left-over pastry. If egg-based fillings are poured in when the pastry is still hot, they will set slightly on the pastry, thereby sealing it, and helping to prevent leaks.

Pâte Feuilletée
Flaky Pastry

I really enjoy making flaky pastry. I like seeing it at its various stages, watching it change from merely flour, butter and salt into layers of magically light pastry. The way it is folded and rolled produces over a thousand layers of dough sandwiched between ultra-thin layers of butter. When this type of pastry is cooked, air and moisture heat up to form steam which causes the layers to rise. This pastry is given six rollings and foldings which produce 1,458 layers of dough and it is these layers which make flaky pastry so light.

Do not try to make it during a heatwave, as the butter would melt, but at the same time, I do not think that one needs such cold conditions as many recipes imply. Restaurant kitchens are often excruciatingly hot, and this is why they need separate areas or complete kitchens for their pastry making, which are very cool in comparison. If the butter is very cold and hard, I find it difficult to roll out the pastry. In fact, butters vary in texture, and I prefer one which has a slightly rubbery, pliable feel to it, such as unsalted Wheelbarrow. I cook with, and serve on the tables, an unsalted Normandy butter, but for this recipe I prefer the Dutch one.

8¾ oz (250g) plain flour
1 teaspoon salt
10½ oz (300g) unsalted butter, at room temperature but still quite
hard

1. Place the flour, salt and 1¾ oz (50g) of the butter in the bowl of your food processor, fitted with the cutting blade, and process until the butter has disappeared and is evenly dispersed throughout the flour.
2. Add just under 5 fl.oz (150ml) very cold water and process for 30 seconds or so, or until the dough forms a ball. Do not over-mix.
3. Turn out on to a lightly floured surface, form into a ball, flatten slightly, then make large cuts in lines in one direction, then at an angle so that you are forming diamonds. This helps the dough to relax quickly. Place inside a plastic bag and refrigerate for an hour.

4. Meanwhile, place the remaining block of butter on a large piece of cling film, cover with another, then press it very firmly to break it up. Ease it into a shape 6 in (15cm) square, with neat, square corners. If the room is very hot, refrigerate; if not, leave it out until the dough has rested.

5. Remove the dough from its bag, and place on a lightly floured work surface. Gently tease it into a square shape with square corners and roll it out into a 10 in (20cm) square.

6. Place the butter in the centre, having given it a quarter turn so that the points of the butter are half-way along the edges of the dough, and slightly in from the edge.

7. Fold the corners of the dough in towards the centre over the butter, so that the butter is completely covered. Press down gently with your rolling pin to seal the edges. Brush off any excess flour which may prevent the dough from sticking together.

8. Keeping the corners as square as possible, roll the dough into a long strip. Lift it now and again to make sure that it is not sticking, and sprinkle the surface with a little more flour. Roll in the one direction, without turning the dough round or over.

9. Mark the strip into three even lengths, then fold the bottom third, the one nearest you, over the centre section, then lift the top third over the centre. Line them up so that the edges and corners match perfectly, then press the edges together with your rolling pin to seal them.

10. Lift it up, lightly flour the surface again and give the pastry a quarter turn in an anti-clockwise direction, so that the folded edges are now lying on the left and right.

11. Roll out once again, using light but forceful strokes in the one direction only. Fold as before, seal the edges, then carefully place in a large plastic bag. Place on a tray and refrigerate for at least half an hour.

12. Remove, give the pastry an anti-clockwise quarter turn again (place it back on the surface in the same position as you finished with last) and roll out again. Fold, seal, give it another quarter turn and repeat. After this you will have completed four rollings. Cover and refrigerate for another half hour.

13. Repeat stage 12, after which the pastry will have had all six rollings, and, after a rest, will be ready to use. Keep covered, in the refrigerator, until needed.

Once you become confident, make double the quantity and freeze half. It will not be quite as good as fresh, but it is a useful standby.

Genoise

Sponge Cake

This recipe will make two sponges, so use one for the 'cheesecake' on page 176, and freeze the other for use at a later date.

Makes 2 sponges

3 eggs, size 2
7 oz (200g) caster sugar
1 oz (25g) unsalted butter
4 oz (100g) self-raising flour
1 tablespoon cornflour
1 heaped teaspoon baking powder

1. Preheat the oven to 350°F (180°C) Gas 4. Lightly brush two 8 in (20cm) sandwich tins with melted butter, cut out Bakewell paper or greaseproof paper to fit the base, position inside and butter that also.
2. Break the eggs into a large bowl, whisk with an electric hand-held mixer (or a free-standing one) until they begin to thicken. Gradually add the sugar and continue to whisk until light in texture and colour.
3. Bring 4 tablespoons of water and the butter to the boil in a small pan.
4. Meanwhile, sieve the flour and cornflour over the mousse-like eggs and fold in using a large metal spoon.
5. Sieve the baking powder over the top, quickly followed by the hot buttery liquid, then, after a few seconds, fold all the ingredients together carefully.
6. Divide between the two tins, level the top, then bake on the middle shelf of the preheated oven for 15 minutes, by which time they will be risen, golden brown, and will spring back if pressed gently in the centre.
7. Remove from the oven, allow to cool slightly, then turn out. To avoid marking the top with the lines of the cooling tray, turn out on to a clean teatowel, remove the paper, then invert on to the cooling tray. Allow to cool.

Pain aux Raisins
Sultana Soda Bread

Bread is not normally a difficult thing to make, but soda bread, which is made without yeast, is a piece of cake! Providing that you can get buttermilk, you could knock this up in minutes as the other ingredients will probably be in your store cupboard already. If you find buttermilk difficult to obtain, thin down natural yogurt with a little milk. It is a sweet bread but, when toasted, complements cheese very well and goat's cheese in particular. Serve a couple of slices per person along with the St Chevrier and rocket salad on page 153. It will be easier to slice if it is not too fresh.

Makes 2 loaves

1 lb (450g) plain flour
2 level teaspoons bicarbonate of soda
2 level teaspoons cream of tartar
1 level teaspoon salt
3 oz (75g) caster sugar
4 oz (100g) sultanas
1 egg, size 2
10 fl.oz (300ml) buttermilk

1. Preheat oven to 375°F (190°C) Gas 5.
2. Sieve the first five ingredients into a bowl. Add the sultanas, mix together, then make a well in the centre of the ingredients.
3. Beat the egg and buttermilk together, then pour into the well, and gently mix into the dry ingredients, using a wooden spoon. Now that the raising agents have been activated by the liquids, work quickly so that the baking process can start as soon as possible.
4. Flour your work surface and the palms of your hands, empty the dough out on to the surface, and pat into an even shape. Cut in two and shape each half into a neat oval, 1½ in (4cm) deep.
5. Lightly butter a baking tray and lay the two loaves side by side on it, without letting them touch.
6. Bake on the middle shelf of the preheated oven for 35 minutes. Remove, cool slightly, then transfer on to a cooling tray.

Pain Complet
Wholemeal Soda Bread

This is another loaf which can be made quickly and easily. I rather like the loose soft texture and distinctive taste of soda bread. You can ring the changes by adding 3 oz (75g) coarse oatmeal which gives a lovely nutty taste and texture, and if serving it with a strong cheese such as Münster or ripe Camembert, you could add a tablespoon of caraway or celery seeds.

Makes 2 loaves

8 oz (225g) wholemeal flour
8 oz (225g) plain flour
1 teaspoon bicarbonate of soda
3 teaspoons baking powder
1 teaspoon salt
1-2 oz (25-50g) caster sugar, depending on taste (omit altogether if you would rather)
1 egg, size 2
12 fl.oz (450ml) buttermilk

1. Preheat the oven to 375°F (190°C) Gas 5.
2. Place the wholemeal flour in a bowl, then sieve in the remaining dry ingredients. Mix evenly and make a well in the centre.
3. Beat the egg and buttermilk together, pour into the well and stir with a wooden spoon, until a fairly soft dough is formed.
4. Turn out on to a floured work surface, then shape and bake as instructed in the recipe for Sultana Soda Bread, but in this case bake for 45 minutes. Remove from the oven and cool.

Pain aux Noix et Raisins
Walnut and Sultana Bread

We are lucky enough to have a wonderful home bakery in the village, where I can buy fresh yeast, flours and bread, as well as cereals, pulses, dried fruits, etc. This is my version of a lovely loaf which they make.

When you are making bread, remember that warmth is important. Yeast develops at a temperature that is roughly blood heat, but too high a temperature destroys it, making it inactive. Low temperatures retard its growth, so you can use this as a method of controlling the rate at which you prove it. For instance, you could prove bread slowly in the refrigerator overnight, or you could freeze bread or rolls which have been proved once, then shaped, ready to be thawed, proved and baked. I prefer to use fresh yeast, but dried yeast is a useful standby to have in your store cupboard.

Makes 2 loaves

1 oz (25g) fresh yeast
1 oz (25g) caster sugar
1 oz (25g) unsalted butter
12 oz (350g) wholemeal flour
4 oz (100g) granary flour
1 teaspoon salt
1 teaspoon walnut oil
2 oz (50g) walnuts, chopped
5 oz (150g) sultanas
1 egg yolk

1. Measure out 10 fl.oz (300ml) of warm water (mix boiled water and cold water rather than use hot tap water). It should feel very slightly warm to the touch.

2. Place the yeast in a small bowl, add 1 teaspoon of the sugar and mash together. Add a quarter of the water and leave in a warm place for 10 minutes until it becomes frothy.

3. Meanwhile, place the butter, cut up roughly, in the bowl of your food processor fitted with the cutting blade. Add the flours, remaining sugar and the salt. Blend until the butter is dispersed throughout the flour.

4. When the yeast is frothy, pour it, plus the rest of the water, into the dry ingredients. Process until a smooth ball of dough is formed.

5. Place a teaspoon of walnut oil in a large plastic bag, shake it so that the surface is evenly oiled, then add the dough.

6. Seal at the top of the bag, leaving plenty of space for the dough to expand. Leave in a warm place until doubled in size which will take approximately 45 minutes.

7. Preheat the oven to 450°F (230°C) Gas 8.

8. Lightly dust your work surface with flour. Empty the dough on to it, punch it down to a height of ¾ in (2cm) and scatter the walnuts and sultanas over it. Knead these into the dough and, when evenly dispersed, cut into two pieces

9. Roll each piece (like plasticine, not with a rolling pin) into a long sausage shape, 14 in (35cm) long. Place on a lightly buttered baking tray, leaving space between them. If necessary, use two trays.

10. Cover with a clean teatowel (or cut open the oiled bag and use that), and leave to prove in a warm place until doubled in size (just the width, not the length, I am glad to say!).

11. Brush the top and sides with the egg yolk beaten with a few drops of water. Bake on the middle shelf of the preheated oven for 20 minutes, reducing the temperature to 425°F (220°C) Gas 7 after 10 minutes, by which time the loaves will be a deep golden brown.

12. Remove and transfer on to a cooling tray.

Brioche aux Raisins
Sultana Brioche

Omit the sultanas if you prefer a plain brioche, but the sweetness of the dried fruit matches the richness of *foie gras* perfectly (see page 56). Make double the recipe and freeze one if you like. Brioche recipes tend to be messy as the dough is much softer than normal bread dough, but this recipe, made in a food processor, is much easier to handle.

Makes 1 loaf

3 tablespoons milk
½ oz (15g) fresh yeast
1 oz (25g) plus 1 teaspoon caster sugar
9 oz (250g) strong plain flour
2 oz (50g) unsalted butter
¾ teaspoon salt
2 eggs, size 2
1 teaspoon oil
2 oz (50g) sultanas
1 egg yolk, size 2

1. Gently warm the milk to blood heat. Pour into a bowl and add the yeast. Mash it into the milk, then add the teaspoon of sugar and 1 oz (25g) of the flour. Allow to sit for 20 minutes in a warm place to prove.
2. Place the remaining flour, the remaining sugar, the butter and the salt into your processor fitted with the cutting blade. Blend until the butter is incorporated into the flour.
3. When the yeast is frothy, add it and the eggs to the flour, and process for 1 minute by which time the dough will have formed a ball.
4. Turn out on to a lightly floured surface and knead for a minute.
5. Rub the oil into a large plastic bag, place the dough inside and seal the top allowing plenty of space for it to expand. Prove in a warm place for 1-1½ hours until doubled in size.
6. Turn out on to a lightly floured surface, knock down by punching it, and sprinkle the sultanas over the surface. Knead them into the dough so that they are evenly distributed.

7.   Lightly butter a 2 lb (900g) loaf tin (I use a Le Creuset cast-iron ter-rine as I like the shape). Flatten the dough into a rectangle the same length as the tin. Roll it up, then place, seam downwards, in the tin, pressing it in evenly. Cover with the plastic bag and allow to prove in a warm place for 30-45 minutes until risen.

8.   Preheat the oven to 400°F (200°C) Gas 6.

9.   Once the dough is ready, use the egg yolk, mixed with a little cold water, to brush over the top of the brioche. Do not allow any to touch the tin as this would spoil its even rising.

10.   Bake in the preheated oven for 25 minutes by which time it will be golden brown.

11.   Remove, slide a knife around the loaf and turn out on to a cooling tray to cool.

'Muffins' aux Framboises
Raspberry Muffins

On the second last day of our one and only trip (so far) to America, I discovered muffins. I had managed to avoid them up until then, but on that particular day we had Sunday Brunch at Campton Place in San Francisco. Along with all the other goodies came warm, soft banana muffins and warm, soft bran and raisin muffins. They were wonderful! In reality I know that they are no more than small sweet cakes which should be eaten in small quantities, but on that occasion I ate rather more than I ought to have. It was a good thing that I did not succumb on the first day of the trip, otherwise my clothes would have become rather tight!

I make many variations, but I have chosen these muffins as rasp-berries are so very Scottish. They are best eaten warm, and when they are split open the smell of hot raspberries is heavenly. Freeze the rasp-berries slightly as this prevents them from being broken up too much when mixing them with the batter. Large paper cases are available, as are metal trays of muffin cups.

Makes 12 muffins

12 oz (350g) plain flour
3 level teaspoons baking powder
1 level teaspoon salt
3 oz (75g) caster sugar
½ oz (15g) bran
finely grated rind of 1 lemon
3 eggs, size 2
3 oz (75g) unsalted butter, melted
8 tablespoons milk
8 oz (225g) fresh raspberries, frozen (see note above)

1. Preheat oven to 400°F (200°C) Gas 6. Lightly brush twelve muffin tins with butter, or place twelve large paper cases into deep bun tins.
2. Sieve the flour, baking powder, salt and caster sugar into a bowl. Add the bran and the lemon rind. Stir together and make a well in the centre.
3. Beat the eggs, melted butter and milk together and pour into the well. Gently but quickly mix together, just enough to mix the ingredients, but no more.
4. Add the frozen raspberries and, mixing as little as possible, stir until they are fairly evenly distributed.
5. Using a tablespoon, spoon into the tins or paper cases.
6. Bake in the centre of the preheated oven for 15-20 minutes, until risen and pale golden on top.
7. Remove from the oven, allow to cool slightly, then transfer on to a cooling tray. Eat while still warm.

Biscuits d'Avoine

Oatcakes

Proper oatcakes are normally made with medium oatmeal, lard or bacon fat, and are cooked on the direct heat of a griddle, but these are a richer, sweeter version cooked in the oven. Coarse oatmeal mixed in with the rolled oats gives a lovely rough texture, or alternatively it can be sprinkled over the rolled-out dough and pressed in, to give an attractive look to the biscuits. Store any leftovers in an airtight container.

Makes 36

4 oz (100g) plain flour
1 oz (25g) caster sugar
¼ teaspoon salt
¼ teaspoon bicarbonate of soda
4 oz (100g) rolled oats
1 oz (25g) coarse oatmeal
1½ oz (40g) unsalted butter
1½ oz (40g) Cookeen or similar white fat
4 tablespoons milk

1.   Preheat the oven to 400°F (200°C) Gas 6.
2.   Sieve the first four ingredients into the bowl of your food processor, fitted with the cutting blade. Add the oats and oatmeal (omit the oatmeal if you would rather sprinkle it over the tops of the biscuits).
3.   Cut the fats into smallish pieces and add to the other ingredients, then process until they are evenly distributed. Add the milk and continue to process until the dough starts to come together.
4.   Turn the dough out on to a lightly floured surface and knead until a smooth dough is formed. Do not overdo this as the dough will toughen, but knead just long enough to get rid of cracks.
5.   Using a lightly floured rolling pin, roll the dough out until it is ⅛ in (3mm) thick. Using a plain 2½ in (6cm) cutter, stamp out rounds as close together as possible. The more you cut from the first rolling, the better, as the results from the re-rolled scraps are never as good.
   If you have held on to the medium oatmeal to sprinkle over the biscuits, do so at the rolled-out-to-⅛ in (3mm) stage. Press them in gently with your rolling pin, before cutting out the biscuits.
6.   Place the biscuits on a lightly buttered baking tray (or two). Prick each one with a fork, then bake on the middle shelf of the preheated oven for 10 minutes.
7.   Remove, ease off with a palette knife or fish slice and cool on a cooling tray. When cold, store in an airtight tin.

Sablé

Shortbread

Cut into thin wedges, this is lovely served with syllabub or other creamy sweets. This recipe produces a light crumbly texture and, if baked in a loose-bottomed, crinkled-edge flan tin, looks very pretty cut into wedges. Unusually for shortbread, the butter is melted first before adding it to the dry ingredients.

Makes 8-16 pieces

6 oz (175g) plain flour
2 oz (50g) cornflour
2 oz (50g) caster sugar
5½ oz (165g) unsalted butter

1.   Preheat the oven to 300°F (150°C) Gas 2.
2.   Sieve the dry ingredients into a bowl. Make a 'well' in the middle.
3.   Melt the butter in a pan, and when liquid, but not too hot, pour it into the well. Gently stir the mixture together, using a wooden spoon, until all the ingredients are evenly mixed.
4.   Turn out into an 8-8½ in (20-21cm) flan tin with a removable base, and press evenly over the surface, pushing it right into the crinkles of the tin. At this stage the surface will be fairly rough, so smooth it over with a palette knife. It should be approximately ½ in (1cm) thick. Prick all over with a fork, then bake on the middle shelf for 1¼ hours by which time it should be lightly coloured.
5.   Remove from the oven, sprinkle with extra caster sugar, and, while still hot, cut into sections. Use a large pointed knife and section by cutting in half first of all, then quarter, then cut into as many sections as you wish, depending on the size you would like. I like to cut it into sixteen thin sections, but it depends on whether you would be serving it as an accompaniment to a sweet, or as a piece of shortbread.
6.   Cool on a baking tray, still in the tin. To serve, slip the sides of the tin down and, using a knife to re-cut the sections again, gently ease out the required number of pieces. Store in an airtight tin.

6oz - 175gms   Plain Flour   28

2oz - 50gr   Cornflour

2oz   50gr.   Caster Sugar   ✓ OK

5½ oz . 160gr.   unsalt butter.

            ⅄   SHORT BREAD ⅄
_____

Cornflour.

Butter .

                                    S

POSTSCRIPT

When I left school in 1969, I realised for the first time that I could put on weight very easily. I had been very athletic at school and seemed to be able to consume enormous quantities of sweets and crisps without any problems. At college, however, the only energy required was to climb the stairs and to walk to the bus stop. The pounds just crept on and on, until something had to be done about it (I had only put on a stone, but to me that was horrendous). That was the start of many diets, and because of this and also because I studied nutrition at college, I have been very nutrition-conscious for the past 20 years.

This may seem incredible to many as the food at La Potinière is far from being low-fat or low-calorie. It is rich and many may read the recipes in horror when they see how much butter and cream is used. My defence is that this is not food for everyday eating, it is special occasion food. If one eats in a careful, well-balanced way most of the time, a treat such as a dinner party or a meal out at a restaurant certainly will not do any harm. If you want to adapt the recipes for everyday eating, you could do so by cutting down on butter, by using a lower-fat substitute for cream such as Greek yogurt or fromage frais, but the results will not be the same. Experiment if you wish, but if you want the same results as mine, follow the recipes given.

Never before has there been such an opportunity for healthy eating. Manufacturers have taken to heart the masses of publicity on the need to cut down on fat, salt and sugar, and have responded well to the situation. Many foods now are labelled with the nutritional content and whether or not there are any additives. There is still a need for more details but at least a start has been made.

From a low-fat point of view, there are many substitutes for cream and butter. Personally, I feel there is no real substitute for butter, and rather than change to a lower-fat alternative, I have not eaten butter or any other spread for years. Naturally, if entertaining or being entertained, I have eaten it if it is included in dishes which have been cooked with it, but cutting it out most of the time seems such an easy way to save hundreds of calories and a great deal of fat. If you eat interesting bread, then butter is not necessary; if you grill or bake meat rather than frying; if you say goodbye to chips, crisps or roast potatoes, you will automatically cut down on your fat consumption. By altering your everyday eating habits, the occasional special meal will not harm you.

Cream, with a fat content of between 18 and 48 per cent and between 60 and 130 calories per ounce really ought to be used sparingly. I have used it in my recipes as, once again, I look on them as recipes you will use occasionally, not every day. For everyday substitutes for cream there is quite a range. Greek yogurt with a fat content of about 10 per cent and a calorific value of about 37 per ounce (25g) is a great saving, and a super substitute for cream in some desserts or when used as a garnish to puddings. Instead of pouring cream on your strawberries, a spoonful of Greek yogurt will make a wonderful alternative. However, do not be fooled that you are being virtuous by eating this type of yogurt instead of low-fat yogurt. Low-fat yogurts range in fat content from 0.1 to 3.5 per cent. The only way to tell is by reading the carton, where you can also check on the sugar content which varies quite a bit.

Fromage frais is my favourite low-fat substitute. The one I eat is so low in fat and calories, I find it hard to believe it is so delicious. Though thick and creamy in texture, it has a fat content of only 0.3 per cent and a calorific value of only 14 per ounce! I like to eat it with fresh fruit such as kiwi and raspberries sprinkled with bran, which sounds awfully uninteresting, but is in fact lovely and makes a very healthy breakfast. Again do not assume that all fromage frais are the same. They vary from very low fat, 0.3 per cent, to 40 per cent fat which is equivalent to whipping cream.

By eating yogurt or fromage frais, you will automatically cut down on calories and fat, but someone who is used to eating low-fat natural yogurt will find Greek yogurt extremely rich, and likewise with low- or high-fat fromage frais. Look at the information on the packs, experiment and decide what taste, texture and fat content suits you best.

WINE

However simple or elaborate your table setting may be, there are some fundamental rules which one should heed if wine is to be taken seriously.

Always sniff the empty glass before allowing wine to be poured into it. A tiny trace of detergent or a foreign odour from a polishing cloth which you thought was clean would be a disaster for the wine, but is averted by this precaution. After polishing each glass, I hold it up to an electric bulb to check for marks, and I have a quick sniff. Even then, however, a clean glass could pick up a taint, in a cupboard which has been recently painted, for example, so do check.

We collect glassware, and admire skilful cutting, engraving or colouring; but for fine wine, we favour plain crystal glasses. At home these are Baccarat and Sèvres, brought back one or two at a time from our trips to France. In the restaurant they are also delicate and French, if not quite so precious. Because we run La Potiniére on our own, and are careful, we can use the kind of tableware we enjoy. Accordingly the majority of our crockery was made for us in Limoges, and those glasses usually far outvalue the wine drunk from them. Their fine stems and generous bowls enhance and facilitate the enjoyment of sight and smell.

Having not distorted the appearance of the wine by the choice of glass, it is important to provide a plain white background so that the colour might be truly appreciated. For this reason we always use white napkins. At home we rarely use a tablecloth as our dining table is an attractive piece of early nineteenth-century mahogany, and at La Potinière the tablecloths are pale pink, so without the napkins there would be no way of seeing the wine's real colour. If this seems a very fussy detail, it at least avoids the fuss of trying to look at a wine against a shirt cuff or the back of a calling card, which, elsewhere, I often find myself forced to do.

213

We used to provide an unusual blackcurrant soap at the washbasin in the restaurant toilet, which many enjoyed and commented upon. One day, however, someone remarked that he was surprised that a restaurant offering such wines as ours should have such a strongly scented soap. How right he was. It was not the soap we ourselves use, and I had not thought of its side effects; but a hand smelling strongly of blackcurrant, or any other, scent holding a glass of wine destroys many of the wine's subtle aromas. Accordingly, in this age of 'designer' toiletries in smart restaurants, we now provide very mildly scented soap.

The other destroyer of subtle smells and much else is smoke. From the day we opened we disallowed smoking in the restaurant until coffee time and I never had any hesitation in enforcing this rule. Although smoking restrictions in restaurants are commonplace now, in 1975 we felt like pioneers. *The Times* referred to it as a 'fetish', and it caused more bad feeling and lost us more customers than anything else; but we persevered, and the majority respected our wishes. Because of our set menus and times, permitting someone to smoke with his coffee was not going to offend another in mid meal, since everyone finishes at the same time. We would prefer that nobody smoked even then, but the few remaining smoking clients that we have have complied so decently all those years that I am not going to turn on them now.

Throughout our 'campaign' there has, not surprisingly, been a considerable amount of discussion on the subject at the restaurant's tables. One comment, however, put any other before or since in the shade. It was uttered in the unmistakable piercing tones of a dear client of ours who, herself in her seventies, had a husband a quarter of a century older. He was with her when the whole restaurant was stunned by her revelation that 'My husband hasn't smoked since 1898'!

'Start Me Up'

In our student days, Hilary occasionally prepared some dishes on an outside catering basis, for other people's entertaining. For one such a commission she was asked to produce a Boeuf Bourguignon and given a bottle of wine with which to prepare it. The wine was a Barton and Guestier Bordeaux Superior of 1966 and my immediate reaction was that this was too good to cook with. (I hasten to add that my opinions have changed considerably since then, and we believe in using good wine in the cooking at La Potinière.) In an act of dishonesty of which I am still a little ashamed, I confiscated the bottle and substituted a simple Beaujolais, which was our usual level for drinking. I could have argued that this was more geographically correct for the dish, but my motive was not so high minded.

On the first suitable occasion, the claret was broached. It was, as one might expect, an unremarkable but sound example of generic Bordeaux; but for me it was a revelation. It had depth of flavour and complexity which I had not experienced before, and I was hooked. I knew a door had opened on to a vast and fascinating new territory for me and I determined to learn all that I could about the subject. I set about my education in a very methodical way. I decided to concentrate on one area at a time, and since it was a bottle of Bordeaux which had fired my enthusiasm, I should start with Bordeaux. I read as much as I could lay my hands on – technical books on wine, romantic books on wine, historical books on wine. Best of all at that time was Hugh Johnson's *Wine,* which was the happiest combination of fact and feelings.

As I read I tasted, again methodically, wines from different districts and communes. I even made some wine myself, not because I had any interest in drinking it, but for the sake of witnessing the process. Of course, I eventually ventured into other areas and other countries, but Bordeaux was my first love and, despite my regular seductions by other grapes or soils, has always kept its hold on me.

For our flat in Glasgow I built a wine rack which had a twenty-five-bottle capacity. I mean, who could ever need to store more than twenty-five bottles? By its first anniversary it was a small corner of the rapidly growing 'cellar'. This growth was accelerated by the collapse of the international market for Bordeaux, when all the big merchants were selling off their huge stocks very cheaply. It was a unique opportunity to extend my wine education by regularly tasting classed growth clarets which hitherto would have been unaffordable.

The other source of fine wines which I was so lucky to be able to take advantage of was the magnificent cellar of Houstoun House. Apart from producing the most interesting food in Scotland at the time, Keith Knight had created a wine list which must surely have been the best in Britain. It was a real wine lover's list both for its incomparable range and quality, and for the generosity of its modest pricing. Just as the style of Houstoun's daily changing set menu was to be the prototype for our own restaurant, so Houstoun's wine list was to be an inspiration to me when the time came. I hope we have, in the inter-vening years, managed to convey to Keith and Penny Knight how grateful we are for their example.

'You Can't Always Get What You Want'

For anybody who ever drinks wine it is important to learn a little about the subject. A little knowledge in this case is a very useful thing if used without pretension. To become very interested in wine, however, is a commitment one should approach with great caution. Of course, it doesn't work that way. It is a fascinating pursuit and those who are sensitive to its appeal become fascinated, but drinking wine can seriously damage your wealth.

It was not always so. When I first became obsessed, great wines were an expensive luxury, but affordable. It is meaningless to quote actual prices from twenty years ago, but with very limited funds we were able to taste good wines regularly and great wines occasionally. Now, despite being better off financially than we were then, we are less able to afford great wines. In the interim fine wine has become an in-vestment commodity and has been ruined for the amateur, in much the same way as paintings and other collectable items have been. When Christie's revived the wine auction in 1966 it was the beginning of the end. Suddenly, whatever price somebody somewhere was prepared to pay became the base auction rate for a given wine, and prices rapidly escalated. Producers of the best performers understandably wanted a piece of the action and prices rose at source. Speculators with no in-terest in drinking jumped at such promising investments. Only the wine lover with limited resources was left behind. Even many a wine lover with limitless resources would, I hope, have opted out, trying to retain some perspective as to the true value of a bottle of wine. If I had really wanted to make money out of wine I should have done so by sending the whole cellar to auction at any time, but I have always re-fused to become involved in wine speculation except from the point of view of future drinking potential. To do so I always felt would be self-defeating in the long run, and I could hardly condemn the practice while contributing to it.

Fortunately, the constant improvement in wine-making technology is producing more and better wines than before in all corners of the globe, and Britain is the ideal place to enjoy them. As a country in a very minor league as far as wine production is concerned, we have no chauvinism to overcome and can openly appreciate good wine from wherever. More and more this means that the accepted wisdom on wine has to be continually reviewed, and developing one's own palate is what matters most. With confidence in one's own taste and an open mind it should always be possible to stay ahead of the speculators who have to rely on well-known names.

Although at the beginning I was insatiable for literature on wine and could readily have answered questions on all aspects of oenology, it was the constant tasting that was of real value. Now, rather like school algebra or Greek grammar, I have retained very little of the written facts, although some distant understanding of origins remains. I go entirely by taste now and it is all that matters. It is vital that any wine drinker should develop this sense. It doesn't matter if it disagrees with the taste of others, and indeed discussion and disagreement often reveal more in a wine than consensus of opinion. Listen to everyone, but make up your own mind. Tasting blind, particularly in company, is invaluable. There need be no embarrassment about 'getting it wrong', as one soon realises that the more you learn the less you feel you know. To consider a wine of unknown provenance or quality requires so much more concentration on smell and taste than when the label is visible that one gets more from the wine and remembers more after.

If the occasion is appropriate I write extensive notes. I rarely refer back to them and certainly do not intend to publish them, but again their real value is their discipline. To write meaningful notes one is forced to concentrate on the wine and to find words for what one sees there. If serious wine tasting does not mentally exhaust you, you are not trying hard enough.

Many people think that only French wines are available at La Potinière. Hardly surprising when there are only French wines on the list. However, those who know me better or discuss wine with me soon realise that the list is just the organised and visible front to a much more random assortment. This is not any pretence at being a 'French' restaurant with a French wine list. French wines are the wines I know best. At the end of the day they are the wines I love best. My interest started with French wine and the vast majority of my experience of tasting wine and visiting vineyards and *vignerons* has been French. In the early years I assiduously built a cellar of French wines and created a balanced list of the classic wines of that country and have maintained it to this day.

However, I have continually, with an open mind, looked at wines from other countries and bought those which have impressed me most. Such a personal selection, a kind of 'edited highlights' of other countries' endeavours, was always too random to make a balanced list. I have too much respect for wine-makers in other countries to tag on a couple of dozen wines from America or Italy at the end of a four hundred strong French list and pretend that this was representative. I should like to do these countries visible justice, but to my organised mind this would mean far more bins than I could handle, and even more problems keeping the list up to date than I have at present. I nevertheless continue to sell a surprising amount of 'foreign' wine to receptive clients, list or no list.

When the Egon Ronay *Guide* awarded us 'Cellar of the Year' for 1990 there was some slight embarrassment because the award was sponsored for the first time by the California Wine Institute and my list didn't contain any Californian wines. I am very grateful to them for being so unbiased, but the fact is for ten years I have been selling superb Californian wines. My first taste of a serious Californian wine just happened to be Martha's Vineyard 1973, so how could I fail to be impressed? It was courtesy of Geoffrey Roberts and shared with him at the bountiful table of a mutual friend. It was served 'blind' as was the custom of the house and, though in the company of first growth clarets and *grand cru* burgundies, was stunning, and a real eye-opener for me.

We have only been to California once and, although we enjoyed the experience and particularly liked the people we met, we have not acquired any great feel for the place. This, of course, may only be a re-sult of too brief an acquaintance; but it does mean that the wines which particularly impress me do so entirely on their performance in the glass. It may be unfair, but the romance of wine is a very important ele-ment. Some wines have led us to their origins, others have been dis-covered because we were there anyway. Either way the association of good wine with its native landscape, with its human creators and with its local cuisine, is vital to its proper appreciation and enjoyment. If the wine comes from a country or district for which one has a particular affection it has a head start.

For this reason I am particularly excited at present by the revolution in Italian wine-making which has gathered pace over the last decade. Italy has a very special place in our hearts because of the beauty which abounds there, in its landscape, architecture and artistic heritage. Whereas we go to France first to eat, then for its many other attractions, we go to Italy primarily for the environment. While I respect the traditional Italian wines, they are in general a style and taste which does very little for me personally. Now, thanks to wine-makers like Angelo Gaja, Fausto Maculan, Maurizio Zanella and others, there are Chardonnays and Cabernets and even Pinot Noirs of real quality and elegance being produced. The aesthetic combination of top-flight wines and their origins in the lovely rolling hilltop vineyards of Piedmont or the profoundly beautiful landscape of Tuscany or Umbria is irresistible to me. The only flaw is in the increasingly silly prices being asked for many of these wines because of small production and international prestige. I love to introduce people to them but sell them at virtually cost price because they are so embarrassingly expensive. I would like to hope that increased production or generosity of spirit might someday cause their producers to bring the price more realistically in line with quality.

Sadly, the assumption that one gets what one pays for cannot be relied upon when buying wine. Even the price at source reflects more the quantity available and the demand, and by the time that price has been distorted and multiplied by importers, auction houses and, worst of all, restaurateurs, it very often bears no relation at all to being a true gauge of quality.

There are very good arguments for a restaurant's mark up on wine. If it has a large stock which is but slowly revolving over a number of years, then the sheer cost of the investment requires some return. Add to that the cost of glasses, decanters and breakages and all the washing and polishing entailed, the time and effort expended on tasting, buying and constructing a list and, where applicable, the cost of relevant staff, and the standard 100 per cent can be readily justified. More and more, however, there are restaurants who shamelessly add 200, 300 or even 400 per cent to the price of a bottle; and many of those same places carry small stocks, regularly topped up by a merchant who has created the list. Thus the restaurateur is relieved of much of the bother of managing a cellar and often doesn't have to pay for the wine until it is sold. No investment, huge profits, almost irresistible.

I, perhaps unfortunately, started as an enthusiastic amateur and have continued to look at wine from a consumer's viewpoint. Thus I have always priced my wines as I should like to meet them elsewhere. The appreciation which we have received from knowledgeable drinkers over the years has sustained us in this approach, but it can be discouraging to hear some who have been impressed by paying a great deal, in some other establishment, for a bottle which they could have drunk for considerably less in ours. A £40 bottle of wine is the memory they treasure, not the taste, or the name, or the fact that a local merchant may be selling it for £12.50!

The old concept of a fair profit seems to have been conveniently mislaid and, for many, a new theory of seeing how much one can charge and get away with has become the practice. Regrettable though this is and, one might hope, eventually self-destructive, it is encouraged to the extent that the Inland Revenue put us through the stress and indignity of an in-depth inquiry a few years ago. Their reason? The inspector had not seen such a low percentage return on wine before! It seems that nowadays this deserves suspicion rather than congratulation.

'Mixed Emotions'

Frustratingly, as a lover of fine food and fine wine, I often find that the two tend to compete rather than complement each other as one might hope or suppose. If both food and wine are of special interest, one of them inevitably suffers. I am regularly caught with my nose buried in a glass while a dish is going cold in front of me, or with my attention absorbed with what is on the plate to the neglect of the wine.

The sensible and time-honoured solution is to drink good but undemanding wine with interesting food and vice versa. There are often occasions, however, when those such as myself have no intention of abandoning one in favour of the other, and the only logical solution which I can suggest (although I have never yet practised) is to have a food course accompanied by mineral water, followed by a wine course, and so on. Certainly it is preferable, if possible, to serve a chosen wine several minutes before the course which it is to accompany rather than simultaneously or just after.

There are comparatively few specific wine and food combinations, despite the endless lists of propositions, which for me are ideal anyway. Those which do succeed include *foie gras* and mature late harvest Tokay d'Alsace, the classic Roquefort and Sauternes, and the salmon dish on page 87 with Alsatian Riesling, again a *vendange tardive*. From these you can see that I think some of the happiest partnerships are of fatty or oily foods with wines which are inherently rich and have some residual sugar. Dry wines often acquire an unpleasant metallic tinge if drunk with such foods. I feel sorry for those who for a special treat accompany smoked salmon with champagne. The two are such traditional symbols of elegance, yet do each other no favours. Eat smoked salmon, drink champagne – but not together.

So-called 'dessert wines' are rarely equipped to stand up to the sweetness of most puddings, and the subtle complexity of good Sauternes or old chenin blanc is better suited to cheese or being sipped on its own. The intensely sweet and slightly fortified Muscats from various parts of the world are a better bet along with dessert. Once again, although I am in favour of drinking champagne at any time, and would like it to be taken more seriously as a wine of many styles and weights, I can only imagine that the old notion of drinking champagne with dessert must belong to an era when the dosage in the wine was considerably sweeter.

At the end of the day it is all a matter of personal taste and it is worth experimenting to see what suits your own palate. It is a fashionable pursuit to try matching fish and seafood with red wines and this can often work very well; and I am continually surprised by the number of people who would not consider choosing a red wine to accompany poultry dishes. The assumption, on the other hand, that red wines are the natural match for any cheese is just as surprising, when whites are often much more appropriate.

Having ruled out champagne twice so far, I must reassure you that for me it is one of the great wines of the world. I was introduced to it, as most are, as a celebratory drink and, in common with most, abused the name by allowing it to anything which sparkled. When I started taking wine seriously, however, I quickly came to appreciate that there were just as many differing styles and qualities of champagne as there are of any of the great appellations. The vintage and the wine-maker are just as significant as in Meursault or Puligny Montrachet, and the wine has the potential to be just as complex and remarkable as the best from those areas. At La Potinière I have always kept the prices of my champagnes low to encourage people to consider it more readily as an accompaniment to a meal or an ideal aperitif at any time, not just birthdays or weddings.

Some of the greatest wines I have ever tasted are from Champagne. In my personal top twenty are certainly such memorable bottles as Krug 1964, Roederer 1945 and Pol Roger 1952, which tasted rather like a gently sparkling Montrachet when drunk in 1982. For consistent excellence there is no champagne house for which I have more regard than the latter and, happily, there is no champagne family for which we have more affection. I still have Pol Roger back to 1906 in the cellar and it is reassuring to see that the discreet and tasteful presentation has not been significantly tampered with this century. Old champagne is a fascination of mine, but although it can yield great delights it is a risky game beyond 20 years of bottle age even in the greatest vintages. I wish I had tasted Krug 1947 and Pol Roger 1928 ten years before I did. Even non-vintage champagne, on the other hand, benefits considerably from at least a year or two's restraint between buying and drinking.

As a final point of interest for those who look on champagne as being expensive, I have in front of me Harvey's wine list from exactly 50 years ago. The 'current' vintages for the lucky customers at that time were 1928 and 1929 and the prices ranged from 184 shillings per dozen for Bollinger to 156 shillings for Ayala. The least expensive non-vintage was Perrier Jouët at 132 shillings. On the same list the first growth clarets from the same years ranged from 114 shillings to 102 shillings, also per dozen, and Yquem 1934 cost much the same. By comparison, at today's prices, champagne is one of the great bargains of the wine world

À la vôtre!